# TIFFIN

*~ for Lakshmi and Tulasi ~*

# TIFFIN

Memories
and Recipes
of Indian
Vegetarian
Food

## RUKMINI SRINIVAS

### ILLUSTRATED BY MOHIT SUNEJA

RUPA

First published by
Rupa Publications India Pvt. Ltd 2015
7/16, Ansari Road, Daryaganj
New Delhi 110002

*Sales centres:*
Allahabad Bengaluru Chennai
Hyderabad Jaipur Kathmandu
Kolkata Mumbai

Food photographs by Nina Gallant in Boston and Mahesh Bhat in Bengaluru
Family photographs from the author's album

Book design by Maithili Doshi Aphale

ISBN: 978-81-291-2390-9

Second impression 2015

10 9 8 7 6 5 4 3 2

Typeset by Rajkumari John

Printed at Rakmo Press Pvt. Ltd., New Delhi

# CONTENTS

*Introduction*

Captain Thomas Williamson, in his *The East India Vade-Mecum,* describes 'tiffin' as a little avant dinner taken at 1.00 or 2.00 p.m., a time which remained unchanged right up until India's independence from British rule. The word 'tiffin' itself is thought to be derived from 'tiffing', an eighteenth-century English slang term for 'sipping'.

Tiffin—luncheon, Anglo-Indian and Hindustani, at least in English—we believe the word to be a local survival of an English colloquial or slang term. Thus, we find in the *Lexicon Balatronicum*, compiled originally by Captain Francis Grose (1785): 'Tiffing, eating or drinking out of mealtime, besides other meanings.'

In the delightful *European in India or Anglo-Indian's Vade-Mecum* by E.C.P. Hull, with a *Medical Guide for Anglo-Indians* by R.S. Mair, published in 1878, I came across this helpful entry for 'tiffin': 'Tiffin, if not made the principal meal of the day, should invariably be light, and consist only of bread or biscuit, fruits and a glass of sherry or claret.' Hull goes on to say, 'Some people make tiffin an excuse for a double dinner, but anyone who eats largely at both these meals, eats more than is necessary. Heavy tiffins make men heavy, sleepy and interfere with due performance of active work in the after-part of the day. Either take a substantial tiffin and a light dinner, or a substantial dinner and a light tiffin.'

K.T. Achaya in *A Historical Dictionary of Indian Food,* 1998, writes: 'Tiffin was a light midday meal enjoyed by 19th century British families stationed in India... In colonial India, when the evening dinner became a heavy daily repast, only a light afternoon meal was necessary. This was called Tiffin, a word which first appears in AD 1807 in Anglo-Indian writing. The word "tiffin" itself is a colloquial English term, which comes from the word "tiffing" for eating and drinking out of mealtimes, and the word "tiff" which was to eat the midday meal. The word "Tiffin" has been adopted particularly in the Madras area for a light afternoon snack of items like the uppama, dosai and vada to the extent that many take it to be an Indian language word.'

Going by these references, 'tiffin' is a play on the time of day and the nature of food served in many homes in India—an informal snack or light meal served at breakfast or with late afternoon tea. Significantly, as dinner time changed and was pushed to later in the evening, there was a change in the nature of the food in India, and 'tiffin', the transition food, became important and continues to be so. Several small commercial eateries known as 'tiffin rooms' became popular—two such in Bangalore (now Bengaluru) that I know of and frequent are the Mavalli Tiffin Room, or MTR, and the Central Tiffin Room. MTR, located on Lalbagh Road in South Bangalore, in the very busy commercial locality adjoining the famous Lalbagh Botanical Garden, is a pilgrimage centre for foodies from all over India and abroad, and has earned its rightful place in the global world of food consumption with its export of packaged spices and ready-to-eat convenience foods.

On the other hand, the Central Tiffin Room in Malleswaram, a suburb in north Bangalore, is low profile and a favourite haunt of the local denizens. Serving only tiffin, just as your mother made it, this small eatery at the junction of two roads is always crowded. But the service is efficient and cordial, and the few minutes' wait is amply rewarded by fresh off-the-fire 'tiffin items', accompanied by rich, fragrant, south Indian style filter coffee with milk and sugar.

Eateries such as these, with their own eclectic fare, dot the cityscape in India. Recently, while travelling by road in south India with my friends Krishna and Aruna Chidambi, we ate at several small and big eateries. Some were several storeys high, while others were very

*With Krishna and Aruna Chidambi*

modest, thatched huts displaying signboards in Tamil that said 'Tippen Taiyaar', meaning, 'Tiffin and Meals Ready'.

In an age when office canteens, eating out joints, take-aways and tuck shops were not as common as they are now, tiffin tended to be made more at home than outside. My mother, whom I lovingly call Amma, spent much time and thought in the preparation of the 'everyday' tiffin for me and my seven sisters. When I was in school between 1932 and 1946, I would leave home by 8.00 a.m., which was too early for me to have a proper breakfast. I could barely down the banana milkshake Appa (my father) made for me. Frequently, the sandwich packed by Amma for the eleven o'clock break would be untouched till lunchtime. Playing or chatting with friends left no time for the snack. Opening my lunchbox, she would be distressed to find that I had eaten only a portion of what she had packed. Little wonder that I was ravenously hungry on my return from school around 4.30 in the evening. The tiffin that Amma made, usually one savoury and one sweet, would be a full meal for me. And, every day, it was a delicious surprise.

My sisters and I had our own lunch 'dabba', a rectangular metal box 10 inches × 5 inches × 2 inches, which would be washed and reused every day. More elaborate meals would be packed into a

*Next to a restaurant board in Tamil Nadu*

stack of such containers made of brass or stainless steel—a tiffin carrier—which was used by the family on picnics or train journeys.

Amma was not only a very good cook, she was innovative and ingenious, and reconstructed recipes of foods she may have tasted years ago. Hers was a simple kitchen with equipment that consisted of two Primus stoves that burned with kerosene oil, two medium-sized stone mortars and pestles for grinding wet and dry fresh curry powders and chutneys, one large stone grinder for grinding rice and lentil batter, a stone quern to grind the rice and lentils into grits, a couple of woks of different sizes, wrought iron griddles, a few soapstone pots (kalchetty), and bronze cooking utensils of various sizes and shapes.

After we were married, my husband Chamu and I travelled every May from Delhi to spend a few weeks with my parents in Tanjore and with his family in Mysore. Lunch was served during the early forenoon in both homes, and tiffin with filter coffee or tea was served in the afternoon. The time for tiffin was elastic and stretched for a few leisurely hours between three and six o'clock, either in the garden in my parents' home in Tanjore or in the wide verandah skirting the front and sides of Chamu's mother's home in Mysore.

*Tulasi and Lakshmi*

In later years, tiffin assumed an even more important role in my family when both my daughters—Lakshmi and Tulasi—left home for studies abroad. Student life is tough anywhere, and more so, away from the support systems one is used to at home. Even for the most adaptable among us, in alien surroundings, eating food that is familiar is comforting. And so letters, phone calls, and later, emails invariably had requests for simple, easy-to-make recipes for food that would stay fresh for a few days in the refrigerator. My daughters had no time for elaborate cooking or four-course lunches and dinners. Along with some traditional recipes for the food I cooked for lunch and dinner,

I sent my daughters many recipes for food that could be translated into easy-to-make, healthy snacks. And as I dug into my memory for those snacks or tiffin, as we refer to them, those 'saviours' from hunger and monotony, I recalled the many anecdotes and narratives about the people and places associated with these recipes. I introduced these characters to my daughters, in the context of tiffin. My replies grew into lengthy stories and my girls loved them. 'Amma, send us more recipes for tiffin,' they wrote, which invariably meant a demand for 'more stories'. Those stories were rambling and multifaceted and they are all here in my book. More recently, they urged me to share with a wider audience all the stories I had told them over a period of nearly two decades. And so, this modest effort resulted in the first, I hope, of a series of jottings on life when I was growing up and the food we ate for tiffin.

All the recipes contained in this book include the food I continue to cook in my kitchen in Boston. There is a growing interest in the UK and the USA in tiffin, the food and its traditional Indian container, the tiffin carrier. Its global popularity is evident from the fact that several Indian restaurants by the name 'Tiffin' have sprouted, in recent years, from London to Philadelphia.

Seven years ago, I started conducting classes on Indian vegetarian cooking in the Boston area at the Cambridge Center for Adult Education (CCAE), and it is heartening to find that the interest in eating and, more importantly, learning to cook Indian vegetarian food at home is increasing. At these fun-filled participatory classes I meet very interesting folks from different walks of life, some of whom are now my dear friends. Friendship through food is a gift that I cherish. I also have a television show on Indian vegetarian cooking, telecast by the local cable television station, which is titled 'The Indian Vegetarian Kitchen: Cooking with Rukka Srinivas'.

This book is written for family, friends and foodies, who I hope will find something in it to savour. Writing it has been a joyful journey back to my childhood, my student life and, in later years, as an adult. It was a chance to relive the happy times with family and friends.

Rukmini Srinivas
Boston and Bangalore

# My Parents and Siblings

Naganathan, my father (Appa to us, his children), was born in 1892 in the village of Thirukarugavur in the fertile deltaic Tanjore district, one of the richest rice-growing regions of south India irrigated by the Cauvery river. He was the eldest of six children, three sons and three daughters, born to an affluent mirasdar (landed gentry) family. Barefoot, he stood five-feet-six-inches tall, was sparingly built, lean and severe in appearance with small deep-set eyes.

I learned from his youngest brother, my uncle Dr Chitappa, that as a young man, Appa was unhappy about and unwilling to compromise on some joint family matters, and left the family home in Thirukarugavur to join the Military Accounts Department in the year 1913, setting aside his admission to the prestigious Presidency College in Madras (now Chennai). In later years, I am told, Appa regretted not having a university education, though that did not deter him from pursuing his love of books. He collected an impressive library of English and Tamil literature classics, and my memory of Appa, from my childhood till he passed on in his mid-seventies, was of him retiring to bed, reading late into the night every single day, with a copy of *A Dictionary of Modern English Usage* by H.W. Fowler, *The Concise Oxford Dictionary* and the *Thirukkural*, a Tamil classic of the Sangam period, authored by the poet Thiruvalluvar, on truth and simplicity in life, on his bedside table. My father's admiration for Fowler led to a correspondence he had for a few years with this great English schoolmaster. My father later gifted his personal copy of *Thirukkural* to my husband Chamu.

Appa joined the Military Accounts Services in 1913 when he was 21 years old, and his first posting was to Quetta (in Pakistan today). He was married a couple of years later in 1915 to Sahayavalli, my Amma.

*Photo taken in Bombay. (L to R) Bombay Chitti with her daughter, Gouri, on her lap, Bombay Chitappa with Leelu, Amma with Mangalam Athai's daughter, Kunju, (seated in front) and Dr Chitappa with Sarasa (seated in front)*

From Quetta Appa was transferred to Karachi, where my eldest sister Kamala was born in 1921. In 1923, he was posted to Bangalore, where my brother Kannan, I and two of my younger sisters, Sarasa and Leelu, were born. After nine years in Bangalore (a city both Appa and Amma called home), in 1932, when I was five years old, Appa left the city for Poona, where we four sisters joined reputed convent schools. We were enrolled in St Mary's School for the first two years, and for the remaining five, at St Helena's School. Both were adjudged the two best schools in the city in those years. The reason for the change in schools was the fact that the tuition fees for Indian children in St Mary's, a school started primarily for the children of British families stationed in India, was double of what the British paid, and Appa realized that he could ill afford it. In 1939, Appa was transferred to Madras and we joined the Good Shepherds Convent School, my only experience of studying in a Catholic educational institution.

Sadly, my brother Kannan's neurological affliction as a young child, and the fact that it was untreatable (still is), changed the course of his life. He could not be admitted to a 'regular' school, and there were no institutions at that time to help disadvantaged children as medical research into such illnesses was in its infancy. My father once told me of his efforts, when Kannan was of school-going age, to admit him in a 'trade' school, but that did not work out. In Kannan's life with us, he did not lack love, care and understanding, but nevertheless, it was a life of frustration and deep sadness, for he was a very sensitive being.

In 1936, there was another addition to the family, Kalyani. Not satisfied with the existing brood, my parents' engineering resulted in the birth of two more beautiful girls, Malathi and Sarala, between the years 1939 and 1941! So now, the Naganathan couple had a total of eight children—seven girls and one boy.

In 1941, the family was uprooted yet again, and this time to Jubbulpore (now Jabalpur). Between 1941 and 1945, Appa's head office was in Jubbulpore, but his work took him to Meerut, Bhopal and Mhow. Appa's last posting in late 1944, before he retired in 1947, was back to Poona, the city that both he and my mother loved.

So we were like a large gypsy family, our parents with their eight children, picking themselves up every two or three years and settling into the customs and culture of different places. But wait, we were in for another surprise when my mother announced in 1950, three years after my father's retirement, that she was going to have another baby! At twenty-three, I was old enough to realize that Amma was in delicate health during this pregnancy. I was worried for her health, but fortunately, things turned out fine and my youngest sister Gita grew up to be a lovely, healthy child who brought much joy to all of us. A couple of years later, when I considered myself old enough for 'adult talk', I teasingly asked Appa if he was not being irresponsible to my mother, to himself and to us, their children, by continuously expanding the family tree. He smiled. 'Rukka, you saw the movie

*Life with Father* with me, and now, let's see *Cheaper by the Dozen* together,' was his response, with a twinkle in his eye. He added, 'Children need love and a sound education, and none of you will be wanting in that.' He kept his promise. I led a happy and contented childhood. My life with Appa was indeed a treasure I continue to enjoy through happy memories.

In the summer of 1947, after Appa retired, he and Amma moved from Poona (now Pune) to Tanjore—not to his natal village in Thirukarugavur but to the district headquarters at Tanjore proper. It was a carefully considered decision that he took, even though he and Amma had grown accustomed to living in Poona.

Moving to Tanjore proved good for the family. Tanjore could boast of a couple of good schools, which was imperative to Appa's decision-making. His children's education was of paramount importance to him. Tanjore, being the 'heart' of Tamil culture, my sisters were trained in classical music: vocal as well as instrumental, playing the veena and the violin in pure Carnatic style. My youngest sister Gita was initiated into the Pandanallur School of Bharatanatyam classical dance when she was about five years old.

Amma's deep interest in music embraced both the Carnatic and Hindustani styles. She was an artist in the sub-genre of south Indian classical vocal music of the Bombay (now Mumbai) radio station, and in Poona, we attended all-night music soirees with Hirabai Barodekar enthralling her audience under shamianas taking over the neighbourhood streets. Between 1939 and 1941, when Appa was posted in Madras, Sarasa and I were initiated into the classical style of Carnatic vocal music. Within a few months of moving to Jubbulpore in 1941, we four sisters—Kamala, Sarasa, Leelu and myself—started our 'home' music lessons, with Sarasa learning to play the sitar, Leelu the tabla, myself vocal music, and Kamala accompanying us on the violin. In addition, Sarasa and I, with help from Amma, would continue practising Carnatic vocal music which we had been introduced to in the two years we had spent in Madras. I remember, on the eve of Appa's retirement and our move from Poona, the Bhashyams, dear friends of my parents, organized an evening of the 'Naganathan orchestra', as they had christened us. They had invited many of our friends to their home in Koregaon Park. I remember the evening culminated with a buffet of Maharashtrian food. Sarasa and I gorged on the mouth-watering delicious-smelling pav bhaaji, soft special buns, fresh corn niblets in a spicy sauce, bhakri, fresh roasted harbare (green chana in pods) with several chutneys, and mango shreekhand.

It is not an exaggeration to say that the greatest gift from our parents was the enjoyment of all things beautiful—be it music, dance, theatre or the culinary arts. The introduction to, and proficiency in, the genre of classical music and dance of south India was a special gift from my mother, who herself was an accomplished vocalist trained in the south Indian tradition of Carnatic music by maestros of the time, Ariyakudi Ramanuja Iyengar and Musiri Subramania Iyer. When they and their colleagues and friends—Narayanaswamy Iyer (violin), the genius Palghat Mani Iyer (mridangam: percussion drum of south India) and a few years later, T.R. Mahalingam (flute)— were my parents' guests, our home reverberated with divine music.

Amma, Sahayavalli (Sahayam to her family and my father), was born in Madurai in 1903, the youngest of five children—two sons and three daughters. Her father Panchapakesa Iyer, an employee of the Madurai Land Records Office, was frequently

*Appa and Amma in Poona*

out of town on business trips. When my maternal grandmother died suddenly, leaving behind my mother who was barely four years old, her maternal uncle, a prominent lawyer in Madurai, and his wife embraced the motherless child into their family.

I remember my mother as not a very tall person. She may have stood about five-feet-two-inches tall, fairly light-skinned, chubby and gentle with a benign, pleasant expression. I have never seen a frown on her face. If indeed she was frustrated at times, she managed never to show her annoyance and frustration. She was the opposite of my father, who exploded with anger on some occasions, albeit briefly and with no malice. Her welcoming nature shone through her face and demeanour. No wonder she had countless friends cutting across age, gender, caste and class. I was not in India when she passed away a decade ago in March 2002. My sisters, Malathi, Sarala and Gita, who were witness to this inevitable loss of ours, described to me the sea of humanity, young and old, who thronged the street in Madras where she had lived with one of my younger sisters, Sarala, and her husband Dinakaran for three decades.

While growing up, I was curious to know how my Amma and Appa met and married—to me, at that time, they were the most ideal couple I had known. Amma had told me a little about her childhood and marriage.

*Panchapakesa Iyer,*
*my paternal grandfater*

I knew Appa and she enjoyed a good relationship. Nevertheless, I felt sorry for her. Her education had been cut short because her family felt she should get married. I now recollect what she once said to me (translated from Tamil), 'I grew up much loved by my father, aunt and uncle. We lived on the outskirts of the temple town of Madurai in a big bungalow, with a cook and other retainers: a gardener, driver and coachman. Uncle owned a car and a Victoria, drawn by two Shetland ponies. I never walked to school. My cousins and I would be driven to school in the car, and in the evenings, we would ride in the horse-drawn Victoria with my aunt to the Meenakshi temple. We spent every summer in the beautiful cottage my uncle had built opposite the lake in Kodaikanal. The present was so beautiful, I never thought of the future. But all this changed when I was barely twelve years old and a student in class 5 in a local school. My father's friend suggested an "alliance", a marriage proposal, for me that my family thought should be clinched without further delay. The "boy" was "from a respectable family and had a good, permanent job". Things happened very fast.

I was married and had to leave Madurai for Thirukarugavur, to my new home and my husband's joint family.' Amma had added, a little wistfully, that she had missed going to school, and wished she had studied at least till class 10. But pre-puberty marriage for girls was the norm among the south Indian Brahmin community at that time, and Amma's was no exception.

My parents' marriage was conventional in the sense that both of them were Tamil Brahmin Shaivites (members of the community that revered and worshipped Lord Shiva), and the marriage proposal was arranged by elders in both the families. But it was unconventional in the fact that my father was determined that he would not select his wife after viewing several prospective brides. He found it churlish to 'view' and reject, saying it was demeaning to the girl who was rejected. Yes, Appa was a man far ahead of his times. He also made his father promise him that horoscopes would not be exchanged and no 'dowry' (gifts in cash or kind) would be asked for nor accepted from the bride's father. The giving of dowry by the bride's family and accepting the same by the groom's family was the unquestioned practice of the times, and surprisingly, even today, some communities follow this tradition.

Appa, at twenty-three, was in no hurry to get married. But this is how it transpired. Soon after he left his home and family in Thirukarugavur and joined office in Quetta, his mother died suddenly, and one of her last wishes, when she was seriously ill with no sign of recovery, was that her eldest son should be married within a year of her death. And so, when my father came home on his annual leave the year his mother died, the formal 'viewing of the bride and betrothal' ceremony was arranged, and some months later, he was married to young Sahayam, my Amma. She had reluctantly left Madurai, the city she called home, to live with her husband's large joint family. She came as a young bride to a house where her husband's father, brothers and sisters, his grand-aunt, aunt, uncle and their children, and other distant relatives lived under the same roof. She stepped into a joint family circle of a household of four generations and twenty-odd members, a world away from the small family of father, uncle, aunt and three cousins she had known in all the years of her young pre-pubescent life. The move was threatening to Amma, to say the least. The loss of her innocent childhood was sudden when she was forced to 'grow up' and take on household chores, helping with the work in the kitchen and looking after the younger children. When she went out, it was only in the company of adult women. A year later, Appa returned to his natal village on a fortnight's leave, and Amma, barely fourteen years of age, accompanied him to Quetta. Her father, my maternal grandfather, came to the Tanjore junction to see his youngest child leave for her future home. All that he knew about Quetta was that it was a 'faraway' city, and took several days to reach.

Thus, with a man she hardly knew and leaving behind all familial connections, Amma left for Quetta as a newly-wed. In Quetta she entered a strange, alien and unfamiliar universe. The landscape, climate, houses, the people, their culture, including their manner of dressing, where both men and women wore loose pants and a loose shirt covering the torso, their language, food, everything was new and so different. But luckily for Amma, her husband was kind and supportive, and the Pushtoon landlady, whom she would learn to call Ammi, was very friendly, kind, gentle and protective of the timid, young and innocent bride. My mother attributed her early lessons in managing the house and cooking to Ammi.

When I once commented on Amma's vegetable biryani with raisins and almonds as being the best I had ever tasted, she told me that her Ammi in Quetta had taught her to cook biryani with vegetables. This was the first 'one-pot' dish she learned.

As a child, Amma had grown up in a liberal environment where she was free to play around in her 'pavadai' and 'chokka' (long skirt and blouse, the traditional and customary attire for a young south Indian girl). In Quetta, however, no respectable woman was seen on the streets without a 'burqa' covering her from head to toe. Even young, pre-teen girls used to decorously cover their heads. Amma's landlady introduced and educated my mother on a woman's attire and deportment in public.

Appa, unlike many husbands from the conservative Tamil Brahmin community, turned out to be a good friend to my mother. He was more than just her husband. Amma soon started looking forward to the weekends when they would trek in the mountains surrounding Quetta. Her first and only experience in life of snow and bitterly cold winters was in Quetta. As she told me, 'I enjoyed living in Quetta.' She talked of the beautiful exotic wild flowers, of sheep with thick, soft coats, of almonds, pistachios, raisins, chilgosa (pine nuts), of the liberal use of saffron in cooking, and of Sufi music which she said gave her much solace.

My father taught my mother to read, write and speak in English and Hindi. Amma had once told me, wistfully going back in time and with pride, that through his office, Appa had arranged for two Tamil magazines to be delivered to their home once a month. That was her lifeline to her culture and her world! She felt utter bliss whenever the magazines would arrive by post, delivered via the high seas. In Poona, too, she would regularly receive copies of *Kalaimagal* and *Ananda Vikatan*.

*Appa and Amma in Tanjore, Amma's sixtieth birthday*

Though my parents were happily married for fifty-three years, they did experience a shared sadness when their second-born, my brother Kannan, was diagnosed with a critical medical condition when he was four years old. He suffered from infantile spasms, resulting in neurological disorders which affected his speech mainly, and his mental growth and development peripherally. In later years I heard from Dr Chitappa that not much was known about this disorder in the early twentieth century. Therefore, little research was conducted into the problem and no treatment could be prescribed for this infantile medical problem. However, contrary to expectations, Kannan grew up to be a

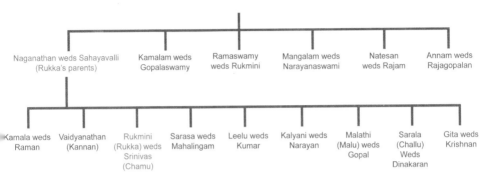

Vishwanathan (paternal grandfather) weds Rukmini
(paternal grandmother)

| Naganathan weds Sahayavalli (Rukka's parents) | Kamalam weds Gopalaswamy | Ramaswamy weds Rukmini | Mangalam weds Narayanaswami | Natesan weds Rajam | Annam weds Rajagopalan |

| Kamala weds Raman | Vaidyanathan (Kannan) | Rukmini (Rukka) weds Srinivas (Chamu) | Sarasa weds Mahalingam | Leelu weds Kumar | Kalyani weds Narayan | Malathi (Malu) weds Gopal | Sarala (Challu) Weds Dinakaran | Gita weds Krishnan |

six-feet tall, strapping young man, very strong in body yet gentle as a lamb in demeanour. My brother passed away a few years ago, within a couple of years of my mother's demise.

Despite the tragedy of her beloved son leading a life of many challenges, Amma did not wear her heart on her sleeve.

All of us nine children, eight daughters and one son, were born between the years 1921 and 1950. I remember my father as a 'hands-on' parent, as is fashionably known in today's times. He bathed and dressed us when we were not old enough to get ready for school, and was always very interested and engaged in all our activities—music, dance, studies, sports events—at school and with our friends. He knew all our teachers at school and they, in turn, were happy to interact with someone as knowledgeable and liberal as him. It was a rare event at school that a parent, a father at that, showed up as frequently as once a fortnight to engage in his children's school activities. This made him popular with the principal and our teachers, be it in Poona, Jubbulpore or Madras. Frequently, I saw him in the school campus leaning on his bicycle and chatting with my principals—Miss Wilson in St Helena's School, Poona, and Miss Levy in Christ Church Girls' High School, Jubbulpore. Sister Rose, otherwise the crochety elderly Mother Superior in Good Shepherds Convent in Madras, would always break into a smile on

## M.N. SRINIVAS' (CHAMU) NATAL FAMILY

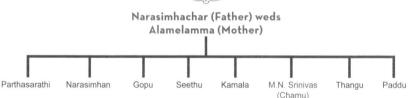

Narasimhachar (Father) weds
Alamelamma (Mother)

| Parthasarathi | Narasimhan | Gopu | Seethu | Kamala | M.N. Srinivas (Chamu) | Thangu | Paddu |

seeing my father and welcome him to the parlour, the school's reception room.

Appa's deep interest in our education continued through my university days, when on his visits to Madras, he would make time to meet my teachers and even keep in touch with some of them. Lucy Thomas, my English professor between the years 1946 and 1948, surprised me once in the corridors of Queen Mary's College, saying she had just received a letter from my father enclosing excerpts from *A Philosophical View of Reform* by Percy Bysshe Shelley, particularly the passages on non-violence in protests. Till date, I do not know what could have prompted him to send her these; it may have been the turbulent political scene in India on the eve of independence.

The year my father passed away in 1968, I was dusting his books in his bedroom and chanced upon two volumes, *Prometheus Unbound* and *Hymn to Intellectual Beauty*. I realized then that my father was born exactly a hundred years after Shelley, and another interesting bit of information was that Shelley strongly advocated vegetarianism and abhorred the inhuman treatment of all living creatures. It was heartening to note that the two men I greatly admired connected at that level too!

I could write volumes about my parents, and particularly of a father who was way ahead of his times. But I shall stop here, for the main scope of this book is to narrate certain vignettes from my life seen through the prism of tiffin. So do join me in my sepia-tinged memories of a fascinating era gone by.

### MY FAMILY

M.N. Srinivas (Chamu) weds Rukmini (Rukka)

| Lakshmi | Tulasi weds Popsi Narasimhan |

*Masala Vadai and Midwifery*

Dr Chitappa, Natesan, my father's youngest brother, a medical officer in rural Tanjore district in the south Indian state of Madras Presidency, now Tamil Nadu, was posted to remote villages. Many a summer, while still in school, I would visit Dr Chitappa during the holidays and spend a few weeks in whichever village he was stationed.

This utterly enjoyable habit of going every year to Dr Chitappa's village began in the summer of 1942 when, as a fifteen-year-old gawky teenager entering the Junior Cambridge class in Christ Church Girls' High School, Jubbulpore (in central India), I went by train to Madras (now Chennai) a port town in south India facing the Bay of Bengal. I had to change trains in Madras and travel by the night boat mail train to the junction of Kumbakonam, on my way to Vedaranyam. This train connected with the ferry service across the Palk Strait from Dhanushkodi, at the southern tip of peninsular India, to Talaimannar, on the northern coast of Ceylon, now Sri Lanka. The long journey by train from Jubbulpore to Kumbakonam, though exciting, was slightly anxiety-ridden for me as this was my first trip unaccompanied by family or friends. True, my younger sister Sarasa and I formed a pair in many adventures,

*Dr Chitappa*

but she did not accompany me on my visit to Dr Chitappa's village for two reasons: she stayed back in Jubbulpore to continue with her sitar lessons, and frankly, she was not interested in spending time in a village. I, on the other hand, had spent time with my uncle in Vedaranyam, Ayyampet, Ammapet, Muthupet, Gandharvakottai and Pandaravadai, to mention a few of the villages where he had lived and worked. I vividly recollect one of my first visits. Till I spotted my uncle, a short, chubby, light-skinned man with a 'kudumi' (Tamil for long strands of hair tied into a knot at the nape of the neck), I anxiously looked for him among the crowd on the dimly lit platform at the Kumbakonam junction. The two hospital orderlies who accompanied him easily spotted me on the platform, for it was not a common sight in those parts to see a teenaged girl with two pigtails and dressed in a knee-length frock, a western dress. At that time, in the villages and small towns of south India, girls of my age wore a pavadai (ankle-length skirt) with a short blouse covering the torso, and a melaaku (a two-yard length of unstitched cloth tucked into the waist and thrown over the left shoulder). This was considered, modest attire, becoming of a teenaged girl. But, like I had mentioned earlier, I was raised in a liberal family and none of us sisters had to submit to societal norms when it came to our sartorial choices.

As I ran towards him, his concern gave way to relief, and he greeted me with, 'Have you been waiting long? How was your journey? Did you sleep a bit on the train?'

The ride to Vedaranyam was fun, the taxi, a black Morris Minor, jerkily moving at a snail's pace on narrow unpaved village roads lined with coconut palms, past many hamlets with street houses and thatched huts nestled in the rich fertile delta of the Cauvery River, where lime-green paddy fields, whispering coconut palm orchards heavy with fruit, and floriculture farms with orange kanakambaram (*Crossandra infundibuliformis*) and white jasmine flowers were part of the landscape. In the foggy dawn, elderly men wrapped in homespun cotton shawls huddled on their haunches in the dusty, thatched front verandahs of village cafés, sipping hot coffee from metal tumblers and enjoying their first beedi smoke for the day. The private taxi, the only one in the village, belonged to Dr Chitappa's friend Velu who, besides running a

taxi service, was the proprietor of the only 'tent cinema' in Vedaranyam. Hooting non-stop, as young children, both boys and girls, took over the road on their way to the village school, the taxi went in a slow procession with some children excitedly running along with and behind it.

Dr Chitappa lived in one of the bigger houses in the village, not too far from his hospital. He usually walked the couple of miles to work, but rode his bicycle when he made 'house calls' before he went to his hospital. His single-storeyed house, built of brick and lime mortar with a tiled roof, stayed cool even during the searing heat of summer. A covered corridor connected the front entrance to a spacious central square courtyard open to the sky. Skirting the courtyard was a twelve-feet-wide covered verandah, on one side of which hung a two-seater mahogany swing, around which were arranged a couple of teakwood chairs with cushions and a rosewood recliner with an intricately plaited rattan seat and back. A reed mat was spread on the floor against the wall. This section of the verandah served as the family room where visitors were also received.

Beyond the courtyard and to the right, adjoining the rear entrance to the house, was the large dimly lit kitchen-cum-pantry. A small grilled window offered a peek into a well-tended herb and vegetable garden around a large, stonelined well.

Dr Chitappa was an enthusiastic and successful gardener, and an avid cook. His

garden was a riot of colours—green tangled
vines spread over the tiled roof, with bright
orange and creamy-white pumpkin flowers and
globular pumpkins. Green and purple aubergines
dangled from neatly planted bushes interspersed
with green chilli plants ringed with beds of
coriander, mint, ginger and turmeric. Curry
leaf bushes lined the back wall. The garden
held other delights for me: ripe bananas, seedy
guavas and tender coconuts with sweet water
and slippery kernels that would slide down the
mouth effortlessly.

Dr Chitappa often tried his hand at cooking
when my aunt was away with her three young
children, visiting her parents. It was only after
my father retired and moved to Tanjore, and
two of Dr Chitappa's daughters joined the same

*Rukka with Dr Chitappa*

school as my sisters and lived with my parents, that I got to know them.

A connoisseur of south Indian food, Dr Chitappa's claim to fame
was his masala vadai, the south Indian falafal; spicy, crunchy, deep-fried
lentil patty, aromatic with herbs and pungent with green chillies and
sharp onions, I remember them as being fabulous! With the making
of masala vadais, the herb garden strayed into the kitchen.

One Sunday, when the clinic was closed and Dr Chitappa had
finished his morning rounds of patients admitted to the small hospital,
he decided to make masala vadai for the afternoon tiffin. It was one of
those weekends when my aunt was away visiting her parents. He put
me to work, assisting him in the prep work. I was told to rinse, dry
and chop all the fresh ingredients—fresh leafy coriander, shiny green
chillies, feathery dill leaves, knobbly sharp ginger, and pink shallots—
while he soaked the lentils for a couple of hours. He then ground them
to a coarse batter in the kalural, the enormous granite stone mortar
with a grinding pestle, fixed to the raised floor near the back entrance
to the house. He sat on a high wooden stool while grinding.

Chitappa preferred to cook in the verandah. Sitting crosslegged on
a slightly raised teakwood plank on the floor, he cooked on a kerosene

Primus stove. Pumping it to a blue flame, he heated up the oil in the wok. While the oil was getting hot, he arranged the bowl of ground batter, the metal colander, a slotted spoon and a smaller bowl of water next to his wooden plank. I sat on a reed mat on the floor, absorbed in one of my first lessons in the art of south Indian vegetarian cooking. I noticed he dipped his fingers in cold water, dried them on the kitchen towel which was neatly folded and resting on his right thigh, took a little of the mix, rolled it in his palm, then patted it lightly with his forefingers, scooped it up and gently slid it into the hot oil. He then patted and slid a few more, turning them over and deepfrying them to a crisp brown. The air was filled with the spicy aroma of the frying of lentils, onions and herbs. Draining the first batch of six vadais in the colander, he asked me, 'Would you like to sample one for salt?' showing me how to break it with the fingers to let out the steam, blow on it to cool it, and dip it in the tomato-mint chutney he had ground in the same stone grinder. So crisp and crunchy outside and soft, warm, flavourful and tasty within, I could have eaten more than just one vadai. The herb garden came alive in every bite. I asked him to try one too.

Soon Mani and Raju, the two hospital orderlies who were hanging around outside, were drawn in by the smell of the vadais. We were enjoying the impromptu party when Pandian, the male nurse from the hospital, stepped in to announce that there was a call from the colony of scavengers and sweepers—a labour case in the Harijan Colony. Dr Chitappa's response was immediate. He hurriedly turned off the stove, covered the bowl of batter, changed into his official clothes—from a cotton sarong (veshti) into trousers and shirt—and told me to get ready, since he did not wish me to stay in the house alone. Pandian picked up Dr Chitappa's medical-kit, stethoscope and a duffel bag with a couple of pails, two flashlights, mugs, towels, soap and disinfectants. Without much delay, we left in a bullock 'bandy', the English corruption of the Tamil 'vandi', a cart or carriage. The hospital midwife joined us, and after a few hours of jerky travel through paddy fields and down dusty country lanes, we reached the Harijan Colony as the sun was setting.

The colony of sweepers was a haphazard cluster of thatched huts and tin sheds across a muddy stream separating and isolating it from the main village. A herd of goats and pigs blocked our path. Dr Chitappa,

Pandian and the midwife got down and walked the short distance to the hut, in front of which a small group had gathered. I followed in the bandy.

I remember the darkness around and the baying and howling in chorus of the pariah dogs (pye dogs) running threateningly towards the bandy and kicking up the dust. The adult men who were gathered outside formed a cordon and guided me to the entrance of the hut, which was lit inside by a flickering lamp, behind which was a framed picture of the Nativity of Christ. By the dim light of the oil lamp, the fire of the hearth and the two powerful shafts of light from the flashlights, Dr Chitappa, assisted by the midwife, examined the young mother who was lying on a reed mat on the mud floor. I sat by her side, stroking her hair and fanning her with a palm-frond fan while her frail body thrashed about and she screamed every now and then. All of a sudden, the screaming stopped and the midwife held up the baby. I was astonished by the suddenness of it all. That was the first time I witnessed the birth of a baby. The tranquillity of the night was pierced by the cries of the newborn infant.

An elderly woman came to the door of the hut as we were ready to leave, folded her hands in a gesture of prayer and gratitude, and offered Dr Chitappa a coconut, a few betel leaves and a couple of bananas.

We left soon after and returned home past midnight. Entering the courtyard, we found the bowl of masala vadai mix overturned and empty. Not a trace of the culprit! Chitappa smiled, adding, 'The rats must have had a field day.' He and I made do with a cup of hot milk and went to bed. But a few days later, he again made his masala vadais and tomato-mint chutney for me, and this time, we both had a leisurely tiffin.

## MASALA VADAI, *aromatic, crisp and spicy lentil fritters, the Indian falafal. I have slightly modified Dr Chitappa's recipe by adding flax seeds.*

### INGREDIENTS TO MAKE 25 VADAIS

* ½ cup tur dal
* 1 cup chana dal
* 1 cup urad dal
* 2 medium onions
* 3 green chillies
* 1-inch piece fresh ginger
* 1 cup freshly chopped coriander leaves and tender stems
* 1 cup freshly chopped dill
* 1 heaped tablespoon flax seeds (optional)
* salt to taste
* 2 cups vegetable oil, for deep-frying
* Bowl of water for dipping fingers

### METHOD

Wash and drain the 3 dals together. Repeat till the water is clear. Soak in a bowl of water for three hours.

Drain and set aside, covered.

Chop 1 onion into quarters. Chop the other in half and cut into thin slices. In a food processor, coarse grind the dals with the quartered onion, green chillies and ginger, without adding water. Empty into a bowl.

Mix in the sliced onion, coriander, dill, salt and flax seeds, if you are using them.

Taste for salt.

Divide and shape the ground mix into 25 balls. Set aside, covered.

Heat the oil in a wok on medium heat.

Wet your fingers and palms in the bowl of water. Pick up 1 ball of mix, place it in the palm of one hand, gently pat with the fingers of the other hand, lift and slide it into the hot oil. Slide in 6 to 8 at a time and fry to a golden brown, turning over a couple of times.

Drain in a colander.

Increase the heat to medium-high after frying each batch of vadais, but halfway through, lower the heat. The idea is that in the process of frying, the crust should not brown too soon, leaving the inside uncooked.

Serve hot or at room temperature.

*The masala vadais should be crisp on the outside and cooked soft in the inside. My friends in Boston enjoy them with margaritas.*

# TOMATO-MINT CHUTNEY, *fresh-smelling and visually appealing, this chutney pairs well with rice and Indian bread as well. I use the chutney as a sandwich spread too.*

## INGREDIENTS TO MAKE 1 CUP

* 3 tablespoons oil
* 1 teaspoon brown mustard seeds
* 2 medium-size ripe tomatoes, chopped
* 1 cup loosely packed mint leaves
* 3 dried red chillies
* 1 teaspoon turmeric powder
* ¼ teaspoon asafoetida powder (optional)
* 2 cloves garlic, coarsely chopped
* 1 cup chopped coriander leaves
* salt to taste
* 1 teaspoon sugar

## METHOD

Heat the oil in a heavy saucepan on medium heat.

Lower heat and add mustard seeds, and when they stop popping, add chopped tomatoes and other ingredients.

Stir and cook to a thick sauce. Cool.

Grind in a blender to a smooth chutney. You could also pulse a couple of times to leave a few chunks of tomatoes. Scrape out all the ground chutney with a spatula. Stir and taste for salt.

Will stay fresh for 3 days if refrigerated.

A small stone mortar and pestle works well for me for grinding small quantities.

## A Victorian Meat Grinder in an Indian Vegetarian Kitchen

Between the years 1913 and 1947, Appa worked for the British defence administration in India in the Military Accounts Department. His first posting was to Quetta near the Afghanistan border. Appa was a man of many interests, ranging from philosophy to gardening, birdwatching to cooking, collecting antique furniture to reading classical Tamil and English literature. On his retirement he donated his entire library of English literature classics to the Fergusson College in Poona.

Appa, like his brother, my uncle Dr Chitappa, enjoyed cooking, but was more interested in the flavours and tastes of food from other parts of India and, in a limited way, from other countries, too. When he joined the Military Accounts Department in Quetta, his friends and colleagues hailed from different parts of India and England, and sharing food with them exposed him to the wealth and variety of Indian and British cuisine. Though Appa remained vegetarian, the food in our home was always an eclectic mix.

In 1937, when we lived in the city of Poona, my father worked in the Southern Command office of the Military Accounts Department on Susie Sorabji Road, just a 10-minute walk from our school, St Helena's. The canteen in the Southern Command office was a large dining room with a well organized kitchen, where delicious soups were made, and occasionally my sisters Kamala, Sarasa and I would join Appa for lunch. The menu boasted of a large spread, but my favourites were the hot soup of the day, which was either tomato or fresh corn soup and Welsh Rabbit(Welsh Rarebit) or a vegetable au gratin. Even today, I can recollect the taste and smell of real butter, Polson's butter, and the melted sharp English Cheddar cheese oozing from the sides of warm toasted bread slices. Welsh Rarebit remains one of my favourite snacks but I now spike it with green chillies. Sarasa almost always ordered potato croquettes with soup, and Kamala preferred a light lunch of soup and green salad. She envied us our big lunch but added, she did not dare fall asleep in the first period after lunch, which for her was arithmetic. For Sarasa and me, it was a library period or a crafts class. Neither of those classes needed the concentration of working out sums in arithmetic. The pastries and plum cakes in Appa's office canteen were also fabulous, and Appa always sent a mint-chocolate pastry, Leelu's favourite, packed for her—as a kindergarten student was not permitted to leave school during lunch hours.

St Helena's School has a very special place in my life because of the dedicated and caring teachers I was fortunate to learn from. I did not realize it at the time. I was not a diligent student like my younger sister Sarasa, who was two years my junior. I spent time studying only the subjects I liked, like nature study, English and French, and while I submitted the homework for these on time, a subject like arithmetic would give me a headache and invariably, I would end up with an 'incomplete' remark from the teacher, three or four times a week. To add to my distaste of the subject, we had two periods of arithmetic on the same day, twice a week! When I was a student in the fourth standard, I was bogged down by 'bill sums', where we students were introduced to the concept of fractions. My father tried to make the concept more realistic for me by introducing shopping lists and bills for groceries for the family as an example; it did not help much. This distaste for arithmetic continued throughout my school days. I was only too happy to move into liberal arts and humanities when I joined Queen Mary's College in Madras.

As I said earlier, my father's interest in cooking was in trying out new recipes that we were not familiar with in our home; once in a while, he would treat us to a fresh salad of lettuce with segments of oranges and walnuts in a vinaigrette dressing. Vinegar was alien to south Indian cooking and my mother did not like the sour fermented smell and taste of vinegar, so he frequently substituted it with lemon juice.

And so it was that Appa, on one of his visits to his other younger brother in Bombay (now Mumbai), returned home bearing a heavy, silver-coated metal Victorian meat grinder. It had a big flywheel on one side, with a wooden handle capped with burgundy-coloured leather embossed with the name of the manufacturing company in the Midlands in the UK. Amma was mystified by his purchase and asked him, 'What are we going to do with this?' Appa soon unveiled his plan.

One Sunday a month, after our family lunch, my father would host a bridge party for four of his friends. Amma would invariably make snacks for the group—a light tiffin. But on one such Sunday, Appa got busy. My sister Sarasa, around eight years of age at the time, and I, two years older than her, watched as he shifted a square, heavy, teakwood side table from the living room to the kitchen. With knit brows and pursed lips, he set about unpacking the meat grinder, washing the parts and drying them with the tea-towel that was slung over his shoulder. He assembled the grinder and fixed it to the table. Inspired by some Victorian recipes for meat cutlets he had been reading, he had decided to make vegetarian versions for the bridge players. He looked very professional in his white apron!

He took a couple of carrots and potatoes, a handful of french beans, some cabbage leaves, a few green chillies, an onion, a couple of garlic cloves and mint leaves from the wicker baskets, washed all the vegetables carefully, quartered the potatoes, cut the carrots into 2-inch lengths, and stacked all of them neatly on a wooden tray. He then started feeding one piece at a time into the meat grinder while one of us turned the flywheel. He patted the vegetable mix into thick juicy discs which he shallow-fried brown and crunchy on the outside and soft and mushy within.

My sister and I excitedly took over feeding the vegetables and turning the flywheel. If any vegetable got stuck, Appa would halt the process while he undid the central screw, cleaned out the barrel, and put it back together. The timing was perfect, and as the last batch of cutlets was being fried, the bridge players walked in. The cutlets were accompanied by a tart, orange and green chilli relish, that Amma made, followed by piping hot south Indian filter coffee. I think Appa's friends stayed longer than usual that Sunday.

Making cutlets with Appa was such fun! From then on, we frequently had vegetable cutlets for tiffin over weekends. Squatting on the reed mat in the verandah enjoying the cutlets, we would tell Appa how our week went at school. As the years went by and we sisters got married and moved far away, the accompanying recipe was one that made its way into our households.

In 1968, Appa passed away. He was gone the day before I reached Tanjore in Tamil Nadu, where he and Amma had moved from Poona on his retirement. I regret that I missed seeing him by a few hours. One summer,a few years later, I was visiting Amma for a few days, and she handed me a heavy cardboard box, adding, 'I know you will treasure this.' When I opened it, I saw the large silver-coated flywheel, and pleasant memories of making tiffin cutlets with Appa in Poona came flooding back.

## APPA'S VEGETABLE CUTLETS, *crisp on the outside, soft and textured within, they are packed with the goodness of fresh vegetables. Mint chutney, garlic hummus, tomato salsa (or tomato ketchup) pair well with this flavourful and scrumptious snack. I have modified his recipe by including mushrooms and quinoa flour.*

### INGREDIENTS TO MAKE 25 CUTLETS

* *2 large potatoes, not peeled, cut in 2-inch lengths of 1-inch width*
* *1 medium sweet potato cut in 2-inch lengths of 1-inch width*
* *2 carrots cut in 1-inch lengths*
* *10 green beans cut in halves*
* *¼ cup shelled green peas*
* *¼ cup corn kernels*
* *1 cup coarsely chopped mushrooms (any variety), optional*
* *1 cup coarsely chopped, tightly packed spinach or cabbage leaves, fresh or frozen*
* *2 green chillies*
* *1-inch piece of fresh ginger*
* *1 large onion, quartered*

- ½ cup chopped fresh coriander or mint
- 2 cloves garlic
- 1 teaspoon garam masala powder (optional)
- ½ teaspoon red chilli powder
- 2-3 tablespoons rice flour (you may substitute with all purpose flour, quinoa or millet flour)
- salt to taste
- 1 teaspoon sugar
- ½ tablespoons limejuice
- 2 cups oil for frying

## METHOD

Wash all the vegetables and set them aside. Use the vegetables in any combination you prefer. Each time I make them, they taste different and delicious

Set the grinder or food processor to the 'coarse' position.

Grind the raw vegetables and herbs, feeding each variety separately.

Empty the ground mix into a bowl.

Add the garam masala, if you are using it, red chilli powder, rice flour, salt, sugar and lime juice. Mix and add salt to taste.

Wet your fingers in a bowl of water and divide the mix into 25 equal portions.

Roll each portion into a ball and gently flatten it to form a patty, either in the palm of your hand or on a sheet of wax paper. If the mix does not hold and cannot be rolled into a ball, sprinkle and mix in more flour, just enough to make it hold. If the mix is too dry and crumbly, sprinkle a little water and mix to hold.

Make several patties and keep them aside on a platter covered with a damp kitchen towel. Do not stack them on top of each other.

Heat oil in a wok on medium heat, but not to smoking point. Gently slide in 6 patties at a time and fry until they are golden-brown, while turning over on both sides.

Remove with a slotted spoon and drain in a colander.

Serve hot with orange rind-green chilli relish.

# AMMA'S ORANGE RIND-GREEN CHILLI RELISH,
*a refreshing burst of citrus in a sweet and spicy sauce.*

## INGREDIENTS TO MAKE APPROXIMATELY 2 CUPS

- 3 oranges or 4 clementines
- 3 tablespoons oil
- ½ teaspoon brown mustard seeds
- 2 green chillies, finely chopped
- 10 curry leaves, torn in half
- 1 tablespoon fresh ginger, grated

- ½ teaspoon turmeric powder
- ½ teaspoon asafoetida powder, optional
- 2 tablespoons brown sugar or jaggery
- ½ cup water
- 1 teaspoon lemon juice
- salt to taste

## METHOD

Wash and peel the oranges. Save half the peel. Separate the orange segments, remove the membrane, threads, pith and seeds. Cut each segment in 3 pieces and transfer to a bowl. Julienne the peel into 1-inch strips and add to the bowl with the orange segments.

Heat the oil in a wok on medium heat, but not to smoking point. Add the mustard seeds, and when they start popping, lower the heat.

Toss in the green chillies, curry leaves, ginger, turmeric powder and asafoetida powder, if you are using it. Stir once.

Add the julienned orange peel and orange segments. Stir and cook for 2 minutes on low heat.

Add sugar, salt and water. Stir and cook for another 5 minutes or more on medium heat till it cooks to a loose jam.

Stir in the lemon juice, remove from stove and set aside to cool. Bottle and refrigerate.

# AMMA'S GARAM MASALA (DRY SPICE POWDER)

### INGREDIENTS TO MAKE APPROXIMATELY 1 CUP

- ¼ cup cumin seeds
- ¼ cup coriander seeds
- 2 teaspoons cardamom seeds
- 3-inch stick of cinnamon, broken in small pieces
- 1 teaspoon cloves
- 1 teaspoon black peppercorns
- 6 bay leaves
- 1 teaspoon fennel seeds
- 1 teaspoon nutmeg, grated
- 1 tablespoon mace pieces

## METHOD

In a spice grinder, grind all the ingredients into a fine powder and store in an airtight jar in a cool space. Will stay fresh for several weeks.

Several brands of garam masala are available today in Indian grocery stores and I do have a jar ready, but I prefer to grind my blend of spices fresh. It makes a difference.

## In Somwar Peth, Poona, for Potato Bhaaji and Bhakri

Most Sunday mornings, Appa and I would cycle to a different part of the city of Poona, and that is how I became familiar with the city and its environs. I learned to ride a bicycle when I was eight years old. The black Hercules 'gent's bike' was a birthday gift from Appa and it was my new toy. I would swing my leg over the central bar while leaning my bicycle against the gatepost and off we would go. I remember cycling through the Bund gardens across the bridge spanning the Mula-Mutha River to the Yerwada jail, which was a tourist site, historically important because Mahatma Gandhi was imprisoned there by the British several times. Another spot we frequently rode to was the foot of the Parvati Hill, a picturesque rugged outcrop about 2,000 feet high, named after the seventeenth century temple of Parvati and her consort Devdeveshwara. Throughout the week, pilgrims crowded the hill, which was also a favourite destination for trekkers. I vividly remember the one time I was cycling down, and in trying to avoid a group of children, I fell down and bruised my knees. When I returned home, Amma, the loving nurse that she was, washed my knees and applied a poultice of soft cooked rice flour mixed with a pinch of turmeric powder, water and castor oil. Miraculously, the healing was quick and complete. Many 'home remedies' such as this one are gentle and efficacious without any adverse effects.

In Poona, we lived in the suburban Saraswath Colony, which was part of the cosmopolitan cantonment area, with big bungalows and well-maintained gardens. My mother was a keen gardener and was part of a small group of passionate gardeners in our locality. My interest in gardening began early in life when I would accompany Amma to gardens and flower shows. Poona was truly a 'garden city'.

Most of the residents of Saraswath Colony were young professionals—doctors, architects, engineers, journalists and the like—from different parts of India. I grew up with friends who spoke Bengali, Hindi, Konkani, Malayalam, Marathi, Punjabi and Urdu. We children often ate at each others' homes and shared our lunch when in school. At a very young age, I was introduced to the many colours, flavours and tastes of India. Amma would often deconstruct meals she had eaten at a friend's home and recreate the dish with her unique touch.

Occasionally on weekends, my father and I would ride to Sathe's Restaurant in Somwar Peth, a Maharashtrian neighbourhood in downtown Poona. Sathe's was famous for its millet bhakri, a flatbread served with spicy potato bhaaji (lemony potato curry) and moong sprouts usal (warm, sprouted moong-bean salad). Decades later, I got to taste bhakri in Belgaum and in Bangalore, at the Kamat Yatri Nivas, which serves authentic bhakri with eggplant curry, a signature food from Maharashtra and north Karnataka.

The urban landscape of Somwar Peth was a hazardous yet interesting maze of narrow streets where children played cricket, unmindful of the cows and bulls relaxing in the middle of the road. To add to the chaos, pedestrians, cyclists and tongas clogged the space, dodging each other.

Old houses, many with balconies facing the street, were divided into small tenements and were occupied by all manner of businesses—haberdashers, tailors, pawnbrokers, newspaper and magazine vendors, ironmongers, thrift shops which bought and sold used brass and copper kitchenware and used second-hand bicycle parts, to name a few, and stalls that sold spices, home-made spice powders, fresh sugarcane juice and home-made biscuits.

Cycling down the narrow crowded lanes was impossible for me, and so, from the round 'thana' (a rotary with a police station) where the traffic policeman stood, Appa and I would walk, leading our bicycles to Sathe's Restaurant half a mile away.

Once there, we would prop our bicycles against the wide wooden platform, below the blue painted restaurant signboard with its garlanded posters of Lakshmi, the goddess of wealth, standing on a blooming pink lotus, and Shivaji, the legendary Maratha hero, riding a white stallion.

Customers would start gathering in front of Sathe's by noon every day and the last stragglers would leave past midnight when the shutters came down. Inside the restaurant there was standing room for fifteen customers addicted to Sathe's bhakri and potato bhaaji. Standing on the street, leaning against the platform and sharing cramped space with the bicycles, was another group of about the same number.

Sathe's was a family-run business. Senior Sathe in his mid-sixties, was the owner and cashier of the restaurant, which had been in business

*Street scene in Somwar Peth, Poona*

for over three decades. Tall and wiry with a shock of silvery-white hair framing his tanned face, he looked down his black horn-rimmed spectacles at every customer who walked up the steps. Kusum, his wife, was the chef sweating over a firewood stove, turning out batch after batch of the one-of-a-kind potato bhaaji and sprouts usal. Their teenaged son, Ashok, was both waiter and manager. Kusum's brother was the bhakri (flatbread) maker, and, as I discovered many decades later, patting out the bhakri by hand and cooking it is an art in itself. It is an example of regional cuisine at its best—comparable to the makki ki roti (corn flatbread) of Punjab.

The four had perfected a system whereby the customer was served in the most efficient way. As soon as a customer showed up, Ashok would fill a fresh leaf cup with one bhakri, a generous helping of the aromatic bhaaji and sprouts usal, and hand it out. As the satisfied customer, after his second or third 'leaf cup', walked towards the cashier's table, Ashok would shout to his father in Marathi and Sathe would charge the customer after making a quick mental calculation. How did Ashok remember to tally the number of 'leaf cups' with each of his customers with not even a pencil and a slip of paper? I wondered as I waited my turn.

I looked forward to the treat of sniffing the aroma inside the restaurant and eating the warm potato bhaaji, spiked with spicy chilli, tart with a squeeze of lime, and sweet with the taste of freshly grated coconut. No water was served at Sathe's, but his cousin did brisk business by installing a sugarcane press on the front verandah of Sathe's restaurant. The combination of the tart and spicy potato with the crunchy masala sprouts usal, washed down with the freshly pressed sweet sugarcane juice, and the pleasure of my father's company made for the perfect day!

Much of the fun for me was to stand with the others on the street and eat, but frequently, Father would request a few leaf cups to be packed for taking home. Ashok would wrap our parcel of leaf cups in a sheet of the local Marathi newspaper. The surprise for Mother and my sisters was the thermos of cool sugarcane juice.

POTATO BHAAJI, *tossed warm, spicy potato salad serves both as an appetizer and a side dish for lunch and dinner. I think it pairs well with the south Indian dosai, the lentil crêpe that has travelled far and wide. I was introduced to it as 'street food' in Poona.*

## INGREDIENTS TO MAKE 4 SERVINGS

* 4 cups water
* ½ teaspoon turmeric powder
* 1 teaspoon mild red chilli powder (gives colour and not much heat)
* 4 medium potatoes, peeled and cubed into small pieces
* 4 green chillies, any variety
* ½ cup fresh coriander, including the tender stems, coarsely chopped
* 1 tablespoon coriander seeds
* 1 tablespoon fennel seeds
* 1 tablespoon cumin seeds
* 1 teaspoon brown sugar or grated jaggery
* 1 tablespoon oil
* 1 tablespoon lime juice
* ½ cup shredded coconut, fresh or frozen
* salt to taste

## METHOD

Boil water in a deep saucepan, adding turmeric and chilli powders and salt.
    Add potatoes and cook till just tender but not mushy. Drain.
Toss, cover and set aside in a bowl.
    Coarsely crush green chillies, coriander leaves, and coriander, fennel and cumin seeds together. (I use a mortar and pestle.) Add to the potatoes and toss gently to coat them with the herbal mix. Sprinkle the brown sugar or jaggery.
    Warm up the oil in a wok or saucepan over medium heat.
    Turn off stove, and to the warm oil in the wok, add the potato mix and lime juice, and toss. Cover and set aside for 5 minutes for the flavours to come together.

    Garnish with grated coconut and serve at room temperature.

**SPROUTS USAL,** *high in protein, easy to assemble crunchy salad, it can be made with an array of sprouted beans and lentils. A little planning of two or three days is needed for the lentils to sprout. You can also buy ready-to-cook sprouts.*

## INGREDIENTS TO MAKE 6 SERVINGS

- 1 cup whole moong beans
- ¼ cup whole moth
- ¼ cup whole black chana
- ¼ cup whole masoor
- 2 teaspoons oil
- ½ teaspoon brown mustard seeds
- 2 green chillies, slit lengthwise in half
- 1-inch piece fresh ginger with skin, julienned
- 10 curry leaves, torn in half
- ¼ teaspoon turmeric powder
- ½ teaspoon brown sugar or grated jaggery
- ¼ cup shredded coconut, fresh or frozen
- ¼ cup coriander leaves, including the tender stems, chopped
- 1 large onion, minced
- 1 lemon, cut in 8 wedges
- ¼ cup water
- salt to taste

## METHOD

You have an option of any one or a combination of beans and lentils, depending on choice and availability. And if you are planning on sprouting the beans at home, you can sprout in a 'sprout farm' by following the instructions, or sprout the traditional way.

Sprouting the Traditional Way

Rinse lentils and drain water. Repeat twice. Soak in fresh water for 6 hours.

Drain water and transfer soaked lentils to a cotton cheesecloth, tie securely into a bundle and hang in a dark cupboard or any dark space for two days to encourage sprouting, or

Drain water and transfer to a container, closing it with a tight lid. Store in a dark place for 24 hours. Check for sprouting, toss and close lid. Check again after 24 hours.

Rinse sprouts gently, drain and use.

### Preparing the Usal

Heat oil in a wok on medium heat, but not to smoking point. Lower heat. Add the mustard seeds, and when they splutter and pop, add the green chillies, ginger, curry leaves and turmeric powder. Stir once.

Toss in the sprouts, salt and brown sugar or jaggery. Stir once again. Add the water.

Raise the heat to medium, and cook with a cover till soft. Remove lid frequently, stir and check.

Lower heat and cook without the cover, stirring frequently, till the water has evaporated.

Turn off heat. Cover wok and let it rest.

Garnish each serving with half a teaspoon each of shredded coconut, chopped coriander, chopped raw onion and with a lemon wedge on the side.

Serve warm or at room temperature.

## The Impromptu Tea Party Aboard the Deccan Queen

Every summer from 1934 till 1939, my younger sister Sarasa and I would spend several weeks during the school summer holidays with our uncle, my father's younger brother Ramaswamy, and his wife Rukmini, who lived in the suburb of Dadar in Bombay. Because of where they lived, we called him 'Bombay Chitappa' and her 'Bombay Chitti'.

Bombay Chitappa was a tall, handsome man, and to my young mind, he resembled a film star. As a senior executive in the marketing department of Volkart Brothers, he frequently went to Europe on work, and at that time, he was the only relative I knew who travelled back and forth from Bombay to Switzerland, Germany, Italy and England. He returned home from his trips with gifts of chiffon material, European cheeses, chocolates, wine and marzipan paste, which was the special ingredient in a rice payasam (milk pudding) my aunt made.

Bombay Chitappa was indulgent as an uncle. Rarely did he deny any request of ours, whether it was a weekend stay in the hill station of Matheran where one of the sports was pony-riding, a trip to the Karla caves near Lonavla, a day out at the Vajreshwari hot springs, or an evening stroll on the Juhu beach, culminating with a stop for ice cream. Sarasa and I looked forward to our holidays in Bombay. My elder sister Kamala often stayed behind in Poona to spend time with her group of friends, and my younger sisters Leelu and Kalyani were a little too young to travel without my mother.

My father would see Sarasa, a six-year-old and me, an eight-year-old, seated in our compartment of the Deccan Queen at the Poona railway station and request a couple of adult fellow passengers to keep an eye on us. Then he would leave. Bombay Chitappa usually met our train at Dadar station and took us home in a horse-drawn Victoria. We preferred the ride in the Victoria listening to the measured 'tlot-tlot' accompanying us to driving home in his car.

Part of the excitement of the Bombay holiday for me at this young age was the adventure of travelling unescorted from Poona on the Deccan Queen, a fast commuter train between Poona and Bombay, not to mention the feeling of being grown-up with the responsibility of 'taking care' of a younger sibling. This sense of responsibility continued through our college days when, in 1947, Sarasa also joined Queen Mary's College in Madras, and the two of us remained close even after we were married. Sarasa lived in Bombay, but would spend a few weeks every summer with me in Bangalore after Chamu and I moved from Delhi.

The journey from Poona to Bombay lasted about three hours, as the train went puffing up and across the hilly ranges of the Western Ghats. The landscape of the Sahyadri Ranges was magnificent and awe-inspiring. The sheer cliffs, green with tropical rainforests, fell steeply away from the train track. All we could see from the train windows was the canopy of trees and glimpses of misty ravines and shimmering waterfalls. Frequently, the train entered a tunnel with a sharp, long hoot, and the entire compartment with many holidaying youngsters would let out excited screams.

There were very few stops on this train journey. As the train steamed into Karjat, a small station in the ghat section, tribal girls and boys rushed towards us selling small leaf cups of black karvand hill berries (*Carissa congesta*). All transactions took place through the compartment windows, watched by the langur monkeys hanging about the station platforms, their youngsters clinging to the mothers' bellies. On more than one occasion we lost all the fruit with us to the langurs, who would pounce at the critical moment with a shrill screech and grab the leaf cups of fruit from our hands. The attack was so sudden that there was no way we could be prepared for it.

As soon as our train steamed out of Poona station, Sarasa and I

*The Deccan Queen snaking its way through the picturesque Western Ghats, shown here entering a tunnel in the ghats with a steep slope on one side*

eagerly awaited the first stop for the local delicacies that were sold on the platform—the sweet, crunchy bars of sesame, coconut and peanut chikki (brittle), and packets of chiwda (flavourful fried mixture of lentils and rice flakes) with lots of raisins, cashews, peanuts and roasted coconut slivers. Packets of dates and dried mango pulp were a treat. We ate all the way to Bombay. The train ride was one delicious tea party for the two of us.

Chandru, our cousin who was a student at the J.J. School of Art, came to receive us at the train station, once, in a horse-drawn Victoria. He knew of our craze for movies and movie stars. We really did not know how often he went to the movies or what his preferences were. But this time he surprised us with, 'Do you want to see Nargis? She lives in a building on our way home.' Nargis was one of the most romantic and beautiful stars in the Bombay film world. An aura of mysterious tragedy made her even more beautiful. Chandru instructed the coachman to stop the Victoria outside a modest building, and we joined a group of bystanders on the street who were all waiting patiently, looking up at a first-floor balcony. It seemed unlikely that such a famous movie star would grant us a 'darshan', but Chandru was pretty certain he had seen her there before. As though to save him from embarrassment, a slim, elegant, almost ethereal young woman dressed in white appeared briefly at the balcony. Some young men in the crowd threw flowers and whistled when they spotted her. Nargis was truly beautiful.

Later, Bombay Chitti wondered why we were delayed. Was the train running late or worse still, was there an accident on the way? Chandru kept his counsel.

It was tiffin time when we reached home and Chitti treated us to batata poha, a Bombay delicacy of beaten rice flakes with boiled potatoes dressed in fresh herbs. And to wash it down, we drank several glasses of freshly churned buttermilk tempered with crushed ginger and asafoetida. She was surprised at our small appetites, but Sarasa and I kept mum about the party on the train.

# BATATA POHA, *flattened rice flakes cooked moist with herbed potatoes, easy and quick to prepare, light on the stomach and low on calories, it comes in handy for breakfast or afternoon tiffin. Can be refrigerated for a day, reheated and served again the next day.*

## INGREDIENTS TO MAKE 4 SERVINGS

* 2 cups poha (flattened rice flakes, the thick variety)
* 1 teaspoon coriander seeds
* 4 tablespoons oil
* ½ teaspoon black mustard seeds
* 1 teaspoon chana dal
* 10 cashew nut halves
* 2 medium onions, finely diced
* 10 curry leaves, torn in pieces
* 1 tablespoon fresh ginger, minced
* ½ teaspoon turmeric powder
* 2 medium potatoes, peeled, cubed (small) and soft-boiled
* ½ cup shelled and blanched peas, fresh or frozen
* 3 green chillies (any variety), slit lengthwise and diced
* ½ cup loosely packed, fresh coriander leaves with tender stems, roughly chopped
* ½ teaspoon sugar
* ¼ cup roasted peanuts, coarsely crushed
* ¼ cup grated coconut, fresh or frozen
* juice of half a lime
* salt to taste

## METHOD

Rinse rice flakes in cold water, drain and soak in water for less than one minute. Squeeze out water, break the lumps with a fork, and set aside in a bowl. Flakes should be moist but not soggy.

Coarsely grind the coriander seeds in a spice grinder and add to the contents of the bowl. You could also pound the seeds in a mortar and pestle. Heat the oil in a wok on medium heat, but not to smoking point. Add mustard seeds, and when they start popping, add chana dal and cashew nuts. Stir and roast till they change colour slightly.

Stir in the onions, curry leaves, ginger and turmeric powder and sauté till onions turn translucent. Add potatoes, peas, chillies, coriander leaves, salt and sugar. Toss to mix, taking care not to mash the potatoes.

Turn the stove to medium low. Add the rice flakes to the wok, drizzle the lime juice and toss, lifting from the bottom up till the flakes are well coated with the vegetables and herbs. Turn off the heat. Garnish with the peanuts and coconut.

Fluff up with a fork and serve warm or at room temperature.

# TANGY, COOL BUTTERMILK

## INGREDIENTS FOR 4 CUPS

* 1 cup yogurt
* 3 cups water
* salt to taste
* ½-inch piece fresh ginger, minced
* ⅛ teaspoon asafoetida powder
* a few mint leaves to garnish each serving

## METHOD

Whisk all the ingredients together, except the mint leaves.

Chill and serve with a mint leaf or two in each glass.

In the midst of our hectic school life, my parents as well as my uncles and aunts encouraged all of us children in the performing arts. Music, dance, drama and recitation filled our growing years with joy. We were a family musical theatre group and we put up plays at home and at short notice, usually during the summer vacation when we spent time in Bombay with Bombay Chitappa and Chitti.

*Father (middle) with his brothers,
(L) Natesan and (R) Ramaswamy*

Fifteen of us, four cousins who lived in Bombay, Sarasa and myself from Poona and nine of our friends from the neighbourhood in Dadar, were cast in every performance. Tall and lanky, I was cast as the good and noble prince Rama or the blind and bearded king Dasharatha in our stage production of the Ramayana. At other times, I played the wicked witch or the equally wicked stepmother in *Rapunzel* and *Cinderella*. My younger sister Sarasa, petite with light curly hair, played Sita, Snow White or Cinderella. One friend of mine, who was tall, heavy and threatening in her gait, had no other role to play except that of the demon king Ravana, and with her face, arms and legs smeared with black paste and circles of red around the eyes, she looked evil and even more threatening on stage. We grew up with the belief that Ravana had no redeeming qualities.

Kamala, my older sister, a trained professional violinist, along with our cousin Chandru, who at that time was an art student at the Bombay J.J. School of Art, worked tirelessly behind the scenes to make the plays a success. They were the scriptwriters, directors and producers. Chandru created posters, with the photographs of the 'stars', to be distributed to the audience comprising our family, friends and neighbours. Kamala was the choreographer, costumier, make-up artist and music in-charge. Suitable parts were decided upon for each one of the fifteen cousins and friends, and we were given a week's time for the first rehearsal. The entire production was executed on a very tight budget, with a small donation from my father and Chitappa.

*Rukka standing in the middle while staging Oscar Wilde's play,*
The Importance of Being Earnest

The enclosed balcony at the entrance to Chitappa's house was the workshop where the rehearsals were held. A section of the adjoining formal living room, the hall in my uncle's home, was the stage, and the rest of the space in the living room was arranged for the audience. Kamala worked feverishly, cutting, pasting and decorating. For weeks in advance, we collected brown paper, coloured paper, ribbons, crêpe paper, balloons, tinsel, cardboard, odd lengths of cloth, bamboo

*Sita's swayamvar in the Ramayana*

poles, and paper flowers, and Kamala would transform all of these into glittering crowns, bracelets, tiaras, wands, sceptres, necklaces, waistbands, garlands and costumes. Our everyday shoes covered with gold and silver foil were transformed to be worthy of the royalty we were for the evening.

Chandru spent days and nights painting screens and building elaborate sets. We would all be roped in to help him. Our younger cousins were deputed to bring branches of trees for the 'onstage' forest. On one occasion, my Bombay Chitappa had to intervene when a neighbour complained that some boys had gone on the rampage and his garden had been denuded. That unfortunate incident taught us to substitute the real branches with painted cardboard cut-outs that were held on the stage by younger friends who had no other role in the plays. The 'stage' was built of wooden benches of uneven height, loaned to us by various neighbours, and treading on them was a skill we acquired over time, although Chandru did his best to minimize the disparity in height. Separating the stage from the audience was an improvised curtain of white bedlinen.

Rehearsals were taken very seriously. My sister Sarasa, a very enthusiastic performer, would often appear on stage before her cue. In the key scene of the Ramayana, where Rama bends and breaks the unstringable bow and wins Sita's hand in marriage, Sarasa as Sita would run onto the stage and fling a garland around my neck, her Rama for the evening, symbolizing his victory over all the other suitors, well before I had even begun the arduous task of lifting the giant bow! She had to be told repeatedly to be patient. Subduing our younger friends playing the roles of the devoted army of monkeys was a no-win situation for Kamala, who would instruct them sternly to wait, crouching beneath the stage, until their cue was given. Frequently, her instructions went unheeded, and the audience would break into laughter when the scene called for serious reflection.

There was always an audience of about twenty admiring family members and friends who filled the living room to capacity. During the interval and between the acts, Bombay Chitti and Amma, with help from their friends, served delicious tiffin. We actors had to wait until the play was over to sample the delights that came from the kitchen: flaky pea samosas dipped in a sweet and sour chutney; sojji halwa, seductively soft semolina fudge; idada, white-speckled, steamed lentil cakes; thayir vadai, tart and spongy savoury lentil doughnuts swimming in a pool of aromatic yogurt sauce; vegetable upma; and in summer, slices of sweet, flavorful alphonso mangoes, the prized fruit of the Ratnagiri region in Maharashtra. And at the end of the perfect day, my father would treat us all to marzipan from the exclusive Italian bakery Monginis in downtown Bombay.

# DELHI-STYLE PEA SAMOSAS, *curried, herb-scented peas in a crisp and flaky fried pastry cone.*

Once, my mother's friend Manju from Delhi happened to be in Bombay the day we performed, and she came over with samosas she had made. Her recipe is one of our family favourites.

Samosas are an all-India favourite too. I know of colleagues at the Delhi School of Economics who made a meal of them. They drove straight to a snack joint in Kashmiri Gate every evening for a plate of samosas. It certainly was an addiction!

The potato-filled cones can be made and frozen 2–3 weeks ahead. Leave them to thaw at room temperature for 15 minutes before frying. When I am strapped for time to make the dough, I use filo sheets for the shell which saves me precious minutes. Wonton wrappers are also good.

## INGREDIENTS TO MAKE THE PASTRY DOUGH FOR 30 SHELLS

* *1½ cups flour, divided (I use half wholewheat and half all-purpose flour)*
* *1 teaspoon salt*
* *4 tablespoons melted unsalted butter or warm oil*
* *1 tablespoon plain yogurt*
* *5–6 tablespoons cold water*
* *2 teaspoons cornstarch, for later use, to seal cone wrappers*
* *2 cups oil, for frying the samosas*

## METHOD TO MIX THE DOUGH FOR THE PASTRY SHELL

Sift 1 cup of flour and salt into a bowl.

Pour in the melted butter and mix to a crumbly pea-like mixture, pressing the fat against the flour. Add yogurt and a little water, if needed, and mix to a stiff dough.

Transfer the dough to the work-board and knead well.

Wrap the dough in plastic and refrigerate, while you prepare the filling.

## INGREDIENTS TO MAKE THE FILLING

* *1 cup shelled green peas, boiled soft and drained*
* *3 medium potatoes, boiled and peeled*
* *2 tablespoons oil*
* *½ cup carrots, finely chopped*
* *1 teaspoon cumin seeds*
* *1 teaspoon coriander seeds, coarsely crushed*
* *1 teaspoon minced ginger*
* *1 teaspoon red chilli powder*
* *1 teaspoon garam masala powder*
* *1 cup fresh coriander leaves with tender stems, finely chopped*

- *10–12 fresh mint leaves, finely chopped (optional)*
- *1 teaspoon lime juice*
- *salt to taste*

## METHOD TO MAKE THE FILLING

Coarsely mash the potatoes and peas together, leaving a few chunks of potatoes. Set aside.

Warm 2 tablespoons oil in a wok on medium heat. Add the carrots and stir-fry for 2 minutes.

Toss in cumin and coriander seeds. Stir once.

Lower the heat and add the mashed potatoes and peas, and all the other ingredients. Fold all the ingredients to combine well, and cook for 1 minute.

Add salt to taste and transfer to a bowl. Set aside to cool.

## METHOD TO MAKE THE SAMOSAS

Take out the bowl of dough from the refrigerator and let it rest on the work-board for 10 minutes. Knead the dough a couple of times, and divide into 3 equal parts. Roll each part into a ball and keep covered.

Combine the cornstarch with a little water in a bowl to make a thin paste.

Dust the work-board lightly with flour, place one ball of dough on it and roll it with the fingers of both your hands into an inch-thick rope. Cut the rope into 5 equal parts.

Roll each part into a smooth ball, cover with a damp kitchen towel, and set aside.

Take one ball at a time and, on a lightly floured board, roll into a 5-inch disc with a rolling pin. Cut each disc in half. Each half will make a samosa cone.

Take half a disc at a time, moisten the semicircular edge with a little of the cornstarch paste and seal well, placing one half of the edge over the other. You now have a cone-shaped wrapper with one open side.

Fill the cone through the open side with 1 heaped tablespoon of the vegetable mix.

Seal with a smear of the cornstarch paste, pressing down firmly.

Make and fill 5 cones at a time. Keep them covered with a kitchen cloth.

Heat 2 cups oil in a wok or 3-quart saucepan on medium-high heat.

Reduce the heat to medium and fry 5 cones at a time for 2–3 minutes to a crisp golden-brown, turning them over with a slotted spoon.

Drain the fried samosas in a colander lined with paper towels.

Lower the heat further, and make and stuff 5 more cones.

Raise the heat to medium and fry them. Drain and add them to the samosas in the colander.

Repeat the process with the remaining balls of dough.

Samosas are best eaten hot.

If the edges of the wrapper are not sealed firmly, the samosas can open up when they are being fried, and the oil will seep in, making them soggy. Oily, soggy samosas are a disaster.

Using wonton wrappers saves time. Working with one wrapper at a time, while you keep the remaining wrappers covered with a damp kitchen towel, place 1 heaped tablespoon of the potato mix either diagonally or horizontally, covering half the space. Brush the edges with the cornstarch paste and seal them firmly. Make 5 samosas at a time and fry them following the instructions given above.

If you are using filo dough to make the samosas, spread melted butter on a sheet, place 3 sheets, each spread with butter, one over the other, and cut in 2-inch squares. Place the potato-pea filling on one half of the square, fold with the other half, seal the edges firmly with the cornstarch paste, and deep-fry or bake in an oven at 350°F for about 5 minutes or till they are brown. These will be rectangular in shape.

I have further cut the making time by lining a greased baking dish with 3 layers of filo sheets buttered as above, spreading a layer of potato filling and topping it over with 3 more buttered filo sheets and baking for 3 minutes in an oven at 350 degrees. When the filo sheets turn a very pale cream colour and are still soft, I remove the baking dish from the oven, cut the layers in 2-inch squares, replace in oven, and bake till golden-brown, about 3 minutes. I keep a close watch to see that they do not burn.

## RAISIN-TAMARIND CHUTNEY, *sweet and tart, this easy-to-make relish lures you into eating more samosas. The leftover chutney makes a tangy sandwich spread.*

### INGREDIENTS TO MAKE APPROXIMATELY 1 CUP

* 2½ cups tamarind juice
* ½ cup brown sugar or grated jaggery
* 1 teaspoon cumin seeds, lightly toasted
* 3 tablespoons raisins
* 1 teaspoon red chilli powder
* 6 pitted dates, chopped coarse
* salt to taste

### METHOD

To extract the tamarind juice, soak an apricot-size ball of tamarind in 2 cups warm water. Let it rest for 10 minutes and then, with your fingers, squeeze the pulp in the water. Pass through a strainer to remove fibres.

Now, boil the tamarind juice in a deep pan on medium heat. Add the remaining ingredients, and stir till the juice thickens to a sauce. It would take about 10 minutes.

Transfer to a blender and grind to a smooth texture. Set aside in a bowl to cool.

*EASY SOJJI HALWA, also known as sheera in Maharashtra and kesari bhath in Karnataka. This warm, divinely aromatic, soft semolina pudding, more like a sweet polenta, continues to be the favoured sweet tiffin in my family. Sojji halwa is literally divine, since my mother would frequently cook it as an offering to her favourite deity.*

Little did I know as a ten-year-old that decades later, after I was married, I would make sojji halwa at least twice a week for my family. My spouse Chamu would ask with his disarming smile, 'Rukka, would it be too much of a bother to make sojji halwa?' He would eat maybe a couple of teaspoons of the halwa, but it was his favourite. A colleague of Chamu's and a friend of the family, Professor I.P. Desai, liked it too. Whenever he stayed at our house in Delhi, he preferred a breakfast of sheera (sojji halwa) and chapattis (wheat flatbread). He firmly believed he had devised a breakfast combination which had kept him healthy for decades.

## INGREDIENTS TO MAKE 4–6 SERVINGS

- ½ cup ghee, divided
- 6 unsalted cashew nuts, broken in halves
- 1 tablespoon seedless raisins
- 1 cup fine sooji (semolina / farina / regular cream of wheat)
- 2 cloves
- ½ cup water mixed with 1 cup milk
- ¾ cup sugar
- 1 teaspoon cardamom, powdered
- pinch of saffron strands soaked in 2 teaspoons milk
- 2 tablespoons honey

Friends from England and America prefer the halwa a little less sweet.

## METHOD

Warm up 2 tablespoons ghee in a wok or 2-quart heavy pan on medium heat.

Add the cashew nut pieces and raisins, and fry till cashews turn light brown and the raisins plump up. Drain with a slotted spoon and set aside in a bowl.

Add 2 tablespoons ghee to the wok. Add the cloves and sooji. Roast the sooji for 2 minutes while stirring continuously.

Lower the heat to medium low and, to the roasted sooji, add the water and milk mixture in a steady stream. While pouring the liquid, stir with the other hand to prevent lumps from forming.

Raise the heat to medium and cook the sooji by softly lifting from the bottom up to prevent burning.

Cook till all the liquid is absorbed and the sooji grains are swollen and soft.

Add the remaining 4 tablespoons ghee and sugar. Stir to prevent burning and cook for about 10 minutes or till the sugar syrup is absorbed.

Combine the cardamom powder, roasted cashew nuts and raisins with the cooked sooji.

Blend the saffron milk and honey into the sooji. Fold through a couple of times and remove from the stove. Transfer to a serving bowl.

Best served warm.

Can be refrigerated for 3-4 days, reheated and served.

Balls of halwa scooped out with an ice cream scoop and rolled over a platter of toasted melon seeds have an interesting crunch.

*Sojji halwa can be made in a jiffy; can also be refrigerated, reheated and served.*

## JYOTSNA'S IDADA (WHITE DHOKLA), *soft and airy steamed cakes of ground rice and lentil batter are not only a popular snack in many homes in Gujarat and Maharashtra, but also a tasty side dish for a meal.*

My Bombay aunt Rukmini and her Gujarati neighbour and friend Jyotsna Ben were in a cosy 'food exchange' relationship. Both Jyotsna and her husband Mr Mehta welcomed south Indian delicacies like dosai, vegetable upma and Mysore pak.

Jyotsna Ben cooked idada every morning for her family. Mr Mehta, a textile factory owner, had been raised on his mother's idada for breakfast, and Jyotsna was happy to continue the tradition. Occasionally, she would send a few cubes across, and my cousins and I craved for more of the spongy, tart savoury delicacy.

Although the basic ingredients are the same as for the popular south Indian rice idli, the addition of black pepper and herbs makes a difference.

You will need an idli steamer with a lid, and fitted with a stand to hold the inner plates. You could use a double boiler which can hold an inner plate with a rim and a lid, or you could use a poaching dish for steaming the idada.

### INGREDIENTS TO MAKE 6 SERVINGS

- 1½ cups rice
- ½ cup urad dal
- 1 teaspoon salt
- 2 green chillies
- ¼ cup coriander leaves with tender stems, chopped
- ½-inch piece fresh ginger
- ½ teaspoon cracked black pepper
- ½ teaspoon asafoetida powder

- *4 tablespoons sour yogurt*
- *1 teaspoon soda bicarbonate*
- *1 tablespoon oil, to grease the steamer cups*
- *water to grind*

## METHOD TO MAKE THE BATTER

Wash and rinse the rice and dal together. Drain the water. Repeat till the water is clear and not cloudy. Soak in lukewarm water for four hours.

Grind the rice and dal together in a blender to a coarse batter of dropping consistency, adding a little water at a time. Start with a cup of water. Occasionally stop the blender to push down the batter from the sides with a spatula, and start grinding again.

Empty the batter into a large bowl. Stir in the salt and yogurt.

## METHOD TO STEAM THE IDADA

Make a coarse paste of the green chillies, coriander leaves and ginger, and add to the batter. Shake in the black pepper and asafoetida powder.

Grease the cups or the plate that will hold the batter, and set aside.

Set the steamer on medium-high heat. Pour water in the lower pan to a depth of 2 inches. Bring the water to a boil.

Combine the soda bicarbonate into the batter and whisk briskly to a froth.

Spoon the batter immediately into the greased cups or the plate with a rim, filling them ¾ th, and place the stand with the cups into the pan of boiling water.

Cover and steam for 5 minutes. Test by inserting a toothpick, which should come out clean.

Turn off the stove, remove the lid and gently lift the containers with the cooked idada.

Let them rest for 2 minutes on the kitchen counter. Ease the edges of the steamed idada with the wet blunt edge of a knife or spatula. Transfer them to a serving dish. Keep covered with a moist kitchen towel.

If you have used a plate instead of cups to steam the batter, ease the edges and invert the plate onto a larger platter, tap on the top to ease the steamed idada. It will drop.

Let it rest for 2 minutes.

Cut into 1-inch squares and transfer to a serving dish.

## INGREDIENTS FOR THE TEMPERING

- *1 tablespoon oil*
- *¼ teaspoon brown mustard seeds*

## METHOD

Warm up 1 tablespoon oil in a small pan on medium heat. Add the mustard seeds, and when they pop, drizzle the oil with the mustard seeds over the idada pieces.

Best served warm or at room temperature. Serve with a coconut-tomato chutney or store-bought sweet and sour mango chunda (grated mango in a spicy sugar syrup).

Leftover idada pieces can be refrigerated for 2 days, warmed in a microwave and served.

## COCONUT TOMATO CHUTNEY, *when tomatoes were in season, Amma used them for that extra colour and taste.*

### INGREDIENTS TO MAKE 1 CUP OF CHUTNEY

* *2 tablespoons oil*
* *½ medium-sized onion, coarsely chopped*
* *1 green chilli, any variety, broken in half*
* *½-inch piece fresh ginger, chopped*
* *1 medium ripe tomato, chopped*
* *¼ cup grated coconut, fresh or frozen*
* *½ teaspoon salt*
* *½ cup mint leaves, finely chopped*

### METHOD

Heat the oil in a wok on medium heat. Add the chopped onion. Stir and cook for 1 minute.

Add the green chilli, ginger and chopped tomatoes, and stir for one minute. Turn off the stove. Cover the wok and let the ingredients rest for a minute or two. Transfer the ingredients to a blender.

Add the coconut, salt and enough water to grind to a smooth consistency.

Transfer the chutney to a serving bowl. Garnish with chopped mint leaves.

## TANGY THAYIR VADAI, *spongy, soft, savoury ground lentil doughnuts, oozing with aromatic yogurt sauce.*

Shape the vadais in the palm of your hand or get yourself a vadai-making press, available in Indian stores.

For me, spooned-out batter balls, that are called bondas, after they are fried and soaked in yogurt sauce, taste equally good and take less time to make.

## INGREDIENTS TO MAKE THE BATTER FOR 15-20 VADAIS

- ❀ *1 cup urad dal*
- ❀ *2 green chillies*
- ❀ *½-inch piece ginger*
- ❀ *¼ cup water; use as much as you need*
- ❀ *1 teaspoon salt*
- ❀ *½ teaspoon soda bicarbonate*
- ❀ *1½ cups oil, to fry the vadais*

## METHOD TO MAKE THE BATTER

Wash and rinse the urad dal, then drain the water. Repeat till the water is clear. Soak the dal in 3 cups water for 2 hours. Drain.

Grind the dal in a blender to a satiny smooth batter of dropping consistency, adding the green chillies, ginger and water, 1 tablespoon at a time. You may not need all the water.

Transfer to a bowl, add salt, mix well, and set aside, covered, while you make the sauce.

## INGREDIENTS TO MAKE 3 CUPS OF YOGURT SAUCE

- ❀ *¼ cup shredded coconut, fresh or frozen*
- ❀ *2 green chillies*
- ❀ *½ teaspoon salt*
- ❀ *½ cup buttermilk*
- ❀ *2 cups plain yogurt*
- ❀ *½ cup water*

## METHOD TO MAKE YOGURT SAUCE

In a blender, grind the coconut and green chillies to a smooth paste, adding salt and water.

Empty the paste into a large shallow bowl, scraping the sides of the blender with a spatula.

Combine the buttermilk and yogurt with the contents in the bowl.

Whisk and mix well. Set aside.

## INGREDIENTS FOR THE TEMPERING AND GARNISHING OF THE SAUCE

- ❀ *1 teaspoon oil*
- ❀ *1 teaspoon brown mustard seeds*
- ❀ *6 curry leaves, torn in pieces*
- ❀ *¼ cup fresh coriander leaves, chopped and set aside for later use*

* ¼ *cup grated carrots (optional)*

## METHOD FOR TEMPERING AND GARNISHING OF YOGURT SAUCE

Warm up 1 teaspoon oil in a small wok or pan on medium heat. Add the mustard seeds, and when they splutter and pop, turn off the stove.

Stir in the curry leaves which will crackle and flavour the oil.

Empty this oil into the bowl of yogurt, and stir to mix.

## METHOD TO MAKE THE VADAIS

You will need a bowl of hot water and the tempered yogurt sauce handy, not too far from the stove. You will also need 2 slotted spoons and a wooden spatula.

Heat the oil in a wok or fryer on medium heat.

Add the soda bicarbonate to the batter and stir briskly.

Test if the oil is ready by dropping a teaspoon of batter into the oil. The blob of batter should swell with a sizzle and rise to the surface.

Take 1 tablespoon of batter and gently slide it into the oil with the aid of another spoon.

Slide in 6 for each batch.

Fry evenly to a light brown, turning over a couple of times with a slotted spoon.

Drain and immediately drop the vadais into the bowl of hot water. Let them rest for a minute.

Remove each vadai with a slotted spoon, and with a wooden spatula, gently press to squeeze out the water, but do not flatten the vadai.

Drop the pressed vadai into the yogurt sauce, spooning the sauce over to submerge it.

Repeat this process of draining and soaking in the yogurt sauce for all 6 vadais.

Fry several batches, briefly soak the vadais in hot water first, press the water out and then drop them in the bowl of yogurt sauce.

If the bowl becomes too crowded, transfer the soaked vadais to a serving platter, taking care to see that they don't fall apart. Pour a little of the spiced yogurt sauce over the vadais.

When all the vadais are transferred to the serving platter, garnish with chopped coriander and grated carrots, if you are using the latter.

# Pound Day at St Helena's School

As mentioned earlier, between the years 1932 and 1939, my sisters, Kamala, Sarasa and Leelu, and I studied for a couple of years at St Mary's School, and later, for a little over four years at St Helena's School, both in Poona. I remember Father telling me that St Mary's School was founded some time in the 1860s, and that it was one of the two best schools in the city. It was an Anglican school founded specifically for the education of the daughters of British Army officers stationed in Poona. Though my father was very satisfied with the education his children received and we sisters were all very happy in the school, in a couple of years he admitted all four of us to St Helena's School because he could not afford the high school fees, as Indian children had to pay double the fees charged from British children in St Mary's.

St Helena's, along with St Mary's, was rated one of the two best schools in the city. The school was founded as an Anglo-Indian educational institution for girls in the year 1907 by Susie Sorabji, after whom the street on which the school is located is named, and as I learnt later, the school gets its name from its principal donor, Helen Gold from Canada. St Helena's School, on Susie Sorabji Road, was within walking distance from our home in Saraswath Colony and a short distance away from the offices of the Southern Command where Appa worked. Occasionally, my sisters and I had a lunch of hot soup, mini sandwiches and pudding with Appa in his office dining room. I think transferring to St Helena's was good for more than one reason. I made friends across communities, languages, castes, religions and cultures. Secondly, as I said, the school was within walking distance from our home in Saraswath Colony and several children in our neighbourhood studied in the same school, so my mother felt comfortable to know that we were in a group while walking to and from school. Thirdly, my sisters and I loved the snacks, hot soups and entrées we ate for lunch at Appa's office canteen.

The entrance gate to our school was guarded by a 'darban', a tall, well-built ex-service man whose sole duty, it seemed to me, was to close the gates on students who arrived a few minutes late for school. He was lenient with younger children and would let them sneak in. If I did manage to soften the old codger and race to my classroom through the long corridor, I would most definitely run into the vice-principal who would haul me up to the principal's office, where it was comforting to find some of my friends already there. I was not alone. The punishment meted out to latecomers was one of the two choices: to stay behind for an hour after school on a Friday and help out either in the school library or in the garden. In practice, as we found out, there was no choice for the defaulter; the principal's secretary handed each of us a slip with a date and 'library' or 'garden' stamped on it.

What I came to admire about St Helena's were the 'special days' in a year set aside for charity. I remember the Pound Day celebrations, when every student was required to donate a pound of a dry food ingredient. During the time allotted to each class, we would go with our class teacher to the principal's office where each one deposited her food packet and collected a 'thank you' note for our parents. The recipients of our gifts were the children of a local orphanage.

Though the observance of Pound Day was meant to teach us the joys of giving and sharing, it turned out to be more of a competition among the students vying with one another to be noticed by their peers for their special donation. A bar of chocolate or a box of halwa was worthy of attention; a pound of rice was sneered at. As soon as we received the notice from the school requesting contributions for the Pound Day, Sarasa and I would start working on our parents to give us something other than rice. And so it was that I always contributed a ribboned box of a pound of Darjeeling tea, and Sarasa a pound of sugar. On the walk to school, there would be much discussion amongst the students about the food each one had brought. 'What did you bring?' was the question on everyone's lips. Some seniors would try and exchange their modest contributions with younger students who had brought brightly packaged boxes of caramel toffee or imported canned food.

Pound Day at St Helena's was special for another reason. On this day, the primary, middle and senior school students and their teachers shared lunch in the lunch pavilion, and Amma always cooked something special. She would send a stack of wholewheat masala parathas, and peas and corn usal (warm spicy salad).

## POUND DAY MASALA PARATHA, *aromatic, griddle-cooked wholewheat flour flatbread.*

### INGREDIENTS TO MAKE 10 PARATHAS

* 2½ cups wholewheat flour, divided
* 1 teaspoon turmeric powder
* 1 teaspoon salt
* 3 green chillies, any variety
* 2 cloves garlic
* 1 tablespoon ginger, finely grated
* ½ cup loosely packed fresh coriander, finely chopped
* ¼ cup plain yogurt
* water, to mix the flour
* 3 tablespoons oil
* ½ cup melted ghee

## METHOD TO MIX DOUGH

Sift 2 cups of flour with the turmeric powder and salt.

Grind green chillies, garlic, ginger and chopped coriander to a fine paste, adding water. Add the paste to the sifted flour in the bowl.

Add yogurt and knead to a soft dough. If needed, add a little more water and knead. Transfer the ball of dough to a work-board.

Add the oil, 1 tablespoon at a time, and knead to incorporate all the oil into the dough. Transfer the dough back to the bowl, cover with a damp cloth, and let it rest for 10 minutes.

## METHOD TO MAKE THE PARATHAS

Transfer the dough to the work-table, knead and roll into a rope with your fingers. Divide the dough equally into 10 portions and roll into balls. Keep covered in a bowl.

Roll one ball of dough at a time into a 6-inch disc, dusting a little flour if needed. Brush with ghee. Sprinkle 1 teaspoon of flour evenly over the greased side. Fold to make a semicircle. Fold again to make a triangle.

Repeat with the remaining balls of dough. Set the triangles aside, covered, in a bowl. Dust more flour on the board, and with a rolling pin, roll 4 triangles at a time, as thin as you can while maintaining the shape. Keep them covered with a kitchen towel.

Heat a heavy skillet or wrought iron griddle on medium heat.

Cook one side of the paratha till mottled with pale brown spots. Brush the uncooked side with ghee and flip over with a spatula. Cook this side till mottled.

Brush with ghee and remove from griddle. Transfer to a flat dish.

Cook the remaining parathas.

Lower the heat while you roll out the next batch of 4 parathas. Continue cooking as before.

# PEAS AND CORN USAL, *a warm, spicy salad garnished with shredded coconut.*

## INGREDIENTS TO MAKE 6 SERVINGS

* **5 cups water**
* **1 teaspoon salt**
* **4 cups shelled green peas, fresh or frozen**
* **2 cups corn niblets, fresh or frozen**
* **2 green chillies, slit lengthwise; more, if you prefer it spicier**
* **1 cup loosely packed fresh coriander leaves with tender stems, chopped**
* **1 tablespoon lime juice**

- *2 medium tomatoes, sliced thin*
- *½ cup shredded coconut*
- *½ teaspoon garam masala powder (optional)*

METHOD

Boil the water in a deep pan on medium heat. Add salt, peas, corn niblets and green chillies. Stir once and cook for 2 minutes. Turn off the stove.

Drain and transfer to a bowl. While still warm, add coriander leaves, lime juice, tomatoes, shredded coconut and garam masala, if you are using it. Toss to mix well.

Serve warm or at room temperature with parathas.

Stays fresh when refrigerated. Warm up and serve as a stand-alone snack too.

*Fun and Fasting with Annam Athai*

My school vacations were punctuated either by visits to my uncles' homes in Bombay or Tanjore, or visits from relatives with their children to our home. My sisters and I looked forward to this gathering of the extended family, when our modest home overflowed with much cheer and with people who loved to tell stories, cook, eat and laugh together. We would hear of quixotic uncles whose sole purpose in life was to follow the 'good life', and crazy aunts who today would have been diagnosed with advanced dementia but were 'master chefs'. 'Do you remember…?' and that leading question from an aunt would yield hours of discussion among the adults over ingredients that were used, the method of cooking, or the combination of vegetables that they had eaten, perhaps several decades earlier. Many other players long passed away would be resurrected and the family genealogical tree would come alive.

There was none other with a greater memory for culinary gossip or the capacity to tell a story with interesting frills than my father's youngest sister Annapoorni, who, when I first met her in our home in Poona, may have been in her mid-twenties, married and with two children at that time. We called her Annam Athai. Annam Athai was short and plump with curly hair twisted into a bun at the nape of her neck. Her disproportionately broad forehead was adorned with a bright vermilion disc, 'a kumkuma pottu', between her eyebrows. She had a wide smile and a hearty laugh that rang through the entire house.

Annam Athai was a repository of many traditional folk songs that were long forgotten or not in fashion: folk songs that celebrated the festivals, the birth of a child, the coming of age for a girl; bawdy songs sung in chorus during weddings, and mournful dirges for the loss of a dear one. Writing about her brings back fond memories of spending happy times with her.

Annam Athai observed all the feasts and fasts of the Hindu calendar, including fasts for the new moon, full moon, solar and lunar eclipses, Mondays, Thursdays and Saturdays, and the many festivals. With India gaining independence in 1947, she added Republic Day, Independence Day and Gandhiji's birthday to her list of fasts and feasts. Athai was a one-woman show of mythological narratives of gods, goddesses, demons and spirits to mark the days when she observed a fast. She added the many stories of Gandhiji's life and his heroic struggle to win independence for India to her repertoire. I was never tired of her stories of the Indian independence movement and listening to the rousing patriotic lyrics composed by the Tamil poet saint Bharatiyar, which she sang with great gusto.

Beginning with 1947, when my parents moved to Tanjore on Father's retirement, Annam Athai visited frequently. Appa built a spacious, two-storeyed modern bungalow, keeping in mind the fact that he and Amma were now nearer to their relatives in Tanjore district, and in Madurai where Amma's nieces and nephews lived. As was expected, many cousins, aunts and uncles visited my parents and it was then that I realized the meaning of an 'extended' family. Young adult relatives would suddenly turn up to attend official interviews for jobs and spend a couple of days as my parents' 'house guests'. Informing the hosts in advance, in this case my Appa and Amma, of their arrival was not a consideration. They were not strangers and where was the need to be formal? Sarasa and I kept count of around fifty 'relatives' who we would invariably meet on our summer vacations from Queen Mary's College.

Growing up in Poona and Jubbulpore, my social world outside the security and comfort of the presence of Amma, Appa, my sisters and brother was in my vast circle of friends. The face-to-face relationships with other immediate family members was mostly restricted to Bombay Chitappa, Dr Chitappa, Annam Athai and their respective families.

Annam Athai was a frequent guest in my parents' home in Tanjore.

And she felt free to continue to lead her life the way she was used to, mainly because Amma was not overbearing. As I said, Athai observed all the fasts and feasts of the Hindu calendar. On the days of her fast, Annam Athai rose earlier than her usual rising time of 4.00 a.m., when the rest of the household was deep in slumber. Dressed in her nine-yard saree, standing on the platform around the well, she cleansed herself by drawing buckets of water from the well and pouring the cold water over her head. After the ritual bath, she cleaned the family puja altar, decorated each idol and picture with flowers, sandalwood paste and vermilion powder, all the while reciting shlokas (sacred verses), invoking all the deities for their continued blessings on her family and the country. She lit the bronze and silver wick lamps of varying sizes with cotton wicks soaked and floating in sesame oil or melted ghee, and waved one small silver lamp three times in a clockwise circular motion around all the deities, all the while ringing a small brass bell with her left hand. She then prostrated herself before the altar. The wafting fragrance of incense sticks moving to the music of a tinkling bell filled the house. Observing this elaborate ritual took her close to two hours.

Amma was not into observing fasts, but even on the 'no fast' other days, she would perform the puja (worship) much the same way.

During the fast, Athai ate nothing in the daylight hours except... drink several glasses of flavoured buttermilk. The buttermilk, called neer moru in Tamil, was kept in a large stone jar (kalchetty), and we children each got half a glass whenever Athai had hers. In fact, neer moru was an everyday, anytime thirst quencher in the hot summer months. A cool refreshing drink, diluted buttermilk continues to be an addiction of mine. In Tanjore, in the hot summer months, many households, including ours, distributed cool buttermilk to pedestrians from a big 'panai' (earthen pot) kept at the entrance of the house. At the creaking sound of the metal gate being opened, one of us would step out onto the front verandah, to pour one ladle of cool buttermilk into the cupped hands of a thirsty passer-by.

On the days of her fast, Athai did not join us at the everyday meal of cooked rice with vegetables and lentil curries, sauces, yogurt, pickles, salads and relishes. The food she cooked and ate during those days was less complicated to make, took little time and energy, and was light on the stomach. After sundown, Athai had a bath and put together two very tasty dishes, one savoury and the other sweet, both made from aval (flattened rice flakes). The savoury puli aval was soft, tangy and spicy, piquant with the taste of tamarind juice and spices and garnished with crispy peanuts and coconut flakes. The kesari aval, moist and sweet, tinged yellow with aromatic strands of saffron and appetizing with the strong aroma of ground cardamom, complemented the puli aval.

ATHAI'S PULI AVAL, *soft, sweet and sour, flattened rice grains with the added flavour of rasam powder was a speciality of Athai's. Mine is a time-saving version of her recipe as I use store-bought, packaged rasam powder. Athai's original recipe calls for freshly roasted and pounded spices, which undoubtedly add to the flavour of the traditional snack.*

### INGREDIENTS TO MAKE 4 SERVINGS

- 2 cups flattened rice flakes (aval), the thick variety is recommended
- 1 tablespoon black sesame seeds
- 2 tablespoons rasam powder, available in Indian grocery stores
- 1 tablespoon powdered jaggery
- ½ cup tamarind juice
- 3 tablespoons oil
- ½ teaspoon brown mustard seeds
- ½ teaspoon urad dal
- ½ teaspoon turmeric powder
- ½ teaspoon asafoetida powder
- 2 dry red chillies, broken in half
- 10 curry leaves, torn in pieces
- ½ cup loosely packed, unsweetened, dessicated coconut flakes
- ½ cup roasted peanuts, coarsely crushed (optional)
- salt to taste

### METHOD

Blend the aval coarsely in a blender or food processor. Set aside in a bowl.

Dry roast the sesame seeds in a thick-bottomed pan on medium heat until they release their essential oils. Continuous stirring prevents burning and charring of the seeds. Cool and powder coarsely in a coffee grinder. Set aside.

Mix the rasam powder, jaggery, salt and tamarind juice to form a gravy.

Bring the gravy to boil in a heavy pan on high heat. Allow the gravy to cool.

Add a little gravy to the aval in the bowl and mix well, breaking up any lumps. Add the rest of the gravy and toss. The mixed aval should be moist not soggy.

Set aside, covered, for the flavours to be absorbed, for approximately 5-7 minutes. If the mixture is too dry, sprinkle a little warm water and mix.

Heat the oil in a small pan on medium heat and add mustard seeds. As they start to pop, lower the heat, add the urad dal and stir-fry to a light brown colour.

Turn off the heat, add the turmeric and asafoetida powders, red chilli pieces and curry leaves and stir. The curry leaves will splutter, so move away from the stove after adding them. Empty this tempered oil into the aval mixture.

Fold in the coconut, sesame and peanuts, if you are using them.

Leave the bowl of aval, covered, in a cool part of the kitchen for an hour for the flavours to be absorbed. Serve with plain yogurt on the side.

To extract tamarind juice, soak a cherry-sized ball of tamarind pulp in a little over ½ cup warm water for 10 minutes. Squeeze out the juice from the softened pulp with your fingers and pass through a strainer.

## KESARI AVAL, *the easy way! Absolutely no cooking, easy to assemble, this aromatic sweet delicacy can be put together in a matter of minutes.*

### INGREDIENTS TO MAKE 4 SERVINGS

* *2 cups raw aval (the hard variety of beaten rice flakes), soaked in 3 cups of cold water for 3-5 minutes, rinsed and the water squeezed out. Fluff up with a fork.*
* *1 cup shredded coconut, frozen or fresh*
* *1 cup grated jaggery/brown sugar; ½ cup more for a sweeter taste*
* *20 unsalted cashew nut halves, roasted*
* *1 teaspoon cardamom powder*
* *1 teaspoon rose water (optional)*
* *3 tablespoons whole milk, divided*
* *few threads of saffron soaked in 1 tablespoon milk*

### METHOD

Place all the ingredients (except the milk, and rose water) in a bowl. Toss and mix gently from the bottom up, breaking all lumps.

Sprinkle the milk, saffron-infused milk and rose water, if you are using it, 1 teaspoon at a time, and mix. Set aside, covered, for ½ hour while the aval absorbs the divine flavours.

Serve at room temperature.

## Narayana's Saturday Night Bajji

Father was transferred in 1941 to Jubbulpore on a promotion to officer's grade in the Military Accounts Department. The family moved from Madras to Jubbulpore in the Central Indian Provinces, called Madhya Pradesh today, and lived there till 1944 when Appa was transferred back to Poona. The Indian political scene at the time was one of great unrest and protest. The Quit India movement, a call from Mahatma Gandhi, was reverberating throughout the country. Jubbulpore, in the Hindi belt, was in the thick of it.

Reading further, you may wonder what the connection is between my life in school and Narayana's bajjis! This is 'the rambling' I warned you about.

My sisters, Sarasa and Leelu, and I joined Christ Church Girls' High School in Jubbulpore. Though we initially did miss our old school in Poona, we soon got accustomed to our new one. Christ Church, like St Mary's and St Helena's in Poona, was a Christian Anglican educational institution for girls, so we were quite comfortable with the school culture. Wearing the school uniform was mandatory in all the schools I studied in. It inculcated a sense of discipline and community among the students; in St Helena's it was a green shift with yellow piping, black socks and black shoes, in Good Shepherds Convent in Madras we wore a navy-blue pinafore with a white undershirt, white socks and black shoes, and in Christ Church in summer we dressed in a sky-blue pinafore, white shirt, white socks and black shoes, and in winter we changed to a flannel pinafore and maroon cardigan. A solar topee was part of the daily uniform in Christ Church. In addition, the gym uniform was a pair of navy-blue bloomers and yellow shirt. In all the convent schools my sisters and I attended, any transgression of the school uniform would be noticed at the daily morning school assembly and suitable action was taken by the vice-principal. Usually, the student would be sent home and marked 'absent' for the day. Habitual offenders were dealt with more severely, and the parents were notified with a warning that called for suspension from school. As I have observed, in a girls' school, the student generation of the time, albeit with a few exceptions, conformed to the school's rules.

At Christ Church Girls' High School, students passed out of the school on the successful completion of the Senior Cambridge examinations, while St Helena's students graduated with a matriculation degree. Where Christ Church School was different from St Helena's was in the fact that most of the students in Christ Church were Anglo-Indian and the teaching staff was from England or Scotland, whereas in St Helena's the student body was a happy mix of Indians from many communities, including Anglo-Indians and among the teaching faculty, there were two Parsi women, one of whom taught us needlework, which was as important a subject for girls as arithmetic and French. As I remember in Christ Church, in the classes of fifteen to twenty students, there were not more than two Indian Hindu girls in each class; the rest were Anglo-Indians, and a few British girls. Nearly all the middle and high school teachers in Christ Church were British while the kindergarten teachers were Anglo-Indians. There was one other difference in Christ Church. An Anglican church and adjoining cemetery was part of the school campus, and while the cemetery was out of bounds for the schoolchildren, our music class was held in the church. I looked forward to singing in the school choir during the annual Christmas festivities, with piano and organ accompaniments.

While walking to school, as we sisters crossed the bridge from Gol Bazaar to the Jubbulpore cantonment, we entered the land of wide avenues, grim army barracks, church steeples and bells, British bungalows with well-laid gardens, white women and girls in frocks and bobbed hair, and Tommies walking hand-in-hand with their girls or riding pillion on cycles. An air of quiet and planned orderliness prevailed. This was in sharp contrast to the city where the streets were narrower, crowded and noisy. A variety of vehicles along with cars and cycles transported people and goods. Tongas (horse-drawn carriages), bullock carts and rickshaws shared the streets with pedestrians, children, cows, dogs, goats and donkeys. Temple bells ringing and the muezzin's call to the faithful brought us back to our part of the world. This was the colourful, vibrant city area.

Appa rented a spacious bungalow in the suburb of Gol Bazaar, adjoining the city on one side and the cantonment on the other, for three reasons. First, and an important one for us, was that our school was within walking distance from our house; secondly, Amma would feel more comfortable with Indian women, mostly 'stay-at-home' mothers; and thirdly, Appa could cycle to his office in the cantonment area. Should I say we lived at the junction of two different cultures?

Three or four days a week, Appa's close friends—I remember eight or ten of them—would come over to our home and there were serious discussions about 'hartals' and arrests and the unstable political future. I hung around the porch, not quite understanding the seriousness of the political climate, although I did feel the disjuncture between the atmosphere in the 'all-British' school I went to and my family and domestic environment.

However disturbing be the political news during weekdays, nonetheless the weekends were taken over in our home with an evening of music concerts. This was a great way to unwind for my parents who were both connoisseurs of Indian classical music, Hindustani and Carnatic. One of the regulars at the musical evenings was Appa's friend Rajagopala Mama, who came not because of a passionate interest in music but to spend a relaxing time with us. He was a fascinating storyteller who held me captivated with his stories of adventures in World War II when he was stationed in Burma (Myanmar today). I was fifteen years old when I met him, and the stories of his escape to India through the jungles and mountains of Burma made him my hero.

Rajagopala Mama was employed in Rangoon as the manager of a British rubber manufacturing company. With the Japanese invasion of Burma in 1941, his wife and three children, along with thousands of other Indians, were evacuated and left for Madras, but he stayed behind. Some months later, he had to flee Rangoon along with many others. His wife, back home in India, lost all hope of seeing him again. But he was one of the few in his group who made it to the Indian refugee camp in Calcutta after several long months of trekking. Crossing mountains and swollen rivers and ploughing through dense forests, he lost seven of his companions to snakebite and malaria while three of them died of severe exhaustion. He even told me that he had become a cannibal just to survive. I believed him. In 1956, when I was in England with my husband Chamu, I heard similar heart-rending tales of some of his colleagues who escaped from Eastern Europe around the same period.

Rajagopala Mama lived alone in Jubbulpore for over a year before he left to rejoin his family in Madras. My father was instrumental in locating his wife and children. When Mama was in Jubbulpore, on most Saturdays, I would cycle to his house with an invitation from my father asking him to join us for an evening of music, tea and tiffin. He would accept the invitation with 'Rukka, will it be bajjis and coffee?' Bajjis and pakodas (vegetable fritters in a delicate chickpea batter) were Rajagopala Mama's favourites for tiffin. Our cook Narayana's name for Mama was 'Bajji Uncle'.

How Narayana became a member of our family is another story.

One of my father's official duties, after moving to Jubbulpore, was to visit the Bairagarh Italian Prisoners' Camp near Bhopal. He went twice every month to Bairagarh. On one such visit, he was served chai and samosas by a smart young lad, at most in his late teens, who could converse in English, Hindi, Tamil and Kannada. Appa was very impressed by his facility with languages, but what he heard was a heart-rending story. Narayana was born in Coondapur, near Mangalore. He belonged to the Udupi Brahmin community. He had no recollection of his mother who died when he was very young. His father owned a hotel-cum-lodge in Mangalore and young Narayana worked during weekends waiting at tables. When he was a student in class 7, his father died of typhoid and his uncle took charge of the hotel. Things changed suddenly for young Narayana who was told his services at the hotel were no longer needed. Without thinking of the consequences, he ran away from home and from Coondapur. After several days of travelling by train, jumping in and out of trains without a ticket, exhausted and weak, the Bairagarh railway canteen manager found him sleeping on the station platform. This good Samaritan recruited Narayana as his 'chai wallah' (tea vendor) and not only gave him food but also a few annas for the work he did. 'Please take me with you. I can cook and will do whatever is asked of me. I need a home,' begged Narayana, after serving Appa a cup of tea. Unlike Amma, Appa was not normally taken in by sob-stories, but he found Narayana too smart to be just a 'chai wallah'.

The chance Appa took in giving the boy our home address in Jubbulpore turned out to be a good one for us and for Narayana.

Narayana, as it turned out, was no ordinary cook. He worked magic in the kitchen. The food he cooked was delicious and he made mealtimes interesting and fun. Amma was very pleased that her fussy children loved his food, making mealtimes easy and uneventful. And he knew that.

On weekends, Narayana set out on his bike for the grocery store-cum-vegetable market in Gol Bazaar. He would get freshly ground besan (chickpea flour), rice flour and wholewheat flour, as also red chilli powder, turmeric powder and garam masala. Those were the days when packaged groceries were not as freely available as they are today. He would pick up an assortment of fresh vegetables and fruit, including raw mango which was the base for mango fool, a sweet-and-sour refreshing drink. It was believed that mango fool kept summer heatstrokes and bilious attacks at bay.

Narayana took pride in his cooking and his vegetable bajjis disappeared faster than he could make them. He bought the freshest cauliflower heads, greenest raw plantains, tender purple eggplants, firm potatoes and onions, and crunchy lotus roots, and washed and chopped them in bite-size pieces. He then mixed a silky smooth chickpea flour batter flavoured with ground garlic and spiced with red chilli powder. Coating the vegetables in the batter, he deep-fried them, draining them well so they were light and crunchy. Rajagopala Mama would leave, satisfied, late in the night, passing my mother's invitation to stay and have dinner with the family, saying, 'I am so satisfied and so full with the delicious bajjis. Thank you.'

## NARAYANA'S VEGETABLE BAJJIS, *vegetable fritters, similar to tempura, in a casing of chickpea flour batter, but with an aromatic difference.*

I have listed the vegetables that are suitable for bajjis, you may use whichever is available. Submerge sliced plantains and potatoes in cold water to prevent discoloration. Pat dry on towel before use.

I have modified Narayana's recipe by adding garlic for that extra flavour.

Vegetables to be cut in bite-size pieces or slices.

### INGREDIENTS TO MAKE 8 SERVINGS

*Slice vegetables ⅛ inch thick*
* *1 medium potato, sliced*
* *1 onion, peeled and sliced*
* *1 Japanese eggplant, sliced*
* *1 small yam or sweet potato, sliced*
* *1 zucchini, sliced*
* *1 plantain, peeled and sliced*
* *1 yellow squash, sliced*
* *15 florets cauliflower and broccoli*
* *8 or 10 baby spinach leaves*
* *8 or 10 small sprigs of watercress*
* *8 or 10 baby turnip leaves*
* *4 or 5 cabbage leaves, torn in medium-size pieces*
* *1-foot long lotus root, cut in discs*
* *1 green capsicum (bell pepper), cut into 12 wedges, seeds removed*
* *a few green chillies, slit lengthwise in half (the bigger ones are less hot)*

### INGREDIENTS TO MAKE THE BATTER

* *2 cups chickpea flour (besan, gram flour)*
* *½ cup rice flour*
* *1 teaspoon turmeric powder*
* *1 teaspoon red chilli powder*
* *1 teaspoon salt; more if needed*
* *½ teaspoon sugar*
* *2 cloves garlic*
* *1-inch piece fresh ginger, chopped coarse*
* *3 green chillies, chopped coarse*
* *1 cup loosely packed fresh coriander leaves with tender stems, chopped*
* *1 teaspoon ajwain seeds (carom)*
* *2½ cups oil, divided*
* *water, for mixing the batter*

## METHOD TO MIX THE BATTER

Grind garlic, ginger, chillies and coriander leaves to a coarse pesto.

Sift the chickpea flour, rice flour, turmeric and chilli powders, salt and sugar into a bowl. Add the ground pesto and ajwain. DO NOT mix.

Heat 3 tablespoons of oil in a wok till it starts smoking.

Empty the oil into the bowl of flour, pouring it on top of the ground paste. You should hear and smell a delicious aromatic sizzle.

Mix all the ingredients in the bowl, pressing with your fingers to form a sandy, granular mix. (This mix, if refrigerated, stays fresh for four days).

Add ½ cup water and mix briskly, breaking all lumps. Add more water, 2 tablespoons at a time, to form a batter of dropping consistency to coat the vegetables.

## METHOD TO MAKE BAJJIS

Heat 2 cups oil in a wok or a deep-frying pan on medium heat, but not to smoking point. Dip 8 pieces of the same kind of vegetable into the batter, and swirl to coat each piece. Gently drop 1 piece into the hot oil to test the temperature. The 'battered' vegetable should sink and immediately rise to the surface. Fry to a golden brown, turning over frequently with a slotted spoon. Drain.

Drop in the rest of the pieces coated with batter and fry to a golden brown.

Drain and serve crisp and hot with tamarind–date-raisin chutney or tomato ketchup.

The temperature of the oil is crucial to the final product. If the oil is not hot enough, the batter-coated vegetables will not rise to the surface soon enough, and the bajji will be soggy and limp. Again, if the oil is too hot, the batter coating will be burnt brown, while the vegetable inside may remain uncooked. Striking the right balance comes with practice.

After frying one batch, wait for a minute for the oil to regain its temperature.

Adjust the quantity of the dry mix depending on the quantity of vegetables. But if the batter is left over, fry delicious pakodas by dropping teaspoonfuls of the batter into the hot oil, stirring in a few cashew pieces and chopped garlic into the batter.

They are heavenly, and the ideal daytime drink to go with them is mango fool.

# MANGO FOOL, *in our home, it was made like a thin shake which I prefer to the thick custard I have tasted at some parties. A frequently served summer party drink in Jubbulpore was mango fool with a blob of cream.*

## INGREDIENTS TO MAKE 5 SERVINGS

* 2 medium-size raw mangoes, the sour variety preferably
* 1 cup sugar or jaggery or brown sugar; more if you want the drink sweeter
* a pinch of salt
* ½-inch piece of raw ginger, finely grated
* 1 teaspoon cardamom powder
* a few strands of saffron
* 6 cups water
* 1 cup heavy cream (optional)

## METHOD

Boil 4 cups of water in a deep saucepan. Gently drop in the whole raw, unpeeled mangoes. Boil them till very soft. Leave to cool.

With your fingers, squeeze out all the juice and pulp, discarding the stone and peel. Begin squeezing with the peel. Strain.

Return the juice with the pulp to the saucepan and add 2 cups water, more if you prefer a thinner drink. Add the sugar, salt and ginger and bring to a boil. Turn the stove off. Stir in the cardamom powder and saffron. Cover, cool and refrigerate.

Serve with or without cream.

# Holi Feast at the Gol Bazaar Orphanage in Jubbulpore

From 1941 to 1944, Amma and her Bengali friend Mrs Ghosh were both members of the Food Committee at the Jubbulpore Gol Bazaar orphanage for young boys. There may have been twenty-five boys between the ages of five and ten years at the orphanage, which was managed by Amma's friend Vimala Bhagat, a Gandhian social worker. All the boys in the orphanage went to the neighbourhood municipal school. My sister Sarasa and I visited the orphanage frequently with my mother, but during the Hindu festivals of Holi and Diwali and on Christmas Day, we would be there for sure. The young boys would greet us with cries of delight, '*Didi, didi* (Sister, sister),' as they tried to hop onto my bicycle, often falling off in the dust of the playground. Frequently, I was inveigled to pedal one round, circling the inner wall of the orphanage, with two of the youngest, one precariously perched on the handlebar and the other sitting astride on the back seat, with the others running behind pleading for a ride.

I nostalgically remember the annual celebrations at the orphanage during the festival of Holi—the festival of spring celebrated at the end of the winter season, on the last full-moon day of the lunar month of phalgun, some time in late February or March. On Holi day, we celebrated the arrival of spring by dousing friends with coloured water and exchanging sweet delicacies. Playing Holi at the orphanage was a lot of fun. All of us children would wait to pounce on the unwary adults and shout, '*Holi khelo* (Play Holi),' spraying them with coloured water from 'pitchkaris' (water guns) and bottles. We ourselves were soaking wet with coloured water, our arms, faces and hair smeared with red and green powder. Not even a stray dog in the orphanage was spared.

Amma and Mrs Ghosh volunteered every year, both for the Holi and Diwali celebrations, to cook food for the orphanage children and to get pledges from local food merchants for a big feast for them. Most of the pledges for north Indian sweets came from the owners of neighbourhood sweetmeat (confectionery) shops frequented by local residents. These confectioners, known locally as halwais, made Indian savoury delicacies like potato samosas, which were popular, and crisp

onion pakodas, sweets like rich carrot halwa, sharp and tangy ginger toffee, caramelized peanut brittle and a host of mouth-watering milk and cream desserts, including rabadi, which was a favourite sweet at the orphanage. Rabadi, a local version of condensed milk with pistachios and almonds, was one of my favourites too. Our neighbourhood halwai stirred gallons of milk while seated on a low stool before a raging fire. He was a gentle, elderly, avuncular person with a walrus moustache. He was amused by my entranced gaze and, once, he let me try to stir the thick, creamy contents in the vat with the extra long wooden ladle, which weighed a ton. The searing heat from the inferno was unimaginable. After several hours of stirring, two well-built men would each hold one of the two huge wooden handles of the vat and tilt it, emptying a slurry of thick caramel into an immense shallow pan. Fistfuls of raisins and slivers of pistachios and almonds were thrown in, while a long line of patient customers dropped a few annas into a tin metal box and picked up the small clay pots of individual servings of rabadi with a wooden spoon stuck in each. My sister Sarasa and I, on our way back from school, would frequently stop to pick up a few clay pots at the Gol Bazaar rabadi stall. I loved the smell of the 'sweetmeat' shop, of the hot ghee, of caramelizing milk in huge vats, and of fresh samosas being fried. I savoured the smells as much as I did the taste. I remember the halwai's big shed was poorly ventilated; the front portion facing the busy street displayed the mouth-watering delicacies in clay bowls and metal trays, and the back was a smoky hive of activity where the cooks were washing, chopping, grating, grinding, mixing, stirring, braising and frying. The entire production crew was in full view of the customers. The halwai's shop opened at eleven o'clock in the forenoon and by 7.00 p.m., when the shutters were downed, the delicacies were gone and some customers left disappointed.

Besides the rabadi bought from the halwai, Mrs Ghosh and Amma would spend days making home-made Bengali and south Indian sweets and savoury delicacies. Amma made Mysore pak, a nutty, chickpea flour fudge, a popular sweet from south India. She also made rava idlis, spicy steamed semolina cakes with an accompanying coconut chutney, and Mrs Ghosh made malpua, lacy sweet crêpes drowned in a sweet syrup heavy with the aroma of cardamom, and rice payash, a creamy rice pudding sweetened with palm sugar. On the occasion of Holi, Amma made special fresh pomegranate juice for the children. Our cook Narayana peeled several dozen pomegranates on the morning of Holi, gently rubbed and loosened the luminous gems of red rubies, mixed them with a little salt and pressed them in a large wooden bowl, extracting the blood red juice, and mixing it with sugar, crushed ice and lime juice. This was a rare delicacy for our friends in the orphanage. Though pomegranate juice was nowhere near the intoxicating thandai, the drink that adults indulged in during the Holi festival, it was nevertheless a cool, refreshing drink.

Narayana would not only help with the cooking, he also helped to serve the food to the children at the orphanage on festival days. His frequent visits to the orphanage to play cricket with the children endeared him to them and they looked forward to spending time with him.

On the night of Holi, my parents hosted a dinner on our terrace for some of their friends. The highlight of their dinner party was the special drink called thandai, made of a paste of almonds, poppy and melon seeds, cardamom and fennel seeds, black peppercorns and rose petals mixed in milk. Frequently, it was laced with the ground seeds of bhang (*Cannabis sativa*), leaving all the revellers happy and free-spirited. Amma made the same thandai for us but without the bhang.

Years later, in 1960, my husband and I were invited to a Holi dinner party at a friend's home in Delhi where endless rounds of thandai were served. That night, as we happily and mindlessly wove our way home down Cavalry Lane where we lived, it brought back for me happy memories of the celebration of Holi in Jubbulpore.

## AMMA'S SPECIAL MYSORE PAK, *a beehive nutty fudge with marzipan that simply melts in the mouth.*

The controversy around the origins of this rich and decadent confection was brought home to me recently when three of my girlfriends came over for dinner. I had made Mysore pak for dessert. Everyone wanted the recipe. Sita from Mysore claimed that the cooks in the Mysore Maharaja's palace were the innovators of this delicious confectionery, and hence, the name Mysore pak. But Bela from Benaras in north India insisted that this popular sweet was originally made from masoor dal grown in the plains of north India, and so, its origin was most definitely north Indian. She added with a trace of resentment that masoor was corrupted to Mysore. I feared that friendships would be lost that evening. 'Let's leave the controversy for the time being and enjoy the royal treat,' I said, hoping their heated arguments would remain purely academic.

The making of Mysore pak is a test in culinary skill and comes with practice. If the first couple of times you fall short of a porous, crumbly yet soft and 'disintegrating in the mouth' texture, and end up trying to bite through a rock, don't lose heart—try again. It is well worth the effort. The heavenly smell of sweet ghee lingers for long after you have enjoyed one crumbly bite. The crucial stage lies in the last few moments as the 'bubbly lava' forms and you tip it into the serving dish.

### INGREDIENTS TO MAKE ABOUT 15-20 PIECES

* ¼ cup water
* 1¼ cups sugar
* 1 cup chickpea flour, sifted
* 2 cups ghee (clarified butter), divided, at room temperature
* ½ cup almonds, ground
* 1 teaspoon cardamom powder

## METHOD

Melt the ghee and set aside near the stove.

Warm up the water in a heavy wok on medium heat. Add the sugar, stir and cook till the sugar dissolves and starts to bubble. Reduce to a 'one-string' sticky syrup which should take 3–4 minutes of cooking.

Lower the heat and to the syrup add 2 tablespoons flour, followed by 2 tablespoons ghee. Stir continuously to break lumps that form.

Continue to add the rest of the flour and ghee alternately, saving 2 tablespoons of ghee for later use. Raise heat to medium, stir and cook without stopping (you may need an extra hand for this). When the ghee is absorbed, add the ground almonds, cardamom powder and remaining ghee. Continue stirring for 1 minute.

Turn the heat off, lift and tip the frothy and bubbly 'lava' into the baking dish, scraping all the contents of the wok. Shake the baking dish to even out the Mysore pak.

Score into 1-inch squares, or 2 inches x 1 inch rectangles. Allow the pieces to cool and store in an airtight container. They stay fresh at room temperature for 2 or 3 days.

To test for a 'one-string' consistency of the syrup, take a smear of the syrup from the back of the stirring ladle with your index finger. Press on the syrup with your thumb and draw out the syrup, which should form a single string between the finger and thumb.

The time taken between the frothing and pouring of the cooked Mysore pak into the dish is a matter of a few seconds. This is crucial!

# RAVA IDLIS, *soft, steamed savoury semolina cakes.*

The first time I tasted rava idlis, they were made at home in Jubbulpore by Amma. Decades later in the 1960s at the Mavalli Tiffin Rooms, aka MTR, in Bangalore, my husband and I shared a breakfast of rava idlis. MTR is credited with introducing this delicious savoury breakfast dish in their restaurant. The MTR brand of packaged rava idli mix is now available in many grocery stores internationally, and these idlis are as good as those Amma made starting from scratch, besides the fact that the packets save me much time.

I prefer eating rava idlis when they are hot. If steamed in advance, they can be refrigerated for 2–3 days and reheated in the microwave or re-steamed before serving.

## INGREDIENTS TO MAKE ABOUT 12 IDLIS

* *4 tablespoons oil, divided*
* *½ teaspoon brown mustard seeds*
* *½ cup raw cashew nut pieces*
* *2 green chillies, slit lengthwise and chopped fine*
* *10 curry leaves, torn in pieces*
* *½ teaspoon asafoetida powder*
* *½ cup coriander leaves, chopped*
* *2 cups rava (medium size sooji/semolina/cream of wheat)*
* *1 teaspoon salt*
* *2 cups sour yogurt*
* *1 teaspoon baking soda or 1 teaspoon Eno's Fruit Salt*

## METHOD TO MAKE BATTER

Warm up 2 tablespoons oil in a heavy wok on medium heat. Add the mustard seeds.

When the mustard seeds start to splutter and pop, add the cashew nut pieces. Roast to a golden brown. Toss in the green chillies, curry leaves, asafoetida powder and coriander leaves, and stir once.

Add the rava and stir for 2 minutes, roasting the rava lightly till it smells nutty.

Empty the roasted rava into a bowl. Stir and leave to cool for 10 minutes.

Stir salt into 1 cup of yogurt and pour into the bowl of rava. Fold, mix well and set aside for 3 minutes.

## METHOD TO STEAM IDLIS

You will need an idli steamer on a stand of idli trays with depressions that will fit inside or, alternatively, an egg poaching dish.

Grease the cups in the idli trays with a smear of oil. Set aside.

Fill the bottom pan of the idli steamer with water to a depth of 2 inches, and on medium-high heat, bring the water to a boil. Lower the heat to medium.

Fold in the remaining cup of yogurt to the rava mix in the bowl. Add salt to taste. Stir in the baking soda or Eno's Fruit Salt. If the batter is very thick, mix in 1 tablespoon of water.

Fill ¾ of each greased cup with the batter. Place the idli trays inside the steamer. Cover with a tight lid, steam and cook for 5–10 minutes. Test by inserting a toothpick which should come out clean.

Turn the stove off, remove the idli trays from the steamer and set aside for 1 minute on the counter. Run a spatula around the edges of each steamed idli, lift and arrange on a platter.

Turn the heat to medium, add more water to the bottom pan if needed, and repeat the process of steaming the idlis with the rest of the rava mix. Stir and mix the rava batter, adding a little more water if it is too stiff each time you steam a fresh batch of idlis.

Serve with coconut chutney.

## HOLI COCONUT AND PEANUT CHUTNEY, *the peanuts give the onions a subtle sweetness, and the roasted lentils a gritty texture to one of my favourite chutneys.*

### INGREDIENTS TO MAKE APPROXIMATELY 1½ CUPS CHUTNEY

* 1 tablespoon oil
* 1 medium onion, coarsely chopped
* 2 dry red chillies
* 1 tablespoon raw peanuts
* 1 cup shredded coconut, fresh or frozen
* ½ teaspoon salt; more if needed
* 1 teaspoon lemon juice
* water to grind the chutney

### METHOD

Warm up the oil in a small wok or saucepan on medium heat. Add the chopped onion and stir for one minute.

Turn the stove off, add the chillies, peanuts and coconut to the onions, and stir a couple of times.

Empty the contents of the wok into a blender. Add salt, lemon juice and 1 cup water. Grind to a smooth consistency. Add ¼ cup more water, if needed, and grind.

Empty into a serving bowl. Add an additional ¼ cup water to the blender, wash it out, and add to the contents in the bowl. Set aside.

## INGREDIENTS FOR THE TEMPERING

* *1 tablespoon oil*
* *½ teaspoon brown mustard seeds*
* *½ teaspoon urad dal*
* *10 curry leaves, torn in pieces*

## METHOD

Warm up the oil in a wok on medium heat. Toss in the mustard seeds, and when they start to pop, add the urad dal. Stir to a golden brown.

Turn off the heat and add the curry leaves. Allow them to crackle. Stir and empty into the bowl of ground coconut chutney. Add salt to taste. Stir, cover and set aside.

## MRS GHOSH'S MALPURA (MALPUA), *these easy-to-cook light flour crêpes, drenched in golden syrup, are a treat from Bengal.*

Malpuras topped with cream or ice cream for an even richer dessert were an all-time favourite at the YWCA parties in Jubbulpore.

Decades later in the 1980s, while returning home after a day's teaching at Bishop Cotton Boys' School in Bangalore, I often stopped at K.C. Das, the Bengali confectionery outlet on St Marks Road, to get malpuras for my family. K.C. Das is uncompromising in its high standards of making quality Bengali sweets.

## INGREDIENTS TO MAKE THE SYRUP

* *2 cups water*
* *1½ cups brown sugar*
* *1 teaspoon cardamom powder*
* *a few strands of saffron*
* *⅛ teaspoon orange food colour (optional)*
* *¼ cup honey*
* *2 tablespoons rose water*

## METHOD TO MAKE THE SYRUP

This should be a thin golden liquid with the fragrance of a rose garden.

Boil the water in a heavy, shallow saucepan on medium heat.

Add the sugar, lower the heat, stir and cook to a thin syrup. This will take 1–2 minutes. Remove from the stove and set aside.

Stir in the cardamom powder, saffron and orange food colour, if you are using it.

Combine the rose water with honey and mix into the syrup. Set aside.

## INGREDIENTS TO MAKE THE BATTER FOR 10–12 CRÊPES

* *1 cup white flour (I use ½ cup wholewheat flour and ½ cup all-purpose flour)*
* *2 tablespoons fine sooji (rava/semolina/cream of wheat)*
* *4 tablespoons milk powder*
* *¼ teaspoon salt*
* *1 teaspoon baking powder*
* *2 tablespoons sugar*
* *1 tablespoon yogurt*
* *2 cups water; use as much as needed*
* *¼ cup oil mixed with 1 cup melted ghee, the shortening, to shallow-fry the crêpes.*

## METHOD TO MAKE THE BATTER FOR THE CRÊPES

Sift flour, sooji, milk powder, salt and baking soda into a bowl. Add sugar, yogurt and ½ cup water, and whisk briskly, breaking all lumps.

Add another ¼ cup water and more, if needed, to mix to a thin pancake batter.

Set aside, covered, for 30 minutes.

## INGREDIENTS FOR THE GARNISH

¼ cup raw almond and pistachio slivers, mixed. Keep in a bowl for use later.

## METHOD TO MAKE THE MALPURAS

Warm up a 6-inch skillet, an omelette pan or a shallow-fry pan on medium heat.

Pour ½ teaspoon of the shortening and brush it uniformly to coat the entire bottom surface of the skillet.

Lower the heat and pour about ½ cup of the crêpe batter. Immediately lift, tilt and rotate the pan to allow the batter to spread evenly. Do not try to fill up any holes that may form.

Raise the heat to medium and cook uncovered for about 2 minutes, or till you see the edges curling and lifting. Do not cook crisp.

Lift the crêpe, gently easing the edges with a spatula. Flip over, drizzle 1 teaspoon shortening around the edges, and shallow-fry for ½ minute on this side.

Lift the crêpe with a pair of tongs, drain and lay on a platter.

Cook all the malpuras, but do not stack them. Place them alongside each other on a platter.

Ten minutes before serving, warm up the syrup on medium low heat. Turn off the heat. Transfer the malpuras, 2 at a time to the pan of syrup. Keep them dipped in the syrup for 10 minutes. Transfer 2 to each serving plate, drizzle 1 teaspoon of the syrup over each malpura, and garnish with slivers of almonds and pistachios.

# DATE PALM SUGAR RICE PUDDING, *creamy and rich, this special pudding is a signature dessert from Bengal. If palm sugar is not available, you can substitute with jaggery or dark brown sugar. I have, at times, used sweetened condensed milk and less jaggery, which may not be authentic but nevertheless tasty. I have modified Mrs Ghosh's recipe.*

## INGREDIENTS TO MAKE 4 SERVINGS

- ½ cup rice; I use Basmati rice
- 1 cup water
- 4 cups milk, divided
- 2 bay leaves
- 4 cloves
- seeds of 3 small green cardamom pods
- 1 cup date palm sugar
- ¼ cup toasted slivers of unsalted almonds (optional)

## METHOD

Wash the rice and drain the water. Repeat twice.

Cook the rice soft in a 3-quart heavy pan on medium heat, adding the water, 3 cups of milk and bay leaves, and stirring frequently to prevent the milk from boiling over or burning at the bottom.

Add ½ cup more milk, stir and bring to a boil.

Lower heat, add cloves and cardamom seeds and stir in the palm sugar. Cook for about 10 minutes, stirring frequently so it does not stick to the bottom of the pan and burn.

Turn off the heat.

Remove the bay leaves and cloves and stir in the almond slivers, if you are using them.

Transfer to a serving bowl. Spread a film of cling foil over the bowl to prevent a 'skin' from forming. Serve warm or cold.

If the pudding becomes thick on cooling, you may want to stir in ½ cup more milk before serving.

*Appa's Retirement and the Move to Tanjore*

In 1944, Appa was transferred from Jubbulpore, but this time to a city of his choice. He was to retire three years later and had requested a transfer to Poona, the city both he and my mother loved and where they had many friends.

My elder sister Kamala, after completing her tenth grade examinations, decided, much to my father's regret, not to study further, but to pursue her interest in music and, more importantly, in playing the violin. So she went to live with Dr Chitappa in Tanjore, where she learnt from the famous Carnatic violinist Papa Venkataramiah. The rest of the family moved to Poona.

I had just completed the Junior Cambridge examination at Christ Church Girls' High School and was studying in the pre-Senior Cambridge standard when Appa was transferred. So I went back to St Helena's in Poona and studied for the matriculation examination, a totally different system from the Cambridge one. It was not easy for me to move from one system to another, but surprisingly, I passed with credit; and this was all due to Appa who understood the difficulty of shifting midstream and tirelessly helped me with all my subjects. The examination results were announced in the spring of 1946.

I was now ready to join college and was keen on Fergusson or Wadia College in Poona. But Appa explained to me that he was to retire the following year and he and Amma had decided to move to the south to Tanjore. He suggested that maybe I should consider applying to Queen

Mary's College for Women in Madras. I was not very excited about his suggestion and reluctant to apply for admission for two reasons; two of my buddies from St Helena's were accepted at Wadia's and, more importantly, I feared Madras would be too conservative a city for my taste after my earlier experience of the attitude of people in general, and if I may say, the very rigid atmosphere in Good Shepherds Convent when I was a student between the years 1939 and 1941. Two incidents stand out in my memory. My mother's elder sister lived with her family in Madras and her remarks on meeting Sarasa and me said it all. I was twelve years old and Sarasa two years younger. Our aunt was disapproving of the way we had been brought up—dressed in knee-high dresses, not to mention that our hair was braided in two plaits, and above all, the ease with which we mixed with members of the opposite sex. She firmly advised Amma to dress us 'modestly' in a 'pavadai', blouse, and 'melakku', a length of unstitched material draped over the blouse. She added that we may look better in one plait and that we girls were better advised not to mingle freely with boys. In her view, upper middle class, south Indian Brahmin girls had to look and behave in a particular way! My father was outraged at her lack of boundaries and interference in his family affairs. Amma tried unsuccessfully to explain that her sister had spent all her life in south India and most of her married life in Madras; she had had no experience of different regional cultures and she did not know any better. After the initial unpleasant introduction to this aunt, we had little contact with her during the two years of our stay in Madras. My experience at school was no better. While most of the teaching staff were women, the maths and Tamil language teachers were conscientious, gentle, middle-aged south Indian men. It was so obvious that the nuns were 'prowling' around keeping an eye on these two! Without fail, one elderly 'sister', and not the same one every day, was seated at the back of my class for most of the Tamil and maths periods. The joke among the students was that these nuns had to earn their maintenance in the convent.

I don't think my impression of the social culture of Madras was born out of ignorance or prejudice; both in St Helena's School in Poona and in Christ Church Girls' High School in Jubbulpore, the French language and maths classes were taught by young Anglo-Indian men.

And it is no exaggeration to say that in both schools, an atmosphere of trust and discipline free engagement made learning a pleasure for me and my classmates.

We sisters had grown up in cosmopolitan surroundings in Poona and Jubbulpore, and looking back, my memory of Madras was of a stifling, conservative culture. Was I overreacting? But Appa managed to convince me to apply. His argument that I could go 'home' to Tanjore from Madras, not only during the longer vacations but maybe even during some weekends, won the day. Tanjore was just about six hours away from Madras; compare that to a train journey of over forty-eight hours from Poona to Tanjore, all the way from the west of the peninsula to the east, with a couple of precious days lost each way in travel alone.

I was accepted at Queen Mary's College for Women in Madras, and honestly, that was a great relief more to my parents than to me.

Bidding farewell to Poona, my friends and my school was not easy for me.

Touching farewell parties and gifts did not make it any easier, and among the many I remember was a cycle ride with three friends, Shireen Bharucha, Sophia Peters and Kusum Patwardhan, to the foot of Parvati Hill, a hilly outcrop rising over 2,000 feet, just outside the town. Parvati Hill attracted tourists, trekkers and pilgrims to the temples built on top of the hill. We talked and laughed, walked and ran, carefree for the present. Later the same evening, the three of us met at our favourite ice cream bar on Main Street and the girls tearfully bid me farewell, promising to keep in touch and even threatened to visit me in my college. Sophia kept her word. She was visiting her elderly aunt in Bangalore in April of 1948 and suddenly showed up one weekend in my hostel. She spent the day with me and we had a great time, much of it spent talking nostalgically of our Poona schooldays. She was very impressed with Queen Mary's and felt I did right in joining this great institution. I was not very sure at that time.

The other party I remember was the one I attended with my father at the Southern Command office campus; Appa invited me to go with him as I had a nodding acquaintance with many of his colleagues and he knew I would enjoy the official farewell party for him. He was to retire a few months later. It was a formal evening with a few speeches followed by high tea. There was live music with Mr Peterson at the piano.

It was at this party, I realized, that the entire office, including the Comptroller, Appa's senior officers, his colleagues and his juniors, held him in great respect, awe and affection. There were a few speeches, nearly all of them detailing Appa's sense of commitment to his work, his disciplined mentoring of the junior clerical staff, his courage and rationale for disagreeing with certain proposals even at the risk of displeasing his superiors, and above all, his 'marginal notings' written in impeccable English on every official document sent to him, described by one of the speakers as a mini dissertation!

A couple of his junior colleagues gave snapshot glimpses of Appa's short temper and blowing his lid, adding, 'It was a lightning strike that passed over ever so quickly without destruction. Mr Naganathan did not bear grudges. He held us to high standards. We will miss him here at the Southern Command.' This was also the father I knew.

At that farewell function, I also learnt that Appa was offered a post-retirement job at the Army Staff College in Wellington, near Ootacamund in south India, which he declined. He wanted to enjoy his retirement reading, going for long walks and spending time with his family.

It was not uncommon for retiring officers to apply for these cushy post-retirement jobs, so I was touched that Appa had declined this offer, one of his reasons being to spend time with us.

I remember most of the menu for the official farewell high tea party at the Southern Command. As a mark of respect to Appa's food preferences, it was a vegetarian evening. There were two soups, green pea soup and, I think, a mushroom soup, with crackers and cheese, followed by a choice of entrées: trays and platters of tarts, quiches and crêpes, and the grand finale was the chocolate ice cream bomb.

That was one evening which still remains fresh in my memory.

## Deepavali Celebrations in Tanjore

My parents' move to Tanjore was seamless. Amma left with my younger sisters in the summer of 1946 in time for them to join school. I left soon after to join Queen Mary's College in Madras. Appa retired in early 1947 and joined the family in Tanjore. Dr Chitappa's help in this move and in settling the family was enormous.

I took some time adjusting to living in the college hostel, and went frequently over weekends to my parents' new home in Tanjore. In fact, I wonder even now if I ever got used to life in the hostel. After the first long week that followed my joining the college, I went home for the Deepavali festival. In the convent schools I had studied in, I did not have even one day's holiday for a Hindu festival, so this was a welcome change.

The Hindu festival of Diwali, also known as Deepavali in south India, is celebrated every year in the month of October or November, depending on the date of the fifteenth day of the dark fortnight of the waning moon. You could say that this 'Festival of Lights' is celebrated on the New Moon Day three weeks after the ten-day celebration of the Hindu festival of Navarathri, also known as Dussehra.

In north India, the Diwali festival is marked by the lighting of myriads of clay lamps and distributing sweets to friends and family, marking the return of the Hindu god-king Lord Rama with his wife Sita to his kingdom of Ayodhya after his fourteen-year exile, his vanquishing of Ravana, the king of demons, and his victorious homecoming. The celebration signifies victory and hope. It is believed that the lighting of lamps and firing of crackers drives away the forces of evil, bringing back joy in people's lives. Weeks before the festival, in the open spaces in different parts of the city and in the villages, huge effigies of the demon-king Ravana are built and stuffed with crackers and sparklers. On the culminating day of the festival, an enormous crowd of spectators gathers around the effigy, while a performer, playing the role of the god-king Rama, shoots a flaming arrow into the heart of the demon effigy, symbolically 'killing' him. A magnificent display of fireworks lights up the cold, wintry night sky to the thrill and joy of the hundreds of people gathered to witness the annual amazing spectacle.

In south India, the celebration of Deepavali is in commemoration of the victory of Lord Krishna over the demon Narakasura. Here again, victory and hope is celebrated with the lighting of lamps, wearing of new clothes, lighting of sparklers and firecrackers, culminating in a feast with family and friends. In our family, it was customary for the day to begin with an oil bath when, before dawn, we children were asked to sit crosslegged on wooden planks before the family altar facing east, and my mother would smear a couple of teaspoons of medicated sesame oil on our hair and faces. A few drops from a sealed jug of 'Ganga jalam', water from the sacred Ganges river, was added to each one's bath water, since it was supposed to be a purificatory bath. This was the explanation given to us by the elderly women of the family. The bath was followed by the wearing of new clothes and firing crackers. A sumptuous breakfast of rice idlis with coconut chutney, and a variety of sweets, halwas and crunchy savouries followed. It was also the custom in our family to feed and give new clothes, cash and sweets to all the family retainers.

From the year 1947, when my father retired and moved south to Tanjore in Tamil Nadu, not far from his ancestral village, till 1968 when he passed away, the peasant farmers who managed his agricultural lands in his natal village came every year to wish him and my mother a 'Happy Deepavali', bringing paddy, coconuts, jaggery and flowers. In return, my parents would gift them cash, new clothes, sweets and firecrackers for themselves and their families. When my father passed away, my mother sold the Tanjore house and moved to Madras, and that marked the end of two decades of a close bond with agrarian clients and friends.

The first time I took the train to Tanjore to celebrate Deepavali with my extended family is a much cherished memory. Juliet, my room-mate, insisted on seeing me off at the Madras station, comfortably seated in the ladies' compartment in the Boat Mail train (the ladies compartment was Juliet's idea; till then, I was unaware of a segregated compartment for women).

This was a time of gift giving, of new clothes in particular. Amma would get new clothes for all of us; sarees, veshties, pavadais and blouses. If my aunts were visiting with their children, she would buy clothes for them too. This Deepavali I wanted to give my parents a gift. My father was fastidious about many matters; in particular, he was finicky about mattresses. He preferred a soft mattress stuffed with silk cotton, which stayed soft and did not turn lumpy and hard over time, like the ones stuffed with cotton. I surprised him with a specially ordered high-piled silk cotton mattress for his double bed, and four pillows to go with it. He was very pleased with my gift and jokingly admitted that even on his wedding night, he did not have this luxury. I know he used the mattress I gifted him till he passed away in 1968. He, in turn, gave me my first diary in 1946 when I left Poona to join college in Madras, and encouraged me to keep a record of events and jottings on people and places. Appa was a 'diary' person.

When I was married, my husband gave me a diary every year, and now for the past few years, Krishna, my dear friend in Bangalore, never fails to gift me one. I find that perusing a diary of years gone by reintroduces me to the friends and people I knew, not to mention, reliving those times.

My parents' home in Tanjore was a two-storeyed modern bungalow built on a large site, measuring about 120 feet × 300 feet where, over the years, my mother raised a beautiful garden. A distinguishing feature of the house was its wide front verandah where my father spent his mornings reading the newspaper while waiting for the postman (this is the vignette I have of him reclining in his rattan armchair), and in the evenings, he looked forward to meeting his friends to discuss the local and national news over tiffin and coffee served in the verandah by

Amma. This, in a sense, was the 'retired' life he was looking forward to. For the thirty-odd years he was in service, he had travelled from Quetta in northwest India (now in Pakistan) to Madras in the south, packing and moving ever so often. When I asked him if he envied his friend and colleague Thiagarajan, who started service in Madras and retired in the same city after thirty-odd years, he smiled wistfully adding, 'I do believe I had great experiences travelling in spite of the adjustments your mother had to make.'

The house was set back well over 25 feet from the street, the yard space between the house and the compound wall covered by a coconut frond, lean-to thatched roof which, though may have interfered with the beauty of the house, certainly provided shade. Along the front wall of the yard, my mother had planted several bushes with sweet-smelling blooms, and these tall bushes together with the thatched awning gave us a certain sense of privacy. I spent much time with my father in the verandah, giving him all the news and gossip whenever I came home from Queen Mary's College.

Beyond the front verandah and inside, the house was like any modern house, with a formal living room, a guest bedroom, a large family room, and a smaller room which could be used as a study but where my sisters and I had our clothes closets. Adjoining the family room was a store room, a pantry of sorts and a kitchenette with a narrow dining area. A staircase led to two bedrooms and an open terrace on the first floor of the house.

The more attractive part of the house was an extension at the back, built after a year of moving into the house, with a large eco-friendly, 40 feet-square, well-lit and airy kitchen and dining space built of bamboo slats and thatched with coconut fronds. My father's rationale for adding this extra space was, 'Your mother spends a lot of time in the kitchen and we all like to be with her, so why not make the kitchen the central part of the house?'

Beyond the new kitchen and around a stone-lined well lay my mother's back garden. It was a visual and olfactory delight, with rows of fragrant jasmine bushes and tulasi plants (sacred basil) interspersed with bushes of multicoloured white, mauve and pink tubular flowers, known locally as 'December flowers' since they bloomed during the cooler months of the year.

Deepavali in Tanjore was a festival Amma enjoyed. She looked forward to meeting and spending time with many members of the extended family, whose respect and love for her warm and unconditional hospitality grew as the years went by. Appa's youngest brother, Dr Chitappa, and Annam Athai, their youngest sister, along with her children, would visit every year to celebrate Deepavali together as a family, and I, too, would be home from college for a week. This was a happy family reunion. The fortnight before the festival, Amma would begin preparations by making Deepavali lehiya marundu, a herbal fudge to aid digestion after the festival feasting. Intriguingly spicy and sweet, the thick, sticky, gooey, dark chocolate-coloured fudge, oozing a complex smell of all the herbs that went into making it, continues to be a favourite with my family, even after the annual Deepavali festivities are over. In the Tanjore home, the tightly sealed, heavy clay jar of marundu would be kept in a dark corner on one of the lower shelves in the pantry. The longer it was stored, the mellower the taste became. A small portion would be dug out with a long-handled dry wooden spoon, rolled into small golis (balls), and given to us whenever we complained of a stomach ache or indigestion. Often, I feigned an upset stomach to get a goli. There is no other confectionery that can match the Deepavali marundu Amma made.

In preparation for making the marundu, Amma would spend days picking and cleaning, drying, pounding and sifting the pounded herbs, roots, buds, flowers, pods and leaves which went into a large heavy stoneware deep pot that only two of my young adult male cousins could lift. This stoneware pot had grown to a shiny black with decades of marundu making. In fact, it smelt deliciously of marundu.

Sitting on a wooden stool in front of a wood fire, adding jars and jars of ghee, jaggery and honey, Amma stirred the aromatic slurry in the pot with an enormous long-handled wooden ladle. Frequently, my male cousins would be co-opted to help stir the thickening fudge. Midway during the stirring, cardamom powder, poppy seeds, clove and cinnamon powder, raisins, dried ginger powder and chopped dates would be added and cooked on low heat till it all came together in a dense ball. It would take a whole day of uninterrupted stirring to cook this bubbling lava to perfection, the overpowering herbal aroma taking over the house.

One year, Amma looked very tired, so I offered to help her make the marundu. It was then that I realized how numerous the ingredients were and how complex the process. She was very appreciative of my effort and announced to everyone that I had been very patient in stirring the pot for hours so the fudge did not burn. One oft-repeated mantra of hers was that a combination of the freshest, best-quality ingredients coupled with love, patience and a passion for cooking and sharing was the secret to appetizing food.

There is a shortcut today for making the delicious marundu. The ground dry mix is available in many stores in Madras, which cuts the preparation time and labour by no small means. But the purist will continue to make it the traditional way. I have no doubt that in the near future, the marundu mix will be available in grocery stores internationally.

The night before the festival, Amma would be busy cleaning the family puja room, her home altar, decorating it with multicoloured electric lights and flower garlands. The silver and brass heirloom lamps of the household were polished to a high gleam, fitted with cotton wicks and filled with sesame oil, ready to be lit. Small clay lamps flickering on the front porch added a serene, surreal beauty to the surrounding darkness of the new moon night, hours before the break of dawn. Bronze, brass and stainless steel containers filled with sweets and savouries would be arranged before the family altar. The marundu made for the occasion would also be kept in a smaller silver dish.

A tray of multicoloured boxes of firecrackers and sparklers, and wicker trays with new clothes for all the family members were also arranged before the domestic shrine. After the festivities were over, for several weeks, my younger sisters and cousins never missed an opportunity to wear their new clothes, be it for a movie or social visit. A frequently asked question amongst women relatives and friends meeting soon after the festival would be, 'What did you buy? Let's see your Deepavali clothes.'

On the day of the festival, the family priest arrived before dawn to conduct a puja (prayer service) propitiating ancestors and invoking their blessings to protect and bestow the family with health and prosperity.

*Kolam (Rangoli) designs on the ground/floor*

After collecting his fee for his services, the priest would rush off to his next stop. The pre-dawn puja on Deepavali day was of immense significance to believers.

I remember one special Deepavali celebration in Tanjore the year my elder sister Kamala was married. It was customary in many south Indian Hindu families to invite the newly-weds to the bride's parents' home for every festival the first year of their married life together. Kamala and her spouse Raman spent a couple of days celebrating Deepavali with us that year. In addition to the new clothes that all of us were gifted by our parents, Amma slipped on a pair of gold bracelets around Kamala's wrists and Appa gifted Raman a pocket watch. This was a celebration to remember for both my sister and Raman.

None of us slept the night before. There was excitement in the air. We knew we had to be up before dawn for a head bath, before we could wear our new clothes and light the lamps. Amma and my aunts were in the kitchen cooking the family breakfast, and my teenaged cousins Ramu and Balu, the mischievous boys that they were, couldn't wait to light the crackers. On Deepavali day the previous year, Ramu had to be rushed to hospital with burns on his fingers. Appa, with a stern countenance, walked up and down the hallway attempting to maintain control in an otherwise chaotic situation.

After the pre-dawn puja, my sister Kamala rounded us up for a breakfast of steamed Kanchipuram idlis with coconut chutney and a variety of sweets and savouries. Each one of us was handed one marble of the special Deepavali marundu. Later that afternoon, some of us visited friends in the neighbourhood with the sweets my mother had packed for each family.

For weeks in advance, the Tanjore home kitchen was a hive of activity. My aunt Annam arrived a couple of weeks earlier to help make the sweets. Badam halwa (dense soft almond fudge), therattipal (rich, chewy, granular chunks of sweetened milk solids), Karachi halwa (wheat gluten sweet bars), Mysore pak (delectable, sugary chickpea treat), peanut toffee, home-made chocolates with cocoa and condensed milk, coconut toffee, kaju barfi (sweet rhombus-shaped cashew slabs), rava laddus (sweetened semolina balls), boondi (bright orange-syrup drenched pearls of chickpea batter), and many other kinds of barfi and payasam (pudding) would roll out of the kitchen, along with traditional savouries such as aval mixture (beaten rice flakes fried and mixed with herbs and nuts), thenkozhal (fried noodles of rice and lentil flour), naada pakoda (deep-fried, turmeric-yellow ribbons of savoury chickpea batter), khara boondi (spicy, crumbly beads of chickpea flour) and khara sev (aromatic, crunchy, savoury noodles of fried chickpea batter).

My favourites that Deepavali were sticky coconut toffee, therattipal, cashew gulkand barfi, sweet boondi, chocolate mounds with sweetened coconut, crunchy naada pakoda, gulab jamun (deep purple spongy balls of reduced milk solids floating in an aromatic syrup), and Kanchipuram idli, an interesting and tasty version of the regular rice idli which we routinely had at least once a week for tiffin.

Amma had made enough sweets to last the extended family for weeks and for me to take back to college. Friends of mine in the college dormitory, who also went home for the festival, returned with sweets, and the Deepavali goodies party was on every evening for a couple of weeks.

# DEEPAVALI STICKY COCONUT TOFFEE, *Amma's recipe included minced dried figs, dates and orange rind, raising the popular coconut confection to a higher degree of sophistication.*

## INGREDIENTS TO MAKE ABOUT 30 PIECES

* 3 tablespoons water
* 2½ cups sugar
* 3 cups shredded coconut, fresh or frozen
* 2 tablespoons whole milk
* ½ teaspoon cardamom powder
* 4 tablespoon ghee, divided
* ⅛ teaspoon saffron strands soaked in ½ teaspoon milk
* ¼ cup minced dried figs
* ¼ cup pitted dates, minced
* 1 tablespoon orange rind, grated
* 1 teaspoon poppy seeds, lightly toasted
* 30 almond halves, blanched and toasted

## METHOD

Grease a 6-inch square baking dish and set aside.

Heat the water in a wok on medium heat. Add the sugar, stir continuously and cook to a sticky syrup. Fold in the coconut and cardamom powder. Add the milk, stir from the bottom up, and cook till it comes together and starts sticking to the sides. This will take about 10–15 minutes.

Add the ghee, continue stirring rapidly and cook, scraping the sides. Cook till bubbles appear.

Lower heat. Add saffron, figs, dates and orange rind. Stir and cook to a rolling ball. Take care to see that the bottom does not burn.

Empty the mix into the greased dish and smoothen the surface with a spatula. Do not press down too hard or, else, the toffee will become dense.

Scatter the toasted poppy seeds uniformly on the surface.

Cut into 30 squares when still warm, and press an almond half on each square.

Leave to rest at room temperature for 15 minutes. When cool, transfer all the pieces to an airtight container, lifting them with a metal spatula.

Stays fresh for a week at room temperature.

# CASHEW GULKAND BARFI, *the easy way. Also known as kaju katli, this festive, rich, creamy cashew nougat is ready in less than half an hour. Amma made it special by blending in gulkand, a jam of rose petals.*

## INGREDIENTS TO MAKE ABOUT 50 PIECES

* 3 cups raw cashew nuts, ground into powder
* ½ cup water
* 1½ cups sugar
* ¼ cup milk
* 3 tablespoons ghee, divided
* 1 teaspoon rose essence
* 2 tablespoons gulkand (rose jam)

Gulkand is available in Indian grocery stores.

## METHOD

Grease a cookie baking sheet with 1 tablespoon ghee, and set aside.

Heat the water in a heavy wok on medium heat. Add the sugar, stir and cook to a single-thread syrup.

Stir in the cashew nut powder, mixing well to break all lumps that may form. Add the milk, stir and cook till the milk is absorbed.

Add 2 tablespoons ghee, stir and cook for 2–3 minutes.

Turn the stove off and immediately stir in the rose essence and gulkand.

Empty the contents of the wok onto the greased baking sheet, scraping the sides of the wok with a spatula.

Gently even out the surface with a spatula, and leave to cool for 5–7 minutes.

Score diagonally into 1-inch rhombus-shaped pieces.

Remove and store in a canister.

Stays fresh at room temperature for a week.

To test for a single-thread syrup, boil the water and sugar for about 3 minutes, stirring continuously. With your index finger, scrape off a bit of the syrup from the back of the stirring spoon. Press it with your thumb and gently pull the finger and thumb apart.

The syrup should draw out as a single thread.

# NO-FUSS QUICK THERATTIPAL, *this granular caramelized milk fudge, a treat for special occasions, is a much sought after sweet delicacy in south Indian homes.*

In my parents' home, therattipal was mandatory for Deepavali. We children savoured its taste and texture, licking the ball of grainy fudge lodged in the palm of our hand. Amongst us sisters whoever could hold on and lick the fudge ball the longest felt a winner.

While my mother's traditional recipe called for a long and tedious procedure of stirring, sitting for most of one day before a wood stove, boiling several gallons of whole milk down to a gallon of thick fudge which could be rolled into a ball, I now have a 'no-fuss' quick recipe passed on by a neighbour in Arlington.

## INGREDIENTS TO MAKE 4 SERVINGS

* *1 can condensed milk*
* *1 cup riccota cheese*
* *1 cup milk powder*
* *¼ cup milk*
* *½ cup sugar*
* *1 stick unsalted butter*
* *1 teaspoon plain yogurt*
* *1 teaspoon cardamom powder*

## METHOD

In a microwaveable deep bowl, combine all the ingredients. Stir and mix to blend well.

Cook in a microwave for 2 minutes at a time, for 16 minutes in all, removing, stirring and replacing the bowl after every 2 minutes. Watch out to see that the ingredients do not overflow. Depending on the power of your microwave, the time taken could vary by a few minutes.

When the liquid evaporates and the cheese mix turns an attractive fawn colour and smells heavenly of cardamom, the therattipal is ready.

Remove from the microwave and transfer contents to a serving dish.

# SWEET BOONDI, *crunchy, sweet, aromatic beads of chickpea batter garnished with raisins and cashews.*

## INGREDIENTS TO MAKE THE SYRUP

* ½ *cup water*
* *2 cups sugar*
* ½ *teaspoon cardamom powder*
* *pinch of saffron ground in 1 teaspoon water*

## METHOD TO MAKE SYRUP

Warm the water in a wok on medium heat. Add the sugar, stir and cook till you get a syrup of one-thread consistency. Approximate cooking time is 3 minutes.

Turn the stove off and stir in the cardamom powder and ground saffron. Set aside.

To test the syrup for a one-thread consistency, take the back of the stirring ladle, scrape off a smear of the syrup with your index finger, press your thumb against the syrup and draw it away. As you separate the finger and thumb, you should draw a single thread of syrup.

## INGREDIENTS TO MAKE BOONDI FOR 6 PERSONS

* *1 cup chickpea flour (besan/gram flour)*
* *2 tablespoons rice flour*
* *pinch of salt*
* *enough water to mix to a 'dropping' batter*
* *1 cup ghee mixed with ½ cup oil for frying, the shortening*

## INGREDIENTS FOR THE GARNISH

* *15 golden raisins*
* *10 raw cashew nuts, broken in small pieces*
* *2 tablespoons dessicated, unsweetened coconut*

## METHOD TO MIX AND FRY THE BATTER INTO BEADS

Sieve the chickpea flour, rice flour and salt into a bowl. Mix to a smooth batter of dropping consistency, adding as much water as needed. Set aside.

Heat the shortening in a wok on medium heat. Hold a flat slotted spoon about 6 inches above the hot shortening (the slots or holes should be round and small).

Stir and pour 1 ladle of batter on the slotted spoon. Immediately tap the edge of the slotted spoon with another spoon. Continue tapping so that the batter falls into

the hot shortening in small droplets. The droplets of batter will immediately rise to the surface, swelling up into little 'beads'.

Cook them till light brown, turning over frequently. Drain and drop into the syrup. Proceed to fry the rest of the batter and add the beads to the syrup.

Gently fold the fried beads into the syrup. Fry the cashew nuts to a honey colour, drain and add to the beads. Fry the raisins till they plump up, drain and add them to the beads. Turn off the stove. Scatter the dessicated coconut over the beads. Fold the cashew nuts, raisins and coconut into the sweet boondi.

Separate the clusters of boondi into individual beads. Leave to cool.

Having absorbed the syrup, these glistening golden beads are now ready to be transferred to a serving dish.

Boondis will stay crisp for a few days when stored in an airtight container in your kitchen.

# NAADA PAKODA, simply called 'tape' after their visual appearance, these light and crunchy, yellow savoury ribbons of fried chickpea batter are a delicious accompaniment to afternoon tea or coffee, and immensely satisfying when you feel peckish.

The special metal press needed to make naada pakoda is available in most Indian grocery stores in the kitchenware department.

## INGREDIENTS TO SERVE 8 PEOPLE

* 2 cups besan (chickpea/gram flour)
* ½ cup rice flour
* ½ teaspoon turmeric powder
* ½ teaspoon red chilli powder; ½ teaspoon more to make it spicier
* salt to taste
* 1 teaspoon ajwain seeds (carom), powdered fine
* ½ teaspoon asafoetida powder
* water for mixing the dough
* 2½ cups oil, divided

## METHOD

Sift besan, rice flour, salt, and turmeric, chilli, ajwain and asafoetida powders into a bowl. Do not mix.

Heat up ½ cup oil in a wok on medium heat. Pour it over the sifted dry ingredients in the bowl. Mix with fingers, pressing the oil against the ingredients to form a crumbly dry mixture.

Add water, 2 tablespoons at a time, and mix to a stiff cookie dough. Keep covered.
Heat 2 cups oil in a wok on medium heat. Fit the barrel of the press with the appropriate plate for ribbons. Fill half the barrel of the noodle press with some dough. Place the extruding stem over the dough.

Hold the press vertically, about 6 inches above the hot oil in the wok, and press down in a circular motion, so that the ribbons of dough spread out in the oil. Fry, turning the ribbons over till they are light brown in colour and fried crisp. Drain with a slotted spoon and transfer to a paper-lined colander.

Add 1 tablespoon water to the dough and mix, if it is too stiff and difficult to press. Continue to fry the rest of the dough.

Drain, cool and store in airtight containers. Stays fresh for at least a week.

## GULAB JAMUN, *a popular confectionery at the festival of Deepavali, these luscious, deep purple balls of fried milk solids resting in a pool of golden syrup look dramatic. Paired with ice cream, they are a royal treat.*

'Gulab' in Persian is a 'rose', and 'jamun' in Hindi refers to the dark purple berry so abundant during the monsoon rains in India.

For years, I made gulab jamuns Amma's way with 'khoya', the fresh milk solids available in most confectionery stores in India. I now have a recipe using dry milk solids (maava) which works very well.

Making the gulab jamuns a day ahead gives time for them to soak in the syrup, and I serve them at room temperature. They can be refrigerated for a week and reheated.

### INGREDIENTS TO MAKE THE SYRUP

* 2½ cups water
* 2½ cups sugar
* ½ teaspoon cardamom powder
* ¼ teaspoon strands of saffron

### METHOD

Warm the water in a deep pan on medium heat. Add the sugar and other ingredients and boil to a thin syrup.

### INGREDIENTS TO MAKE THE DOUGH FOR 25-30 PIECES

* 1 cup khoya or maava
* 1 cup all-purpose flour

- ¼ *teaspoon baking powder*
- ¼ *teaspoon baking soda*
- ½ *cup water*
- 2 *cups oil for frying*

## METHOD, FIRST STAGE: TO SHAPE THE BALLS OF DOUGH

Combine the dry ingredients in a bowl. Sprinkle water a little at a time and mix to a soft dough. Gently knead and set aside for 10 minutes.

Divide into 25-30 portions and roll gently into balls. Keep covered.

## METHOD, SECOND STAGE: TO FRY AND SOAK

Keep the bowl of syrup near the stove.

Warm the oil in a heavy pan on medium low heat.

Test the temperature of the oil by dropping in a small piece of the dough. It should sink in, and within 1 minute, swell and rise to the surface.

Gently drop 10 'balls' at a time into the hot oil (do not crowd the frying pan as the balls of dough will swell).

Do not stir with a ladle; instead, gently shake the pan horizontally to agitate the shortening.

When the balls of dough rise to the surface, slowly turn them over with a slotted spoon, helping them to brown evenly on all sides.

Fry to a dark brown, drain, and briefly rest them for a minute in a colander before slipping them into the bowl of warm syrup. Ladle a tablespoon of syrup over the gulab jamuns.

Fry all the balls in batches of 10, and after resting each batch for a minute, slip them into the syrup.

If the bowl of syrup gets too crowded with gulab jamuns, carefully lift each gulab jamun you have soaked earlier and transfer to another shallow bowl, and pour a little syrup over them.

## COCONUT CHOCOLATE MOUNDS, *Amma's simple, easy-to-make, delectable rich sweets.*

### INGREDIENTS TO MAKE 30 MOUNDS

- 2 *cans sweetened condensed milk*
- 1 *cup unsweetened dark cocoa powder*
- *a pinch of salt*
- 2 *cups grated dessicated cocoanut (copra)*

- *1 teaspoon vanilla extract*
- *1 tablespoon unsalted butter*
- *½ cup mixed nuts (almonds/walnuts), chopped (optional)*

METHOD

Empty the cans of condensed milk into a heavy skillet.

Add the cocoa powder a little at a time and stir, incorporating it well into the condensed milk. Add the salt, coconut and vanilla, and cook on medium heat, stirring continuously, till it caramelizes and thickens. Stir in the butter. Turn off the heat.

Scoop out 1 teaspoon of the fudge and, sliding it with another spoon, place it in a mound on a sheet of wax paper. Scoop out the rest of the fudge in mounds, press ½ teaspoon chopped nuts on each mound, and leave to cool. Lift gently with a metal spatula and store in an airtight container.

KANCHIPURAM IDLI, *fragrant and mildly pungent, steamed rice-lentil cake with bits of coconut and cashew buried within.*

The township of Kanchipuram in Tamil Nadu is famous for its handwoven silk textiles, more importantly for sarees. But how these special idlis got their name is not clear, except that there are reports that a certain sect of people migrated from Kanchipuram and carried the special recipe with them.

Making Kanchipuram idlis requires preparation time of 24 hours before you plan to serve them, but they are well worth the planning. The fermented batter can be refrigerated, and the idlis steamed within the next two days. The steamed idlis can also be refrigerated for up to 3 days, reheated and served.

To make idlis for breakfast, soak the grains the previous evening, grind post-dinner, and leave the batter overnight. The ideal temperature for fermentation is 70°F. In cold weather, leave the batter in a covered container in the oven with the pilot light on, or in a proofing unit.

INGREDIENTS TO MAKE THE BATTER FOR 20–25 IDLIS

- *1 cup raw rice; any variety without fragrance works well*
- *1 cup parboiled rice*
- *1 cup urad dal*
- *1 tablespoon plain yogurt (used when the temperature is less than 70°F)*
- *1 tablespoon chana dal*
- *¼ cup chopped 'tooth-size' pieces of fresh coconut (my mother's description for the size)*

- ½ teaspoon cracked black pepper
- ½ teaspoon minced fresh ginger
- 12 curry leaves, torn in pieces
- ½ teaspoon asafoetida powder
- 12 raw cashew nuts, broken in pieces
- ¼ cup oil to grease idli cups or depressions in mould
- ¼ cup ghee to smear on steamed idlis
- salt to taste

## METHOD TO MAKE THE BATTER

Mix both varieties of rice in a bowl. Rinse and drain. Rinse till the water is clear. Soak rice in water for 5 hours, and drain.

Do the same with the urad dal, and set aside in a separate bowl.

In a blender, grind half the quantity of rice, adding ½ cup tepid water. Pause frequently and push down on the sides with a spatula. Grind to a thick batter, the texture of cream of rice. Empty into a large bowl. Repeat with the remaining rice, scraping all the contents into the same bowl.

Without washing the blender, grind urad dal to a fine smooth, satiny and fluffy batter, adding ¼ cup of water. Pause frequently and push down the sides with a spatula, and grind. Empty into the bowl with the ground rice.

Wash out the blender with 2 tablespoons of water and add to the bowl. The batter should be a thick pancake consistency.

Stir in salt and yogurt (if you are using it) and set aside, tightly covered, for 8-10 hours or overnight, in a warm area of about 70°F to ferment. Choose a large enough container, as the batter will swell to double its size. Keeping it in a proofing unit with the pilot light on aids the fermentation process.

In hot weather, there is no need to add yogurt to the batter.

## METHOD TO STEAM IDLIS

Soak the chana dal in water for 2 hours before steaming the idlis. Drain and add dal to fermented batter.

Add the other ingredients, except the oil. Add salt to taste. The batter at this tage should be well aerated, thick but of a pouring consistency.

Fill the lower pan of an idli steamer with water up to 2 inches in depth. Bring the water to a boil on medium heat.

Grease the idli cups with a little oil and pour enough batter to fill about ¼ of each cup. Place the idli stand with the filled cups inside the steamer, cover tight and cook. You could steam in a pressure cooker without the weight.

Steam for 10 minutes. Remove lid. Test each idli by inserting a toothpick which should come out clean. Scoop out each idli with a spatula and transfer to a bowl. Cover the bowl with a kitchen towel and set aside.

Repeat process of steaming as many batches of idli as required.

Check the quantity of water in the lower pan of the steamer after steaming each batch, and refill water if needed.

Serve idlis hot or at room temperature, smeared with hot ghee, and with coconut chutney and shallot sambar on the side.

## Krishnan Nair's Appams in Queen Mary's College

When I left Poona in the summer of 1946 to join the liberal arts and humanities department at one of the country's premier women's institutions for graduate studies, the Queen Mary's College in Madras, it was not easy for me to leave the security of home and of loving, caring parents and adoring siblings, not to speak of the city I grew up in.

I took the train from Poona to Madras Central Station, where my mother's cousin met me in the early hours of the morning, gave me an early breakfast and put me in a cycle rickshaw, handing me a sheet of paper with handwritten directions to the college. The two black trunks containing my personal belongings were loaded onto another rickshaw, and I left for my college and new 'home', the college hostel, with trepidation.

I was feeling low, anxious and unsettled, to say the least.

Soon, I was at the imposing gates of the college on Beach Road, overlooking the sandy Marina with the fishermens' boats setting out for the day towards the brilliant sun. The Bay of Bengal was shimmering calm that morning. Little did I know that with the onset of the torrential monsoons, the stormy waves would drive the sea into the college campus.

I liked what I saw when I entered the gates. A canopy of rain tree branches spread across the driveway and a well-laid-out rose garden on the lower terrace of the campus was in bloom.

On arrival, every student had a brief interview with Miss Myers, the principal and warden of the college. I was nervous about the interview but Miss Myers allayed my fears. She was the spitting image of Miss Levy, my English teacher whom I adored at the Christ Church School in Jubbulpore. She asked me a couple of questions about my parents and my family, and wished me well in my studies and for my stay in the hostel. I left her room, thankful for the short interview, which I learnt later was a formality. It was comforting to have met and talked to Miss Myers.

I was south Indian and Tamilian, and Madras should have been 'home' to me, but it was not. I generally found people, including many of my classmates in college, conservative and caste conscious. Poona, by comparison, was cool and liberal. Women had more freedom in Poona, where girls and women rode bicycles to school and work. Though

*Entrance to Queen Mary's College, Madras*

I had brought my bike with me, I rarely felt comfortable riding it in Madras. To add to the feeling of being an 'outsider', I also missed the comfort of familiar home-cooked food.

Queen Mary's College had an excellent reputation for academics, but the hostel food was indifferent in quality and the atmosphere of the dining room uninviting. There were two divisions in the hostel mess; the crowded, noisy 'vegetarian mess' and the orderly 'non-vegetarian dining room'. A vegetarian by upbringing, I preferred to join the vegetarian mess. Soon I realized that more than two-thirds of the hostel inmates had joined the vegetarian mess even though many preferred non-vegetarian food. They had their reasons.

Many in the hostel referred to the food served in the non-vegetarian dining room as 'English food', which translates to omelette and toast for breakfast instead of idli and dosai. They were also uncomfortable with the formality of the dining room and that conversation was conducted in English. They decided they were not going to pay for the tables with table cloths, vases with flowers and uniformed bearers.

In comparison, the appearance and atmosphere of the large

*Rukka and colleagues in Queen Mary's College*

rectangular vegetarian dining hall was chaotic and unappetizing. Six long rectangular wooden tables were arranged parallel to each other and students sat on wooden benches. The dining hall could seat only about forty students at a time, and there were several batches at every meal. There was an unwritten hierarchy among the students; our seniors dined before us. The first two batches of students dined at cleaner tables and the food was hot. The Malayali cooks and servers looked exhausted and overworked; thus, order and cleanliness were very low priorities for them. One of the resident staff did try to improve matters, but the numbers were so large that it was a no-win situation.

The weekday lunch and dinner in the vegetarian mess was ill-planned. On most days, it was potatoes in one form or another. Green vegetables were a rarity.

After the third week of the first term, in my first year in college, Krishnan Nair, an avuncular man in his forties and the head cook in the vegetarian mess, noticing that I ate very little, came up to me and advised me on the importance of eating well—he meant more—in order to be able to study. I told him I did not like the food served for lunch and dinner and that I preferred the breakfast menu. I still remember the weekly breakfast menu—idlis (steamed rice cakes) with coconut chutney and sambar (lentil stew), dosai (rice crêpes) with potato curry and chutney, uthappam (a variant of the dosai), rava dosai (semolina crêpes) with coconut chutney, semolina upma (herbed, cream of wheat polenta), appam (rice pancakes) with vegetable kurma (mixed vegetable stew), and puri (fried Indian wheat bread) with potato curry. My favourite breakfast was the spongy, frilly edged appam that came with the creamy mixed vegetable kurma, with the vegetables disintegrating in a thick, spicy, coconut milk sauce, and puris with a potato curry and spicy pitlo. Krishnan Nair treated me to one more appam and two more puris than was my share.

I would eat heartily at breakfast and deliberately miss lunch. I found no variation or variety in the menu for lunch and dinner. The staple was boiled rice with one dry vegetable curry, sambar with a few vegetables, rasam (a thin soup usually with a tomato puree base), buttermilk and, on some days, appalam (fried lentil wafers). Dessert was served on Sundays and festival days—fruit salad and ice cream on Sundays and payasam (rice pudding) on festivals. After the eclectic fare in my parents' home, I found the hostel menu boring and the food poorly cooked.

In my second year in college, Krishnan Nair suggested that I volunteer as a member of the vegetarian mess committee so I could have some clout in suggesting changes in the menu. I was not reluctant to take on the extra work involved in the membership. In fact, I enjoyed going to Kotwal Chowadi market, the wholesale vegetable and fruit market, with Krishnan Nair once a week, wandering among the mountains of vegetable sacks and fruit baskets. I introduced more vegetables into the menu and started eating better. I also introduced a more substantial evening tiffin, of appam with kurma and puri, and with potato curry instead of the two biscuits or two bajjis (vegetable fritters) that the existing menu provided. The result was an increase in the mess bill, which made me unpopular with some of the students who protested, threatening to stage a one-day hunger strike. It was a delicate balancing act for me between good food and capping the mess bill at the end of the month. Fortunately, this was sorted out without compromising on the quality of the food, and I was re-elected to the student membership for the next few years of my stay in the college.

APPAM, *soft, light crêpe suzette of ground rice with a hint of sweetness of coconut milk. And with the addition of yeast granules, mine is a modified version of Krishnan Nair's recipe for appam.*

### INGREDIENTS TO MAKE 15-20 APPAMS

* *2 cups raw rice*
* *3 tablespoons cooked rice*
* *2 cups coconut milk*
* *2 teaspoons sugar*
* *½ teaspoon yeast granules*
* *¼ cup oil to grease appam griddle*
* *salt to taste*

### METHOD TO MAKE THE BATTER

Wash and rinse the rice. Repeat till the water is clear and not cloudy. Soak the rice in five cups of water for three hours.

Drain and grind to a smooth paste, adding the cooked rice, ¼ cup water and ¼ cup coconut milk. Empty batter into a bowl. Stir in the remaining coconut milk, salt and sugar.

Mix the yeast in 1 tablespoon warm water and add to the batter. Whisk to mix well. Cover and set aside for 4 hours. The batter should be of pouring consistency.

## METHOD TO MAKE APPAMS

Heat an appam wok or shallow saucer-shaped griddle on medium heat. Brush the wok with ⅛ teaspoon of oil.

Pour about ¼ cup batter in the middle of the wok, and immediately tilt and swirl the batter around to spread in the shape of a disc. The edges of the disc should be thin and lacy and the centre thick, with the draining of the batter collecting in the middle. Cover and cook for one minute.

Remove lid and gently ease the edges with a spatula, and lift and remove appam to a serving dish.

Serve hot with a vegetable kurma or coconut chutney.

# VEGETABLE KURMA, *a flavourful stew with a variety of vegetables in a herb and coconut sauce. I have modified Krishnan Nair's recipe by adding ground cashew nuts and poppy seeds, which add to the texture and taste of the kurma.*

## INGREDIENTS TO MAKE 6 SERVINGS

* 1 tablespoon poppy seeds
* 1 cup shredded coconut, fresh or frozen
* ½ teaspoon fresh ginger, grated
* ¼ cup raw cashew nut pieces
* 2 tablespoons oil
* 2 cups peeled shallots, halved, or 2 medium onions, each chopped in 8 wedges
* 3 green cardamom pods, small
* 3 cloves
* 1-inch length cinnamon
* 4 bay leaves
* 2 green chillies, slit lengthwise
* 1 large potato, peeled and cut in 1-inch cubes
* 1 medium carrot, peeled and cut in 1-inch cubes
* ½ cup shelled peas, fresh or frozen
* ½ cup loosely packed fresh coriander leaves and tender stems, chopped
* juice of half a lime (optional)
* salt to taste

## METHOD

Dry roast poppy seeds in a skillet or wok on low heat till the seeds turn a very light brown colour with a nutty aroma. This will take under one minute. Do not over-roast. Stir continuously to prevent burning.

Grind coconut, ginger, cashew nuts and roasted poppy seeds to a fine paste in a blender, adding enough water. Empty into a bowl. Wash out the blender with 1½ cups water and add to the bowl. Cover and set aside.

Heat the oil, but not to smoking point, in a heavy bottomed saucepan on medium heat. Add the onions and sauté till they turn translucent.

Lower the heat, toss in the cardamoms, cloves, cinnamon and bay leaves, and stir a couple of times. Add the green chillies and vegetables. Stir and cook for two minutes, coating the vegetables with the herbed oil.

Add 1½ cups water and salt to taste, and cook the vegetables until soft but not mushy. Add the ground coconut masala, stir and bring to a boil.

Scatter the coriander leaves. Turn off the stove. Stir in lime juice, if you are using it. Cover and leave to rest. Serve after about an hour when the taste and aroma of the ground masala gets absorbed by the vegetables. You may stir in a little hot water if the gravy is too thick.

Kurma is good served hot or at room temperature. I make kurma, not just as an accompaniment to go with appams but also with chapattis (wholewheat flour flatbread), puris (deep-fried wholewheat bread), steamed rice and western-style baked bread. Friends in Berkeley ate kurma like a thick vegetable soup.

The dish stays fresh for 3 days when refrigerated.

PURI, *soft, airy, puffed-up, fried wholewheat bread, puris are an all-time favourite, and my friends in England and America marvel at the way they inflate with pride.*

## INGREDIENTS TO MAKE 15 PURIS

* *2 cups wholewheat flour*
* *½ teaspoon salt*
* *water to mix and knead to a stiff dough*
* *2½ cups oil, divided*

## METHOD TO MIX THE DOUGH AND FRY THE PURIS

Mix flour and salt in a bowl. Add water, a little at a time, to mix to a stiff dough.

Turn out onto a work-board and knead till soft and smooth. Drizzle 1 tablespoon oil and work it into the dough. Roll the dough with your fingers into a rope, and divide into 15 equal portions. Roll into balls. Keep them covered in a bowl.

Heat oil in a wok or frying pan on medium-high heat, but not to smoking point. Lower heat to medium.

Roll each ball with a rolling pin into a 3-inch round. Roll 3 at a time.

Slide each ball gently into the oil and fry, turning over both sides, pressing down slightly with a slotted spoon. Do not crowd the wok. The puri will magically puff up. Fry to a golden brown.

Drain and remove with a slotted spoon onto a colander lined with paper towels.

Serve hot or at room temperature. I also serve puris with coconut chutney, raita and a sweet and sour mango pickle.

POTATO CURRY, *spicy and aromatic, this easy and quick-to-make curry goes well with rice and any kind of bread. I prefer a slightly liquid version of the curry.*

## INGREDIENTS TO MAKE 4 SERVINGS

- 2 large potatoes, cut in half and boiled soft
- 2 tablespoons oil
- ½ teaspoon brown mustard seeds
- ½ teaspoon chana dal
- 2 medium onions, chopped coarse
- 2 green chillies, chopped coarse
- 1-inch piece fresh ginger, chopped fine
- 12 curry leaves, torn in halves
- 1 cup chopped tomatoes
- ¼ teaspoon turmeric powder
- ⅛ teaspoon red chilli powder (optional)
- ¾ cup water; more for a slightly liquid version
- 1 teaspoon lime juice
- ¼ cup fresh coriander with tender stems, chopped
- salt to taste

## METHOD

Peel and mash potatoes coarsely, leaving a few chunks. Set aside.

Heat oil in a wok or saucepan on medium heat. Add mustard seeds, and as they splutter and pop, add chana dal and stir to a golden brown. Toss in chopped onions and sauté till translucent.

Add green chillies, ginger, curry leaves, tomatoes, turmeric powder and red chilli powder (if you are using it), and stir a couple of times.

Add mashed potatoes and salt, and toss for one minute with the sautéed onions and herbs. Pour in the water and bring to a boil. Cook for 2 minutes.

Turn off the heat and stir in the lime juice.

Garnish with coriander and keep covered till ready to serve.

PITLA, *smooth and spicy chickpea flour snack, rich in protein and amazingly easy to whip up. Originally a savoury street food from Maharashtra, it has found its way to far-off destinations. I visited a women's hostel in Trivandrum in the southern state of Kerala and one of the popular sell-out snacks in their canteen was 'pitlo'! It was runny and was served in soup bowls with slices of bread. This is my version with some greens.*

## INGREDIENTS TO MAKE 6 SERVINGS

- 1 cup chickpea flour (gram flour, besan)
- salt to taste
- 3 cups water
- 1 cup buttermilk
- 4 tablespoons oil
- ½ teaspoon brown mustard seeds
- 1 medium onion, chopped fine
- 3 sprigs scallion, chopped
- 3 green chillies, slit lengthwise and chopped fine
- 10 curry leaves, torn in halves
- ½ cup spinach leaves, chopped
- 1 medium tomato, chopped
- ¼ teaspoon turmeric powder
- ½ teaspoon red chilli powder
- ½ cup coriander leaves and tender stems, chopped

## METHOD

Mix chickpea flour, salt, water and buttermilk in a bowl. Mix with fingers, breaking up the lumps. Set aside.

Heat 3 tablespoon oil in a wok on medium heat. Add mustard seeds, and as they splutter and pop, add onion and sauté till translucent. Stir in the scallions, green chillies, curry leaves, spinach, tomato, turmeric and red chilli powder. Stir a couple of times.

Pour in the chickpea flour batter, and stir continuously till it turns soupy and bubbly. The raw smell of the chickpea batter should disappear.

Empty into a serving bowl.

Serve hot.

# The Mobile Canteen on the Madras Marina

Once I had settled down in my college, I started bonding with the nine other girls in the large dormitory. I learned that all, except one, came from small towns near Madras. Sushma Kutty, from Trissur in Kerala, and I were the only two from outside Madras Presidency, now Tamil Nadu. None of them had heard of Poona.

Four of the girls, in ankle-length skirts ('pavadai' in Tamil), and a short blouse with 'melakku', a length of material wrapped over the upper part of the body, looked in their early teens to me. The other five looked older and were dressed in sarees. They all looked disapprovingly at my clothes, a knee-high pleated maroon dress, and two of them had even asked, 'Are you Christian?'

A couple of days later, I shifted to wearing a saree, which helped me blend with the student community in the college.

Ten days later at a hostel meeting, all the new entrants to the intermediate, BA and BSc courses, were allotted tutors and rooms. The tutors were responsible for the good behaviour and academic performance of their wards. They assumed the role of surrogate parents. My tutor, Mrs Mandakini Bai, was the chairperson of the Hindi department. She may have been in her fifties, and was benignly firm and helpful. She was fond of me, maybe because of my fluency in speaking Hindi, and unsuccessful though, had tried to get me to transfer to Hindi from French.

I was allotted a room on the first floor in Stone House Block—a room for two—and my first room-mate was Juliet. I found, when I entered my room with two trunks and a hold-all, she was already unpacked and waiting to see who would share her room. I remember her as being short in stature, just about five feet tall, with a tanned complexion, curly-haired and stockily built. I was very impressed that she could lift my trunks without much effort. As we got talking, I learnt that her parents also lived in Tanjore, which was another reason to bond with her. Juliet and I shared a room for the first year after we joined college in the intermediate class. Over the first couple of weeks, we became good friends, and though the hostel room was small and cramped with two chests of drawers, two writing desks with straight-backed chairs, and two beds against each wall, and hardly any room to move, each one of us had managed a space of our own. Juliet was very adjusting and, as I realized soon, caring too. When my younger sister Sarasa also joined Queen Mary's College in 1947, Juliet helpfully moved to another room in the same block and on the same floor, and we continued to be friends. She left Queen Mary's College at the end of the second year when she joined the Vellore Medical College, and sadly, thereafter, I lost all contact with her. I continued to stay in the students' hostel for the next three years till I completed the Bachelor of Arts (Honours) program in Geography.

My interest in geography, I think, was kindled by Mr Mackintosh who taught nature study as a subject in St Helena's School in Poona, where I had spent eight years. The school curriculum included Nature Study, a fascinating subject which included not only a study of text books but was also combined with field studies. Mr Mackintosh began and ended his lively classes with personal stories of his travels, of the places he had visited and the people he had met. He spoke several Indian languages, besides the many dialects of the British Isles. He brought life to his class and clearly loved what he taught. Broadly, nature study included studies of the relationship between man and the environment in different parts of the globe. As an integral part of the subject, the school also took its students on field trips in and around Poona. My teacher was not only well qualified and widely travelled, he also taught the subject with passion. I looked forward to his classes.

Though I was able to befriend other girls within a few weeks of joining Queen Mary's College, it took me much time to adjust to

*The Marina Beach in Madras*

the indifferent food in the college hostel. Frankly, I found the food unappetizing and often made only a pretence of eating it. This continued for months, which is when the head cook of the vegetarian mess, Krishnan Nair, became concerned about my health. The food in the vegetarian mess of the college hostel was inedible, and within a few weeks of joining the hostel, I was visibly exhausted. I had lost weight and was not able to concentrate on my studies. Juliet echoed Krishnan Nair's thoughts. She was a pragmatic person and her philosophy was, 'Don't sit and moan; do something to improve matters.'

Acting on Juliet's advice, as I mentioned earlier, I volunteered to be an ad-hoc member of the mess committee and tried to reorganize the menu, working within the parameters of cost and affordability, which was no mean task that took up much of my time. Juliet also suggested that in the meantime I buy a tiffin carrier, so I could get snacks or food from the mobile canteen which parked right opposite the college every evening between four and nine o'clock. In a few days, I became an ardent devotee of the red and blue van that provided me with my daily tiffin favourites.

The mobile canteen arrived with great fanfare on the Beach Road, playing loud and cheerful Tamil cinema music. Cloth banners displaying the mouth-watering fare fluttered from the front and back of the van, tempting the beach crowd with crisp brown bondas (fried lentil balls), golden dosai (lentil batter crêpes), bowls of fruit salad and ice cream, and rich brown coffee. Delicious smells beckoned the passers-by along the beachfront. Other vendors doing brisk business selling boiled peanuts, spicy puffed rice, and in summer, raw mango slices dusted with chilli powder and salt, each with his own jingle, dotted the evening beach landscape.

By four o'clock every evening, my thoughts and senses wandered to the aromatic, hot and crunchy Mangalore bondas (spicy fried balls of dough) and hot coffee that was served from the van window. My dorm mates and I preferred to enjoy eating the snacks leisurely in our rooms.

Buying food from outside was not new for the hostelites, and this need was acknowledged and accepted by the hostel tutors as long as no outsiders entered the hostel rooms. The hostel rules were very clear, especially ones that pertained to banning of entry of males to the first and second floors, the residential section of the hostel.

The ferrying of food from the mobile canteen to the hostel fell to the lot of the 'chhokras', the young 'ball picker' lads in the tennis courts of the college. By four o'clock every evening, half a dozen of them would hang about the staircase, knowing well that their services

would be needed. Kullan (in Tamil), which translates to 'Shorty', was my tiffin boy. With his usual question in Tamil, *'Innikku enna venum* (What do you want today)?' he grabbed my tiffin carrier and the cash and scampered off. In about an hour, he did ten dashes to the mobile canteen and back, knowing he would be 'tipped' by that many number of thankful hostelites.

This Pavlovian conditioning was not peculiar to me alone. I was not the only famished slave of the mobile canteen. Soon, a group of my dorm mates assembled on the wide verandah outside our rooms facing the front garden of the college, each with her favourite snack for the evening and ready for an impromptu party. Masala dosai, Mangalore bonda, medu vadai (savoury lentil-batter doughnuts), masala rice (small servings of extremely aromatic, spicy, well-cooked vegetables mixed with rice), and packets of coconut barfi, peanut brittle and semolina fudge would be spread out before us.

I do not know how much the others spent each evening on their tiffin from the mobile canteen. I remember, we were six of us in the group who shared our snacks on most evenings. And there was quite a variety and plenty to go round. My guess is, each of us would have spent about five rupees. Three of our groupmates were Tamil movie buffs, who divided their personal expenses between film tickets on weekends and the mobile canteen on some weekdays. As to me, I felt no guilt in spending on tiffin since I rarely went to the movies.

I give below the recipes of some of my favourites from the mobile canteen.

## MANGALORE BONDA, *crisp fried blobs of batter, speckled with peppery cumin. Best eaten hot!*

### INGREDIENTS TO MAKE 15-20 BONDAS

* 2 cups white flour
* ½ teaspoon salt
* ½ teaspoon cumin seeds
* 1 teaspoon red chilli powder

- ½ cup fresh coriander leaves, chopped
- 2 tablespoons plain yogurt
- water to mix batter
- 2 cups oil for frying

## METHOD

Mix all the ingredients in a bowl, adding enough water to get a batter of dropping consistency. Leave to rest, covered, for ½ hour.

Heat the oil in a wok on medium-high heat, but not to smoking point. Lower the heat to medium. Scoop up 1 teaspoon batter, and with another spoon, slide it into the hot oil. Slide in six more. They will swell and rise to the surface.

Fry to a golden brown, turning over a couple of times.

Drain with a slotted spoon and serve hot with mint-coconut chutney.

## CHEESE BONDAS, my variation of Mangalore bondas with the addition of cheese. This recipe is the closest I could get to the inimitable cheese balls I first tasted in 1956 at one of the restaurants in Fisherman's Wharf in Ghirardelli Square in San Francisco.

### INGREDIENTS TO MAKE 25-30 BONDAS

- 2 cups white flour
- ½ cup wholewheat flour
- 2 tablespoons rava/fine semolina/cream of wheat
- 1 teaspoon red chilli powder
- 1 teaspoon cumin seeds
- ½ cup chopped fresh coriander leaves
- 1 cup mixed hard cheeses, grated (leftover bits of cheddar, gouda or jack. Parmesan or mixed Mexican cheeses work well too)
- ¼ cup plain yogurt
- water to mix batter
- 2 cups oil for frying
- salt to taste; add only if needed

### METHOD

In a large, deep bowl, mix all the ingredients, except yogurt, water and oil.

Add yogurt and 2 tablespoons of water, and mix well to form a loose batter of dropping consistency.

Heat the oil in a wok or deep-frying pan on medium heat, but not to smoking point.
Pick up 1 teaspoon of the batter, and with another spoon, gently slide it into the hot oil. Slide in 5 more and fry till golden-brown, turning over a few times.

Drain on paper towels and serve hot with any sweet, sour or spicy chutney.

## CORN CUTLETS, *when fresh corn is in abundance and you tire of roasting and boiling them, corn cutlets are a delicious alternative.*

### INGREDIENTS TO MAKE 20–25 CUTLETS

* *1 large potato with skin, washed, boiled and mashed coarse*
* *2 cups corn niblets, boiled and drained and the water squeezed out; frozen niblets may be soaked in warm water for about 10 minutes and the water squeezed out*
* *2 green chillies, cut in thin rings*
* *1-inch piece fresh ginger, grated*
* *2 cups chopped coriander leaves with tender stems*
* *1 teaspoon fennel seeds, crushed coarse (optional)*
* *½ teaspoon turmeric powder*
* *1 teaspoon coriander powder*
* *½ teaspoon red chilli powder (optional)*
* *1 teaspoon sugar*
* *1 tablespoon lime juice*
* *¼ cup besan (gram flour, chickpea flour)*
* *¼ cup rice flour*
* *2 cups oil to fry*
* *water to mix*
* *salt to taste*

### METHOD

Empty all the ingredients, except the water and oil, into a large bowl. Mix to blend. Sprinkle water, 1 tablespoon at a time, and mix so that the mixture just holds together. Add salt to taste.

Divide into 20–25 portions and roll loosely into balls.

Heat 2 cups oil in a wok or deep-frying pan on medium heat.

Take 1 ball at a time, and in the palm of your hand, pat gently to a ½-inch thick disc. Test by frying one first. If it falls apart, add an extra tablespoon of rice flour and mix. Gradually slide 6 discs at a time into the hot oil, and fry both sides golden-brown. Drain in a colander lined with paper towels. Complete frying the remaining discs.

Serve hot with a chutney of your choice.

# MINT-COCONUT CHUTNEY, *fresh mint ground with coconut adds colour, as also a fresh, cleansing after-taste.*

## INGREDIENTS TO MAKE 2 CUPS

* *1 cup shredded coconut, fresh or frozen*
* *2 green chillies*
* *½ cup mint leaves*
* *1 tablespoon lime juice*
* *¼ teaspoon sugar*
* *salt to taste*
* *1 cup water; more if needed*

## METHOD

Grind all ingredients in a blender to a smooth paste adding water a little at a time. Empty into a bowl.

# MASALA TOAST, *a popular snack any time of the day, with no toiling over a stove!*

## INGREDIENTS TO MAKE 5 SERVINGS

* *10 slices white bread (day-old bread is better)*
* *½ cup melted butter*
* *1 cup grated carrots*
* *½ cup onions, finely sliced*
* *2 green chillies, sliced in thin rings*
* *¼ cup chopped coriander leaves and tender stems*
* *1 tablespoon coriander seeds, coarsely crushed*
* *1 cup sharp cheddar cheese, grated (optional)*
* *salt to taste*

## METHOD

Trim edges of the slices of bread and butter on one side. Scatter 1 teaspoon carrots evenly on the buttered side. Place a layer of onions over the carrots. Scatter a few chilli rings and ½ teaspoon of chopped coriander on top. Sprinkle a pinch of salt and scatter ½ teaspoon crushed coriander seeds. Drizzle ½ teaspoon melted butter on top. Scatter grated cheese, if you are using it.

Grill under a broiler to a crisp brown.

Cut diagonally. Serve hot and crisp.

# Pudina Pidi Kozhukattai in Poonamallee

Appa's sister Kamalam, my Athai, and her advocate husband, my Athimber, lived in Poonamallee, a fast-developing satellite town on the outskirts of Madras. Kamalam's younger sisters referred to their Athimber, brother-in-law, as 'pleader' Athimber; I have not heard them use the term 'advocate'. All I know about his work is that he represented his clients at the mofussil and district courts, and sometimes, in the high court in Madras. The original name of the village, Poovirundhavalli, I was told, was derived from its small market gardening industry of floriculture ('poovu' in Tamil means flower), growing flaming orange kanakambaram (*Crossandra infundibuliformis*), also known as the firecracker flower, and fragrant pearl-white jasmine flowers for the wholesale flower market in Madras. The pre-dawn buses from Poonamallee arrived in Madras laden with hundreds of baskets of flowers.

Seated, (L) Bombay Chitappa and (R) Poonamallee Athai. Standing, (L) Rukka and (R) Bombay Chitti

While it retained its rural charm with spacious village houses set in gardens that grew both fruit and flowers, Poonamallee was rapidly becoming a satellite town of the city of Madras. Home to many commuters, it took a bus ride of just over an hour and a half for the scene to change from a quiet, laid-back rural haven to a crowded, restless city on the move.

Athai and Athimber's home on the main street was a charming traditional village house, one of seven semi-detached street houses. A covered verandah at the entrance was used as a waiting-room for Athimber's clients before they were ushered into his office chambers. The house was dominated by a spacious, inner square courtyard. A wide covered deck skirted the courtyard, one side of which was converted to an informal living space with a carved wooden traditional swing, a rattan two-seater and a couple of chairs. At night, this section of the deck was converted to a sleeping area, a dormitory where the younger members of the family slept. Two cows and a calf were tethered in a shed in the back garden, and a pye dog, Timmy, kept guard at night in the front verandah.

When I first met her in late 1939, during my father's posting in Madras for two years, Poonamallee Athai was elegantly thin, her face framed with curly hair wound in a knot at the nape of her neck. Small alert eyes and a sharp pronounced nose gave her a bird-like expression. I came to know her better when, in 1946, I joined Queen Mary's College and had a standing invitation from her and Athimber to spend weekends with them. By then, her curly hair had turned completely grey and her eyes seemed cloudy.

Athai's life centred around her family. My mental picture of her is one of a frail little woman spinning around her home doing several domestic chores. She was an orthodox housewife, her life governed by unquestioned caste rules of purity and pollution.

Poonamallee Athai's day began at 4.00 a.m. A bath at the well in the backyard was followed with milking the cows. She filled three or more brass pots with water drawn from the well for use during the day, and carried them to the kitchen. One pot would be cradled along the left side of her waist and the other she carried in her right hand.

The entire household woke up by six o'clock to the warm, smoky smell of wood fire and freshly brewed coffee.

I marvelled at her style of drinking coffee. With her head slightly tilted back, raising the silver tumbler at least two inches above her open mouth, she tipped it ever so slightly, and the steaming coffee poured in a steady stream into her gullet. I would watch her, fascinated, as she swallowed with a gurgling sound and with her mouth open. While Athai drank from her silver coffee tumbler, the rest of the family drank out of 'vengalam' (bronze) tumblers. All the tumblers had a lip, so the liquid poured in a steady stream without spilling over the sides. In reply to my asking her why she ate from a banana leaf and only drank from a silver tumbler, and why she did not sip the coffee, she looked at me lovingly and explained, 'Rukka, you grew up in Poona and in the north. You went to a Christian school. You will not understand. I eat from a banana leaf because it can be thrown away once I eat from it...' The gist of what she explained in Tamil is that cooked food is considered as polluting, and silver is considered a pure metal that cannot be polluted. Athai smiled and added, 'I also drink without my lips touching the tumbler for the same reason. My lips pollute the tumbler when they come in contact with it. Do you also notice, when eating, my fingers avoid touching my mouth as I roll the rice in small balls and throw them into my mouth?' In fact, I noticed she flung the food into her open mouth from a few inches away. The food never missed their mark. Later, I realized that for the likes of her—conservative people from my Tamil Brahmin community—all bodily secretions, not just saliva, are considered polluting.

In Athai's house, it was brunch during weekdays, and breakfast only during weekends and holidays when the courts were not in session. And some weekends, too, when Athai was not well, my cousins and I would walk to the corner hotel for a morning tiffin of idlis and sambar. Brunch, which Athai finished cooking by 9.00 a.m., was usually a lentil-based mixed vegetable stew with steamed rice, a dry vegetable curry, a light tomato rasam (mildly spiced tomato soup), toasted or fried lentil wafers, yogurt and a chutney or pickle. Athimber ate by ten o'clock and left for the law courts.

Very rarely did Athai rest during the day. Her mornings were busy supervising the cowherd, the housemaid and sometimes, attending to her husband's clients by spreading a paai, a reed mat, for them to sit on, or giving them a drink of water. By mid-morning, she had washed the coffee filter, tumblers and other pots and pans she may have used earlier in the day. The maid was not permitted to wash the dishes, and again, this was in keeping with Athai's caste rules. Athai was a member of the Brahmin community which her maid was not, and the same rules of purity and pollution governed this as well.

Athimber returned home around four o'clock, tired after a long day at the courts, and would slump in the recliner. Athai would fuss around him, and he and I would leisurely have home-cooked tiffin and coffee, which is when he relaxed and regaled me with fascinating stories of the machinations of local politicians, the frequent kidnappings and murders associated with land disputes, the petty thefts of domestic cattle and goats, and the messy extramarital affairs of well-known personalities. I thought his was a life full of excitement and variety. He would say with a smile, 'I make up for the predictable monotony of life I lead otherwise.' I remember him fondly for an old English ditty he often sang to me: 'When I was single my pockets would jingle...'

Athai's tiffin was always elaborate, and one of the treats she frequently made was 'pidi kozhukattai', in Tamil, which translates to steamed dumplings. Made of ground rice and lentils flavoured with fresh herbs and spices, Athai's pidi kozhukattais were special, studded with beans and speckled with shredded carrot, chopped green dill and mint that she grew in her kitchen garden. As with many of the best vegetarian dishes, the flavour was enhanced by the freshness of the herbs.

Athai planned the cooking of pidi kozhukattai in two stages. She ground the rice and other dry ingredients in a stone quern to a coarse mix, and stored it away a few days earlier, the closed air of the kitchen and deck smelling like a spice cabinet. That was the first stage. On the day of steaming the pidi kozhukattais, she enlisted me in a number of tasks; first, I broke and grated a couple of coconuts from a pile in the back verandah where they were stacked. Then I churned the milk cream into butter. The week's cream was collected and saved in a deep, heavy soapstone jar, a kalchetty. Next, I helped chop and grate the vegetables and bunches of fresh coriander, sprigs of dill, fenugreek and mint into a fine, feathery, fragrant pile, and finally, I helped Athai shape the pidi kozhukattais by pressing the mix in the palm of the hand to form elongated oval dumplings. Throughout the process, she instructed me minutely, and asked me repeatedly if I had washed my hands and feet, warned me not to touch my hair, mouth, clothes, and so on. She made no compromises. In fact, it felt like she was neurotic.

She carefully arranged the portions in a pan, and steamed them in a shining brass idli steamer. Such was her expertise that with one look at the dumplings and a sniff of the steam, she knew when they were done. Piling a few on a banana leaf, with a big dollop of freshly churned butter streaming down the dumplings, and coconut chutney or pulimilagai, a hot and spicy green chilli relish, on the side, she would urge me to break one open and taste a bite. Pidi kozhukattai continues to be one of my favourite tiffin treats.

Athai's arishi upma, savoury rice couscous, which she produced in a matter of minutes, was also special, with the nutty sweet aroma of fresh home-made cow ghee and the tart lemon pickle she made from home-grown lemons.

PIDI KOZHUKATTAI, *this very satisfying, aromatic and tasty steamed tiffin of ground rice and lentils can substitute for a meal, and is amply rewarding for the labour invested. This 'twice-cooked' tiffin is also healthy, as my Athimber never failed to point out.*

## INGREDIENTS FOR 4 SERVINGS

- 1 cup raw rice
- ¼ cup tur dal
- 1 tablespoon chana dal
- 2 dry red chillies
- ½ teaspoon black peppercorn
- 2 tablespoons oil
- ½ teaspoon brown mustard seeds
- 1 teaspoon chana dal
- 2 green chillies, chopped in thin rings
- 12 curry leaves, torn in pieces
- ¼ teaspoon asafoetida powder
- 2 cups water
- ¾ cup shredded coconut, fresh or frozen
- ¼ cup grated carrots, ¼ cup chopped methi (fenugreek leaves), ¼ cup dill, ¼ cup mint leaves (optional)
- salt to taste

## METHOD FOR THE FIRST STAGE

Dry grind the first 5 ingredients to a coarse consistency, resembling corn grits or coarse semolina.

Dry roast the ground mix on medium low heat in a heavy pan till it is just warm to the touch, stirring continuously for 2 minutes. Empty the roasted mix into a bowl and set aside.

## METHOD FOR THE SECOND STAGE

Heat the oil in a wok on medium heat.

Add mustard seeds, and when they pop, lower the heat, add the chana dal, and roast till the grains turn light golden-brown.

Stir in the green chillies, curry leaves and asafoetida. Add 2 cups water and salt, raise the heat to medium, and bring to a boil.

Add the coconut, herbs and vegetables, if you are using them. Bring to a second boil. Drizzle 1 cup of the ground mix, little by little, stirring and breaking all lumps that may form.

Keep stirring and cooking till all the water is absorbed. If the mix is too dry, sprinkle

1 or 2 tablespoons water and stir, and if too wet, add a little more of the ground mix and stir.

Turn off the stove. Add salt to taste and empty into a bowl. The mix when cooked should be moist enough to hold together.

## METHOD FOR THE THIRD AND FINAL STAGE

Wet your fingers in a bowl of water and take 1 tablespoon of the warm mix, and loosely roll into an oval dumpling in the palm of your hand. Set aside on a platter and keep covered. Roll and make rest of the dumplings.

Fill the bottom pan of a steamer with water to a depth of 2 inches. Set to boil on medium heat.

Grease the steamer plate with a smear of oil. Transfer the dumplings from the platter to the steamer plate and steam, covered, for 5 to 7 minutes. Remove lid and test by inserting a toothpick which should come out clean.

Remove and arrange the pidi kozhukattai on a serving platter.

Steam all the pidi kozhukattais in batches.

Serve with a drizzle of hot melted ghee or butter, and coconut chutney or spicy pulimilagai on the side.

I have made pidi kozhukattai with grated carrots and shelled peas for my American friends in Berkeley. They loved it, but were intimidated by the laborious cooking process. When I broke it up into two stages, first preparing the dry semolina mix in the blender one afternoon, and a few days later, steaming the dumplings, they found it more manageable. The dry mix can be refrigerated for a week.

*THAVALA ADAI, with the same pidi kozhukattai mix, Athai made thavala adai for herself. Brown, crisp and crumbly on the outside, and softly disintegrating when you take a bite, her tiffin tasted delicious. Tearing off large pieces, we both savoured the thavala adai with ghee and chunks of jaggery and pulimilagai.*

## METHOD

Heat a heavy cast-iron griddle on medium low heat. Grease the griddle with ½ teaspoon oil.

Wetting your fingers, pick up about 3 tablespoons of the cooked pidi kozhukattai mix and pat it on the griddle to a ½-inch thick pancake. Poke three or four holes in the pancake with the tip of a teaspoon or your finger. Drizzle ⅛ teaspoon oil in each hole

and ½ teaspoon around the edges.

Raise the heat to medium and cook till the underside is brown and crisp.

Flip over with a spatula, drizzle a little oil again in each hole and around the edges but less than before, and cook till brown. Ease the edges and remove with a metal spatula.

Serve hot with mango or lemon pickle, a lump of jaggery and a dollop of ghee on the side.

## PULIMILAGAI, *a sour and spicy, chilli tamarind preserve which serves as a multipurpose chutney. It livens up rice mixed with yogurt. It is a tangy spread for tomato and cucumber sandwiches. I have modified my Athai's recipe by including green bell peppers in combination with green chillies.*

### INGREDIENTS TO MAKE 1 CUP

* *3 tablespoons oil*
* *½ teaspoon brown mustard seeds*
* *1 cup coarsely chopped green chillies (any variety) and 1 cup finely chopped green bell peppers*
* *¼ teaspoon asafoetida powder*
* *10 curry leaves, torn in halves*
* *¼ teaspoon turmeric powder*
* *2 tablespoons brown sugar or grated jaggery*
* *one golf ball size tamarind pulp soaked in 2 cups of warm water, squeezed and juice extracted*
* *salt to taste*

### METHOD

Heat oil in a wok or deep pan on medium heat, but not to smoking point.

Lower the heat. Add mustard seeds, and as they splutter and pop, add chopped chillies and bell peppers, asafoetida, curry leaves and turmeric powder. Stir for one minute.

Add salt, brown sugar or grated jaggery and tamarind water.

Raise heat to medium and bring to a boil. Cook, stirring occasionally and scraping the sides, till the liquid thickens to sauce consistency.

Cool and refrigerate in an airtight jar.

# KUZHI APPAM, *athai made the most scrumptious banana kuzhi appams, chewy and caramelized. This is a good way to use overripe bananas. Years later, when visiting Solvang in California, I longed for kuzhi appams when I saw the aebleskiver pans. Kuzhi appams are the south Indian version of Danish aebleskivers.*

## INGREDIENTS TO MAKE 6 SERVINGS

* 4 large overripe bananas
* 1 cup grated jaggery or brown sugar
* ¼ cup raisins
* ¼ cup cashew nuts, broken in pieces
* 1 teaspoon cardamom powder
* ⅛ teaspoon nutmeg powder
* ¼ teaspoon salt
* ¾ cup white flour
* 1 tablespoon fine rava/cream of wheat/sooji
* 1 teaspoon baking soda
* ¼ cup milk; use if needed
* 1 cup oil and 1 cup melted ghee combined, the shortening

## METHOD

Peel bananas into a bowl. Add other ingredients, except milk and shortening. Mix gently without mashing bananas too much. If you are using milk, add 1 tablespoon at a time, and mix the batter to a dropping consistency.

Grease the cups in a kuzhi appam griddle with ½ teaspoon shortening for each cup. Place griddle over medium heat. Spoon out enough batter to fill ¾ of each cup. Cook, easing the sides and turning over with a chopstick, till all sides are browned. Add more shortening to cook, if needed. Remove and serve hot.

If you are using a wok, pour the ghee and oil into the wok and heat on medium heat.

Spoon out the batter, 1 tablespoon at a time, into the hot oil. Turn over with a slotted spoon and fry brown.

Remove, drain and serve hot.

ARISHI UPMA, *herbed, cream of rice couscous. This was a no-fuss tiffin in Athai's home. Tasty with yogurt and a sour mango or lime pickle on the side, it is a complete meal.*

### INGREDIENTS TO MAKE 6 SERVINGS

- **2 cups cream of rice, not the instant variety**
- **4 tablespoons oil**
- **1 teaspoon brown mustard seeds**
- **2 teaspoons chana dal**
- **1 teaspoon urad dal**
- **½ cup cashew nut pieces**
- **½ teaspoon peppercorns, crushed coarse**
- **2 dry red chillies, broken in half**
- **½ teaspoon cumin seeds**
- **10 curry leaves, torn in half**
- **½ teaspoon asafoetida powder**
- **4 cups water**
- **½ cup shredded coconut, fresh or frozen**
- **2 tablespoons ghee**
- **salt to taste**

Cream of rice is not always available in Indian grocery stores. To make it at home, grind 3 cups of raw rice (any variety of rice without a strong fragrance) in a spice grinder, 2 tablespoons at a time, to a corn grit texture. Sieve and use only the grit-like part, saving the flour for other uses.

## METHOD

Dry roast the cream of rice in a heavy wok on medium-low heat for 2 minutes. Empty into a bowl.

Warm up the oil in the same wok on medium heat. Toss in the mustard seeds, and when they pop and splutter, add chana dal, urad dal and cashew nut pieces. Roast to a golden colour.

Lower the heat and add peppercorns, red chillies, cumin, curry leaves and asafoetida powder. Stir once. Add the water and salt, raise the heat to medium, and bring to a boil.

Add 2 cups cream of rice in a steady stream, stirring with the other hand. Cook till the water is absorbed. Fold and cook till soft and moist. If it is dry, add 2 tablespoons water, fold and cook for another minute.

Fold in the coconut and ghee. Turn the heat off. Cover and let it rest for 5 minutes to absorb all the flavours.

Serve hot with yogurt and a tangy pickle of your choice.

*Delectable Delights from Palani's Bakery*

It was the summer of 1947, and the annual public Madras University examinations were postponed from early April to the end of May. This was not unusual; one year, there was a postponement when members of the examination board discovered that the question papers had 'leaked'. This was brought to their notice when news spread that a tutorial group had got access to the English and Science question papers ahead of the examination date and was raking in money for providing students with the answers. Another year, we heard that several sets of question papers had been lost. For the student community, this postponement turned everything topsy-turvy. For us 'out-of-towners' who stayed in Queen Mary's College hostel, it was an even more trying time. The vegetarian mess normally closed from the second week of April until early June, when the college reopened for the new academic year. The cooks—mostly Malayali—were on their annual summer leave and head off to their homes in villages in the state of Kerala in south India.

The postponement of our examinations to May, coupled with the absence of the cooks, left us students to fend for ourselves. Some left for their home towns near Madras, and some of us, like me, opted to stay back.

Before the head cook Krishnan Nair left for his village home, I sought his advice on whether I could make some special eating arrangements when the vegetarian mess would not be functioning. He suggested I try out his friend's small eatery, called 'Palani's Bakery', in the

neighbourhood of the Church of Santhome, which was within walking distance of the college.

Palani's Bakery was owned and managed by an elderly, childless couple, Palani and his wife Muthu, who lived in the one-room bakery. The address was No. 12 A, Beach Road, Santhome, and the small tin signboard painted in blue on the yellow door read 'Palani's Bakery, Welcome'.

Palani had inherited the bakery from his father, who had started it in the 1920s. Palani's father baked bread and biscuits for the British residents of Santhome. In 1945, Palani, converted the bakery into a small restaurant. The bakery was well situated on the busy Beach Road opposite the city bus-stop and, in a matter of a few days, became a popular tiffin joint for people going to and returning from work when Palani and Muthu added south Indian vegetarian snacks to the menu, and gradually stopped baking western-style loaves of bread and biscuits.

Palani's Bakery was small and cramped but cheerful. This single-storeyed building with a tiled roof had one dining room which accommodated eight wooden tables and benches during the day. Each table could seat three, with just enough space between two tables for the customers to walk by. Frequently, there was no seat available, so orders were placed for tiffin with a long line of hungry customers either waiting for a seat to fall vacant or to collect their parcel and eat standing in the front verandah. Later, Palani added a few more tables and benches in the verandah. He did not want to lose his long-time clientele.

At night the dining room was converted to Palani's and Muthu's bedroom, with the tables and benches stacked against the back wall and the cotton bedding unrolled on the floor. An enclosed verandah at the back was the kitchen and pantry, a neat, well-organized space. The open front verandah facing the road was a waiting area for the restaurant's clients. While waiting for the bus, people would snack on Palani's food and also get a few idlis packed to take with them for lunch. A bucket filled with water and a mug tied to it was left in the front verandah for customers to wash their hands. The extra minute the bus took to

swerve round the bend of the road saw commuters hopping onto the road clutching their paper parcels. A large red tin drum, painted with the initials P.B. in bright yellow, was left to one side of the bakery on the road, and customers dropped the plantain leaves on which they were served into this waste bin. Every night, the local cowherd would collect all the leaves as feed for his cows. And for this service of cleaning up after the restaurant was closed for the day, he was given a parcel of two idlis and chutney wrapped in a banana leaf.

Every day from 7.00 a.m. until 9.00 p.m., Palani and Muthu served soft, fluffy rice idlis (steamed rice cakes) with a spicy coconut and coriander chutney and creamy shallot/onion sambar (lentil stew). Additionally, on weekends from 12.00 p.m. to 3.00 p.m., Muthu took over the bakery and served flaky, delicate, south Indian parottas (white flour flatbread), which she called Ceylon raeshmi parottas. I don't know why 'Ceylon' but 'raeshmi', which translates to silken, described her parottas well. The parotta, accompanied by a flavourful mixed vegetable stew cooked in rich coconut milk, was a treat.

This modest, clean, one-room restaurant was a find, especially when the vegetarian mess at college closed down during the summer months. For the next five years, even after I had graduated and joined the teaching faculty of the Department of Geography in Queen Mary's College and till I left in 1955 when I was married, I went back to Palani's Bakery for a tasty and affordable tiffin, without the excuse of a postponement of examinations.

Palani gave me two of his recipes for rice idlis. These very soft, delicate, steamed rice and lentil cakes continue to hold a special place as a signature breakfast favourite or anytime snack for south Indians.

His reason for giving me the two recipes was that in the second recipe, store-bought idli rava (cream of rice) is substituted for the raw rice and the parboiled rice. Using idli rava is a time-saving convenience but the idlis are certainly not inferior. I follow his second recipe more frequently now, as the Indian grocery stores in the Boston area sell packaged idli rice rava.

Cooking rice idlis needs some planning, since the idli batter has to ferment. And so, it is best to start the preparation a day in advance. Soak the rice and dal in the forenoon, grind the batter in the evening,

and set it aside, covered, through the night in a warm place at a temperature of about 70°F, to give enough time for fermentation to set in and be complete by the following morning. The remaining batter can be refrigerated and steamed later, but should be used within two days. Batter that is more than three days old can be spread on a griddle to make uthappam, a soft and slightly thick pancake version of dosai, the south Indian rice and lentil crêpe.

# RICE IDLIS, *Palani's first recipe.*

## INGREDIENTS TO MAKE 15 IDLIS

* *1 cup raw rice (use any variety that has no fragrance)*
* *1 cup parboiled rice*
* *1 cup urad dal*
* *2½ cups water, divided*
* *1 teaspoon salt*
* *½ cup coconut milk (fresh coconut milk is preferred to canned milk)*
* *¼ cup oil for smearing on idli moulds*
* *½ cup ghee or ½ cup sesame oil, to smear on the steamed idlis*

## METHOD TO MAKE THE BATTER

Wash and rinse the raw rice and drain the water. Repeat till the water is not cloudy. Soak the rice in tepid water for 5 hours. Drain and set aside.

Do the same for the parboiled rice, and in a third bowl, repeat the procedure for the urad dal. Soak each separately and drain.

Grind the raw rice in a blender, adding ¼ cup water; grind to a thick batter of cream of rice texture, stopping to push down the batter with a spatula from the sides towards the blades. Empty into a large deep bowl scraping the sides of the blender.

Grind the parboiled rice in the same blender without washing it, to a cream of rice texture, adding ½ cup water. Stop and push down the batter from the sides towards the blades, and grind. Empty into the same bowl scraping the sides of the blender.

Grind the urad dal, adding ½ cup water. Grind to a satiny smooth, fluffy batter. Periodically, stop and push batter with a spatula towards the blades, and grind. Empty urad batter into the bowl with ground rice. Scrape the sides of the blender and empty.

Add salt and coconut milk, a little at a time, stir and mix well to a smooth thick pancake batter.

Cover with a tight lid and set aside in a warm place, about 70°F, overnight or for 12 hours, to ferment and double in volume, when it will acquire a sour smell. The batter can also be fermented in a proofing container or in an oven with the pilot light on. Choose a container large enough to hold the fermented batter, which would have doubled in volume.

## METHOD TO EXTRACT COCONUT MILK

Soak 1 cup of shredded coconut in ¾ cup hot water in a bowl. Let it rest for 15 minutes. Squeeze the softened coconut with your fingers to extract the milk, and strain, collecting the milk in another bowl. The residue coconut can be used to make coconut chutney.

## METHOD TO STEAM IDLIS

Fill the bottom pan of an idli steamer with water to a depth of 1 inch.

Grease the idli bowls or moulds with a smear of oil. Whisk the idli batter and ladle into the greased bowls to about ¾ full.

Set the idli steamer on medium-high heat and bring the water to a boil. Place idli stand with bowls of batter into the pan of boiling water, and cover with a tight lid. Steam and cook, covered, for 4 to 5 minutes.

Turn off the stove, remove lid and test each idli by inserting a toothpick, which should come out clean. Ease the idlis, running the blunt edge of a knife or spatula dipped in cold water, remove and place in a bowl. Cover with a kitchen towel.

Repeat this process and make as many idlis as you need, adding more water to the lower pan of the steamer.

Serve the idlis warm or at room temperature, smeared with a dollop of ghee (clarified butter) or a drop of sesame oil, with coconut chutney and onion sambar on the side.

Steamed idlis can be refrigerated for 2 days or frozen for one week, reheated and served.

# RICE IDLIS, *second recipe, substituting the rice grains with cream of rice.*

## INGREDIENTS TO MAKE 15 IDLIS

- *2 cups rice idli rava (cream of rice), available in Indian grocery stores*
- *1 cup urad dal*
- *½ teaspoon methi (fenugreek) seeds*
- *1 teaspoon salt*
- *½ teaspoon baking soda*

## METHOD TO MAKE THE BATTER

Wash and rinse urad dal and fenugreek seeds together, thrice. Soak in a bowl of tepid water for 3 hours, drain and set aside.

Rinse rice idli rava once in cold water, and soak for 10 minutes in just enough water for it to be absorbed by the rava.

Grind the urad dal and fenugreek to a fine, satiny smooth, fluffy batter, adding 1/4 cup water to start with, and 2 tablespoons more, if needed. Stop the blender midway, push batter down the sides towards the blades, and continue to grind till very smooth.

Turn off the blender, add the soaked rice rava to the ground urad batter, and grind for another 2 minutes, adding 2-3 tablespoons of water, if needed. The batter should not be runny.

Empty the batter into a large bowl, large enough to have room for the batter to double in volume after fermentation.

Scrape out all the batter from the blender into the bowl. Wash out the blender with 1 tablespoon water and add this to the bowl, but I repeat, do not make the batter runny. Combine salt with the batter, whisk to mix well and aerate the batter.

Cover and set aside in a warm place (temperature 70°F) overnight or for 12 hours. If after 12 hours the batter is still thick, add 2 tablespoons of water and mix well.

**METHOD TO STEAM THE RICE IDLIS**

Add baking soda to the batter and whisk to incorporate well.

Steam the idlis following the instructions given for the first recipe. Serve the idlis warm or at room temperature, smeared with a dollop of ghee, and with coconut chutney and sambar on the side.

## SHALLOT SAMBAR, *a spicy lentil stew with shallots.*

My experience in Palani's Bakery was that the sambar would be of thicker consistency, but only if I went for a breakfast of idlis before 11.00 a.m. By evening, the same onion sambar would be somewhat diluted.

**INGREDIENTS TO MAKE 5-6 CUPS**

- ½ cup tur dal
- 3 tablespoons oil, divided
- 2 tablespoons chana dal
- 2 tablespoons coriander seeds
- 6 dry red chillies; use fewer for less spicy sambar
- 1-inch cinnamon stick, broken in small bits
- 3 cups peeled whole shallots, or 4 peeled medium onions, chopped coarse
- ½ teaspoon turmeric powder
- 2 medium tomatoes, chopped coarse
- 1 keylime-size tamarind soaked in 1 cup warm water
- 2 tablespoons shredded coconut, fresh or frozen
- ½ teaspoon sugar
- salt to taste

## METHOD TO MAKE SHALLOT SAMBAR

Wash and rinse tur dal twice. In a 3-quart heavy pan on medium heat, cook the dal soft with 4 cups of water. Transfer the cooked dal to a bowl and set aside. Keep the heavy pan aside for using later. If you are cooking dal in a pressure cooker, cook until 4 whistles.

Warm up 1 tablespoon oil in a heavy skillet on medium heat. Lower the heat and add the chana dal, stir and roast to a light golden-brown.

Turn off the stove and add the coriander seeds, red chillies and cinnamon. Stir and roast for one minute. Empty the roasted contents into a blender. Add soaked tamarind along with the water, and coconut. Grind to a fine paste. Do not empty the blender.

Warm up 2 tablespoons oil in the same skillet. Add the shallots or onions and sauté till they are translucent. Transfer half the sautéed onions to the blender and the other half to the 3 quart pan. Pulse the onions with the contents in the blender.

Add the tomatoes to the skillet on medium heat, and stir for a couple of minutes. Turn off heat. Transfer the sautéed tomatoes to the blender. Pulse twice.

Empty the contents of the blender into the 3-quart heavy pan with the sautéed onions.

Wash out the blender with 3 cups water and add to the pan.

Set the pan on medium-high heat, add the salt and sugar, and bring to a boil. Cook for 3 minutes, stirring occasionally.

Lower the heat to medium and cook for 5 minutes or till the sambar thickens a bit. Add the cooked dal and 1 cup water. Stir and bring to the boil once. Turn off stove.

For a thinner sambar, add more water and a little salt (if necessary), and bring to a boil.

## INGREDIENTS FOR THE TEMPERING

* *1 teaspoon oil*
* *1 teaspoon brown mustard seeds*
* *2 green chillies, slit lengthwise*
* *10 curry leaves, torn in pieces*

## METHOD FOR TEMPERING THE SAMBAR

Warm up a small saucepan on medium heat and add the oil. Toss in the mustard seeds, and when they splutter and pop, turn off the stove. Stir in the green chillies and curry leaves, which will crackle and splutter.

Stir and empty into the sambar.

Serve with rice idlis.

Nowadays, I use the MTR brand of packaged sambar powder available in Indian grocery stores. This saves me cooking time.

I cook the tur dal usually in a pressure cooker. In a blender, I grind the soaked tamarind with its water, coconut and tomatoes, and add this to the wok with the sautéed onions. I then boil this, adding the turmeric, salt and sugar and another 2 cups water, till the quantity is reduced by half and I can no longer smell the raw tamarind. At this stage, I add the cooked dal and 2 cups water, stir in 2-3 teaspoons of the sambar powder, and bring the sambar to boil. And finally, I temper it.

## MUTHU'S CEYLON RAESHMI PAROTTA, *griddle-cooked south Indian flaky, layered, silky flatbread.*

The weekend afternoon tiffin of parottas at Palani's Bakery was very popular with the young beach crowd. The sandy Marina Beach stretched beyond the road, a stone's throw away from the bakery, and during weekends it was packed with the locals and tourists who also thronged to Palani's Bakery.

Muthu's weekend raeshmi flatbreads had a reputation for being spicy, and she served them hot off the griddle. In addition to coffee, she served fizzy, aerated bottled drinks, which were stacked in a barrel and chilled with slabs of ice covered with salt and sawdust to keep the ice from melting too fast in the Madras heat. The younger crowd was addicted to the cold drinks.

The process of making the parottas seems daunting, but in actuality, it is quite simple and well worth a try, for the end product is a delicious savoury pastry. Splitting into two stages makes the process less formidable.

**INGREDIENTS TO MAKE 8 PAROTTAS**

* *½ cup loosely packed, chopped, fresh coriander leaves with tender stems*
* *2 green chillies*
* *2½ cups of white flour, divided*
* *¾ teaspoon salt*
* *1 teaspoon red chilli powder*
* *½ teaspoon turmeric powder*
* *½ teaspoon cumin powder*
* *1¼ cup oil, divided*
* *3 tablespoons rice flour*
* *½ teaspoon baking soda*
* *½ teaspoon baking powder*

**METHOD TO MAKE THE DOUGH**

Grind fresh coriander and green chillies to a smooth paste, adding 2 tablespoons of water. Set aside.

Sift 2 cups flour, salt, red chilli powder, turmeric and cumin powder into a bowl.

Add 3 tablespoons oil and mix.

Add the ground paste to the flour, mix to a soft elastic dough, adding a little water, if needed. Transfer the dough to a work-table and knead. If the dough is sticky, dust a little flour and knead.

Roll the dough into a ball with your hand and smear it with 2 tablespoons oil. Set it aside, covered in a bowl, for 30 minutes at room temperature.

## METHOD TO MAKE THE PAROTTAS—THE FIRST STAGE

Combine the rice flour, baking soda, baking powder and ½ cup oil in a shallow bowl. Beat and whisk to a creamy foaming batter. Set aside.

Roll the dough with your palms into a rope. Cut the rope into 8 portions. Roll each portion into a ball, and set aside in a shallow dish covered with a kitchen towel.

Take 1 ball of dough, and on a work-board with your rolling pin, roll into a 4-inch tortilla. Place 1 teaspoon of the creamy batter in the middle and gather the edges of the tortilla together in the middle. Pinch the edges with your fingers and seal them. Roll between the palms of your hands to make a ball.

Dip your fingers in the remaining oil, and pressing outwards from the middle of the ball of dough, stretch it to an even and thin disc. You will need to use both hands. You could use a rolling pin instead and roll it out thin.

This will take a few minutes. Do not worry if there are tears in the tortilla.

Pick up the tortilla on the edge furthest from you and lift it slowly off the work-board.

Lower your hands slowly to bring back the tortilla onto the work-board in folds, one over the other, to form a long ribbon of several folds about 1-inch width.

Lift one end of the folds of ribbon, pressing the other end down with your finger onto the work-board. Wind the ribbon of dough spirally to a tight pinwheel till the entire ribbon is wound. Set aside on a platter, dribbling ¼ teaspoon oil on top of the pinwheel.

Repeat the process with the rest of the balls of dough and keep the pinwheels moist with oil.

## METHOD TO MAKE THE PAROTTAS—THE SECOND STAGE

Take one pinwheel at a time, and with your rolling pin, roll to a disc as thin as you can.

Warm up a skillet on medium heat. Cook the disc on one side till brown spots appear. Flip over and cook the other side. Remove from the skillet and serve while the parotta is still warm.

To save time, while one parotta is cooking, roll out the next.

The pinwheels can be made a day in advance and refrigerated. Bring them back to room temperature before rolling them into parottas.

# MUTHU'S CREAMY, COCONUT MILK, VEGETABLE STEW WITH ONIONS, POTATOES AND BEANS

I have modified the original recipe by adding more vegetables and canned unsweetened coconut milk as a substitute for freshly extracted coconut milk. With warm croutons, it is a hearty soup. Can be served with a bowl of rice too. This soup is so filling that a few crackers is all I ask for.

## INGREDIENTS FOR 6 SERVINGS

- 3 tablespoon oil
- 1 medium onion, chopped coarse
- 3 green cardamom pods
- 3 bay leaves
- 1-inch piece fresh ginger with skin, julienned
- 4 green chillies, slit lengthwise in half
- 10 curry leaves, torn in pieces
- ½ teaspoon turmeric powder
- 1 large potato, unpeeled and cut in medium-size cubes
- ½ teaspoon red chilli powder (optional)
- ½ cup shelled peas
- ½ cup snow peas
- 10 string beans, cut in 2-inch lengths
- 1 medium carrot, diced
- 1 cup baby corn, diced
- 1 cup khol rabi, peeled and cubed
- 1 teaspoon salt; more if needed
- ½ teaspoon sugar (optional)
- 3 cups water; more if needed
- 2 cans unsweetened coconut milk
- ½ cup ground raw cashew powder (optional)

## METHOD

Warm up 3 tablespoons oil in a heavy-bottomed pan on medium heat.

Stir in onion and sauté till it turns translucent.

Lower the heat. Add the green cardamom pods, bay leaves, ginger, green chillies and curry leaves, and stir a couple of times.

Add the turmeric powder, potatoes and red chilli powder, if you are using it, and stir for 1 minute.

Toss in the other vegetables, stir to coat with the herbed oil. Add the salt, water and sugar, if you are using it.

Raise the heat to medium and cook covered, till the vegetables are cooked tender but not mushy. Remove the lid occasionally and check.

Cook uncovered till most of the water has evaporated.

Stir in 2 cans of coconut milk. Turn off stove.

Sprinkle cashew powder (if you are using it) and stir to mix. Keep covered till ready to serve.

I prefer a thinner stew.

If you are pressed for time, much of the cooking can be done 2 days in advance. The onion can be sautéed and cooked with the rest of the vegetables and spices, herbs and salt, adding water. Cool and transfer to a container with a lid. Refrigerate. Take out from the refrigerator 2 hours before serving, add ½ cup water and cook on medium heat. When it comes to a boil, stir in the coconut milk and ground cashew. Turn off the stove.

Serve warm.

# An Eligible Boy, Astrologers and Tiffin

Between the years 1946 and 1955, when I was first a student, and later, a teaching faculty member of Queen Mary's College, I spent my holidays and long weekends with my parents and siblings at Tanjore.

Most of the houses in Rajappa Nagar, where my parents lived, were set in plots of a minimum of half an acre each. There was ample space for a garden, and my mother, an avid gardener, created a front garden with many fragrant flowering plants welcoming the visitor, and a back garden of fruit trees, vegetables and herbs, which gave us the joy of harvesting fresh home-grown produce. She had planted a dozen coconut palms around the boundary walls of the plot, mango trees, a jackfruit tree, one gooseberry bush, a guava tree, several papaya trees and a vegetable garden of delicious seasonal vegetables and herbs.

Enough space was left on one side for a badminton court where my sisters and I played badminton. The house was surrounded with flowering bushes, both tropical annuals and seasonal flowering plants. In a short time, my parents transformed our Tanjore family home, No. 8 Rajappa Nagar, into a garden retreat. Soon, our house was identified by the residents of Rajappa Nagar as 'the garden house'.

The front of the house facing east was bathed in the morning sunlight. To the right of the front entrance gate, Amma had planted a parijata bush (*Nyctanthes arbor-tristis*), commonly known as the coral flower plant, with a profusion of white intoxicatingly fragrant, delicate flowers on coral-coloured stems. The fragile jasmine-like flowers bloomed at night during the months of September to January, leaving the front yard covered with a perfumed floral mat at dawn.

To the left of the entrance passage was a bed of fragrant sontaka, *hedychium multiflora* and *Hedychium coronarium*, members of the ginger family. A profusion of sweet-smelling flowers welcomed visitors during the rainy season, when every stem was bent, laden with snow-white flowers. A competitor was the night-blooming jasmine, leaning against the entrance wall, covered with a profusion of small creamy 'stars' perfuming the lane, and at the far end of the front garden to the left was a row of henna bushes (*Lawsonia inermis*). When the plants flowered twice a year with bunches of fragrant, white, petite flowers, the air smelt so heavenly. But henna was also grown for the leaves, which were gathered a few days before each festival or a special celebration, a birthday or wedding. We girls plucked the henna leaves, ground them into a fine paste, and applied it on the palms and fingers of our hands, drawing intricate designs. When the paste dried a few hours later, it would be washed off to expose the striking orange patterns. Henna paste is also believed to have a cooling effect on the body, besides being a reddish hair dye, actually more burnt sienna than red.

On one of my visits from college, Amma introduced me to Mrs Pasha, who had recently moved from Hyderabad. Her son had joined the orthopaedic department as a junior surgeon in the Vallam Medical College Hospital. Mrs Pasha lived four houses down the road, and came frequently for henna leaves from our garden. Her greying hair was always a reddish orange.

To the right of the front garden a straggling ornamental, Lady Palmer bougainvillea, hedge with dramatic red-and-white blooms marked the yard between our home and our neighbours, the Swamys.

Amma was a passionate gardener. If she was not in the kitchen, we would be sure to find her bending over and straightening the stakes of tender papaya seedlings, or digging extra channels for the well water to reach the farthest edge of the backyard where the herb and vegetable garden was. She grew colacasia yam tubers, chilli peppers, eggplant, and several varieties of squashes, gourds and pumpkins. Herbs like coriander and mint formed border plants. There were also a few drumstick trees (*Moringa oleifera*), their long pods dangling in the air, and a few curry leaf trees (*Murraya koenigii*). The leaves with their distinctive lemony, pungent flavour are indispensable to Indian cuisine, particularly to the cuisine of south India. Amma had planted a clump of banana trees near the well, most of them for the fruit, but she had also planted two varieties earmarked for the leaves on which food was served on special occasions. Any visitor to our home would go on a tour of my mother's garden, and would also be gifted with fresh flowers, fruit and vegetables, and for those interested, Amma would gift plant saplings or bulbs.

The place of pride in the garden went to the bushes of tulasi plants (*Ocimum sanctum*), holy basil, planted right next to the back door of our home. Amma worshipped the sacred tulasi plant every morning and evening, lighting an oil-wick lamp and circumambulating the plant while saying her prayers. In the Hindu tradition, the tulasi plant is invaluable in the home. This was truly my mother's dream garden.

There were between eight to ten houses on our street in Rajappa Nagar. The residents met frequently and were well informed about what was happening in each others' homes. Engagements, marriages, births and religious ceremonies were attended by most, but no one would miss a funeral for fear of being misunderstood.

Mr Swamy, our neighbour, a particularly unctuous one, was a civil engineer who, after his retirement from government service, was appointed a member of a team of experts to restore and maintain the Brihadeeswara Temple, the world-renowned Shaivite temple in Tanjore. His wife Kanakam was a frequent visitor, spending time with my mother, especially when Swamy was out of town on work. Meera, their only child and my friend, was in the last year of medical school at the Stanley Medical College in Madras.

Meera graduated from medical school in 1952, and her parents were keen to see her married by the end of that year. There was added pressure from Swamy's elderly parents, who wished to see their only granddaughter married suitably into a 'good family', with a husband who would take care of her. Kanakam's only conversation with my mother was about 'finding a suitable boy' for Meera who, in turn, would bless the family with grandchildren. There was never any doubt in Swamy's family that Meera would marry the young man of their choice. Meera was slim with a wheatish complexion, and was considered beautiful and attractive with large expressive eyes and full lips. Standing five feet six inches, she was tall by south Indian standards. With her family background, her looks and her professional education, she was a 'prize catch'. This was the general opinion of the Rajappa Nagar community.

News that Meera had graduated was sent to all members of Swamy's extended family and friends, with a request to send horoscopes of 'suitable boys'. Kanakam kept my mother posted with the progress on the search.

'Within a month, over a hundred horoscopes have been received. Swamy has contacted Ganesha Pandithar,' she reported. G.P., as the astrologer was known in Tanjore, was a person of good standing in the realm of analyzing horoscopes. The Swamys were confident he would sort and discard the incompatible ones, and focus on the most 'eligible' young men of the same Brahmin caste as the Swamys. Nothing was more important than finding the right young man to wed Meera. While Kanakam kept my mother informed of the latest developments, she wondered at my parents' composure in the face of the mounting 'disaster' of having seven, possibly over-educated, spinster daughters! (Kamala, my elder sister, was the only one married at that time). Both Kanakam and Mr Swamy could not fathom their neighbours' irresponsible attitude.

G.P. finally zeroed in on one young engineer from Madras who had the right credentials, being the only son to his wealthy parents. The father was a successful businessman. The young prospective groom was four years older than Meera, which was considered a suitable difference in age. G.P. had done his calculations and explained to Mr Swamy why the young engineer's horoscope was eminently compatible with that of Meera's. The two rising planets for a happy married life and for professional success were strong in the boy's horoscope, and were matched a 100 per cent by their counterparts in Meera's horoscope. In his entire professional career of thirty-five years as an astrologer, he had seen very few horoscopes that matched as perfectly as these two did. Mr Swamy was not only pleased, he was convinced of a 'divine intervention' in his family affairs. After the happy occasion of his dear daughter's betrothal, his sleepless nights would be a thing of the past. Preparations were moving according to plan, and both he and

Kanakam had plenty to do before the wedding. G.P. was requested to choose a couple of appropriate and auspicious dates and time for the 'viewing of the bride' event, when the prospective groom and his family would be visiting Swamy and his family. After consultations with the elders in the family, the meeting between the 'girl' and the 'boy' and their families was fixed for a Friday afternoon in August. Fridays were generally considered auspicious. Mr Swamy and Kanakam showed their appreciation for Ganesha Pandithar's involvement with their family by gifting him generously with cash and a silver lamp. The astrologer, on his part, was pleased to see the couple happy and to humbly accept the gifts. More gifts awaited him on the happy occasion of the wedding. As they indicated, the August event was a precursor to a happier one. The marriage between Meera and the engineer boy was a foregone conclusion.

The crucial first face-to-face meeting of the two families was the talk of Rajappa Nagar. Meera's paternal grandparents arrived from the temple town of Madurai a week before the event, and her maternal uncle and aunt drove down from Tiruchirapalli. Two of her teenaged girl cousins were visiting from Hyderabad. Kanakam was in a state of high excitement. My parents were also invited to the event. I was home on a few days' vacation from college and Meera requested me to go over for moral support, saying she was very nervous about 'this whole thing'. I had never heard of a 'bride-viewing ceremony' and was curious to see what would happen. I accompanied Amma, who took a basket of jasmine flowers from our garden for the function. My father, who thought the whole plan demeaning and ill-conceived, stayed home, at the risk of being misunderstood by his neighbours.

That Friday morning Kanakam's house wore a festive look, with fresh mango leaves strung across the entrance to the house, and a beautiful elaborate rice powder 'kolam', ritual auspicious drawing, decorating the front yard. Ribbons of sweet-smelling jasmine flowers were strung in long 'toranam' (strands) at the front entrance and in the 'family puja room', the family shrine.

By three o'clock in the afternoon, the time mentioned by the astrologer as auspicious, a few close friends of the family arrived and soon, the house was packed with invitees. The prospective groom's party of ten members who spanned four generations—grandparents, parents, the groom, his two teenage cousins, a married sister, her spouse and their infant son—joined soon after. On seeing the two cars stop in front of the house, Mr Swamy rushed out to welcome the guests. He excitedly called out to his wife and the call was relayed through the many relatives in the house. Kanakam, dressed in a green silk saree, finally bustled out onto the front porch with a welcoming smile. Meera, in keeping with tradition, was hidden from view, her cousins keeping her company in an anteroom.

The men in the visiting group entered the house, followed by the women, who came bearing gifts of fruit, flowers, coconuts, betel leaves and areca nuts, packets of vermilion and turmeric powder, and trays of home-made sweets. After a formal exchange of pleasantries between the

elders, the visitors settled down to the serious business of 'bride viewing'.

On a cue from her husband, Kanakam went to fetch her daughter, who made her entry flanked by her cousin and aunt. She looked radiant, dressed in a mango-coloured silk sari with strands of jasmine wound round her dark, braided hair. She walked into the room, modestly looking at her toes, as was expected of a prospective bride. Meera's grandmother was pleased with this show of modesty, and she smiled and nodded her head approvingly. She was certain in her mind that Meera, with her poise and demeanour, had already won over all those who mattered. The groom's grandmother said, within everyone's hearing, 'The girl is beautiful, despite her height.'

Meera went round to all the women guests, offering jasmine strands from a silver tray. As she mentioned later to me, she could 'feel' all the eyes scrutinizing her. The groom's mother broke the awkward silence in the room with a compliment, 'These jasmine flowers smell more fragrant than the ones we get in Madras. These must be from your garden.' The conversation shifted to plants and gardens, and Kanakam introduced Amma to the groom's mother as 'the lady with the best garden' in Rajappa Nagar, and there was a general discussion about the several tons of jasmine, roses, and orange kanakambaram cultivated, along with pachauli and fragrant vetiver, in the villages around Tanjore for the flower markets of Madras and beyond. All the women agreed that the 'kadambam' flower strands from Tanjore were famous throughout the south.

As Meera turned to leave the room, the groom's mother invited her to sit next to her, and both she and her husband made unsuccessful attempts to get Meera to talk about her college and medical studies, her hobbies and other interests. Meera remained silent. I found it strange that the young engineer son Raghu, who was supposedly destined to be her future life partner, did no talking at all, but this was convention, and I concluded his behaviour was that of 'a good son'.

Kanakam and Meera's aunt soon appeared with trays of stacked silver plates and bowls of badam halwa, saffron and cardamom-flavoured marzipan fudge, and platters of Mysore bondas, fried balls of herbed lentil batter, for all the guests. The warm aroma of south Indian coffee filled the air. The atmosphere thawed as the conversation turned to food, and everyone talked about how well the snacks were cooked. Raghu's grandmother turned to Meera and asked her if she could cook, a significant question which Meera had been tutored to answer in the affirmative, but she merely shook her head...and the guests concentrated on the delicious tiffin and coffee.

Soon after, the visitors decided to leave. Kanakam rushed about offering return gifts of fruit, flowers, coconuts and home-made sweets, befitting their status. This final ritual marked the end of a tiring day for the Swamys.

Meera's behaviour was puzzling to her family and, after the guests departed, she was subjected to a barrage of questions and comments. Was she 'shy', 'arrogant', 'diffident', 'self-opinionated'? Why was she so uncommunicative? Would this not be interpreted by all who were present as a total lack of respect for the family who would have made such a difference in her life? Or worse still, they might have concluded that she had a speech defect or was unable to speak. Meera remained silent.

The following day, Meera came over to our home. She looked relaxed. Appa asked her how she was, and sensing a non-judgemental presence in him, she said, 'I love my parents, but I will not agree to marry someone who I see for a few minutes one afternoon. The whole exercise was one of protocol and hierarchy.' She said nothing more.

A few months later, Swamy's contract at the temple came to an end and he and Kanakam left Tanjore. My mother told me that when Kanakam came to bid farewell, she was devastated. She was also unforgiving of her husband who had encouraged Meera to study to 'become a doctor', and added they were both paying a heavy price now. 'Meera was always an obedient child. I don't know why she is so rebellious now.' My parents and the Swamys were neighbours and, yet, worlds apart.

Thereafter, I lost touch with Meera. My father passed away some years later, necessitating the sale of our family home in Tanjore.

A decade later, when I lived in Delhi as a young married woman, I met Meera's cousin Lata, the one from Hyderabad. Talking nostalgically about our younger days in Tanjore, I learned that Meera had joined as an intern in one of the hospitals in Bombay. She married a Dr Joseph Thomas, who worked in the same hospital where she was a paediatrician. He was fifteen years her senior and a divorcee with a young child. Swamy and Kanakam were initially heartbroken, but were now living with her in Poona.

Lata added that the family was sorely disappointed with the astrologer. How could he have not seen this coming? All his calculations obviously went wrong. Why was it that what was expected to happen did not? After all, Meera's parents left no stone unturned to please the 'boy's' family.

'Meera took charge of her life and her future,' said Lata.

Some weeks after the Swamys had left Tanjore, my aunt Annam Athai visited my parents and heard of the 'debacle' at the Swamy's residence. She came up with an explanation. She emphatically declared that the tiffin served on this occasion of 'bride-viewing' had flouted tradition and convention. The tiffin to be served on such an occasion, she said, was as important as the rest of the social ritual. And in keeping with centuries-old custom, Kanakam should have served sojji halwa (cream of wheat halwa) and bajji (savoury vegetable fritters), along with coffee. The Swamys, while they consulted the astrologer on the compatibility of horoscopes, had shown no regard for the basic rules of age-old customs in the matter of tiffin to be served on the occasion.

Appa was both amused and annoyed by this explanation trotted out by his sister, and even more exasperated by the cultural and behavioural constraints imposed on society by the self-appointed keepers of 'tradition'.

# KANAKAM'S BADAM HALWA, *saffron-flavoured soft marzipan fudge, with the aroma of cardamom, saffron and nutmeg.*

## INGREDIENTS TO MAKE ABOUT 8 SERVINGS

* 3 cups raw blanched almonds
* 1½ cups whole milk
* 2 cups sugar
* 1½ cups melted ghee (clarified butter)
* pinch of saffron threads soaked in 1 teaspoon of milk
* 2 teaspoons cardamom powder
* 1/10 teaspoon nutmeg powder

## METHOD

Puree the almonds in a blender to a smooth paste, adding ½ cup milk. Empty into a heavy saucepan, scraping the sides of the blender.

Add the sugar, half the quantity of ghee, the remaining milk and mix.

Cook on low heat, stirring continuously, till the aroma of almonds fills the air and the paste thickens and turns a golden-brown. Pour in the rest of the ghee, stir and cook till the ghee is absorbed. Stir continuously from the bottom up to prevent burning at the bottom.

Fold in the saffron, cardamom and nutmeg powder into the cooked almond halwa. Turn the heat off. Empty into a serving dish and serve hot or at room temperature. The warm halwa can be spooned out or scored into squares when cool.

# MYSORE BONDAS, *scrumptious deep-fried balls of lentil batter.*

## INGREDIENTS TO MAKE 4 SERVINGS

* 1 cup urad dal, washed and drained
* 6 peppercorns, cracked
* ¼ cup fresh coconut chopped in 'tooth-size' pieces, (this is my mother's specification for the size)
* ½ teaspoon asafoetida powder
* salt to taste
* 12 curry leaves, torn in pieces
* ¼ cup cashew nuts broken in bits
* 2 cups oil for frying

## METHOD

Grind the dal in a blender to a smooth, fluffy batter, adding ¼ cup water. Empty into a bowl. Mix in all the other ingredients.

Heat the oil in a wok on medium heat. Scoop up 1 teaspoon of batter and slide it with another spoon into the hot oil. Slide in 6 and cook till brown, turning over with a slotted spoon. Drain. Fry the remaining batter.

Serve hot with a chutney of your choice.

## The Farmers' Market in Tanjore

During my holidays, one of my pleasures in Tanjore was cycling through the Pookara veedhi, the street where the flower-sellers lived, to the Poo Santhe, the local farmers' market. The origins of Poo Santhe as a flower market, where neighbouring villagers brought their produce of jasmine and kanakambaram flowers, are blurred, and as time went by, the Poo Santhe grew to include vegetables and even cattle for sale. Itinerant small farmers from the neighbouring villages came with their seasonal fresh produce of deep purple baby eggplants with their thorny sepals intact, dusty-green ridged gourds, white and green striped, four-feet-long dangling snake gourds, tender cluster beans which you could snap with your fingers with a 'cluck', greens that were in season, pungent and shiny green chilli peppers, and hard, pink, sweet potatoes with fresh soil still clinging to them, making them smell of the sweet earth.

The Poo Santhe opened to customers by six o'clock on Sunday mornings, but the bullock carts laden with fresh produce started arriving before dawn. From my bedroom, I could hear the creaking wheels of the bullock carts and the tinkle of bells around the animals' necks, as the caravan of carts passed our home to the Poo Santhe Maidan a couple of miles away.

The maidan was divided into two sections, one for the wholesale transactions, where growers sold sacks of sweet potatoes, onions, baby eggplants, tender okra, shallots, bottle gourds, chilli peppers, round and firm pumpkins and squashes, and wicker baskets of a variety of greens and herbs, all of which would vanish within the hour. The air rang with the farmers' raised voices calling out their price. The other section was for retail customers like us. Bags and baskets of fresh produce would be carted away on bicycles, and young children with headloads of vegetables would greet me as my uncle and I pushed our way in the jostling crowd. Small hillocks of vegetables and bundles of herbs were sold at a fixed price. The air was scented with the fragrance of jasmine flowers as we entered the Santhe, and the fresh smell of coriander leaves, curry leaves and ginger as we left. I loved wandering through, taking in the sights and smells.

What I noticed in the Poo Santhe was the absence of weighing scales and weights, as also of bargaining. All sales were by volume and in units of fixed prices. There were sacks of vegetables, baskets of flowers, bundles of herbs and little hillocks of vegetables, ginger and chillies.

The vegetables at the Santhe were so fresh and tempting that we ended up buying more than we needed for a week, and frequently, Amma would sun-dry the okra, baby eggplants and chillies and store them. Sun-dried vegetables came in handy at home during the monsoon season, when much of the local fresh produce for the market would be lost in the incessant rains and floods, and there wouldn't be much of a variety.

A favourite snack in our family was sweet potato salad with green chutney. I have modified my mother's recipe. Her sweet potatoes were roasted over charcoal embers. I have aromatic memories of the smoky, warm comfort snack I enjoyed every weekend after a trip to the Tanjore Poo Santhe.

## SWEET POTATO SALAD, MY WAY! *you could use a barbecue grill to get the smoky flavour.*

### INGREDIENTS TO MAKE 4 SERVINGS

* *5 medium sweet potatoes*
* *½ teaspoon turmeric powder*
* *½ teaspoon red chilli powder*
* *1 tablespoon powdered gur/jaggery*
* *3 tablespoons shredded coconut*
* *1 teaspoon lime/lemon juice*
* *salt to taste*

### METHOD

Scrub and wash the sweet potatoes. Trim the ends, chop into ½-inch cubes, and boil in just enough water, adding the turmeric and chilli powders and salt. Boil until soft but not mushy. Drain and transfer to a bowl.

Add the remaining ingredients while still warm, toss and serve with chutney.

## AMMA'S EASY GREEN CHUTNEY, *which adds colour and flavour to the salad. The chutney can either be drizzled on top of the salad or served in a bowl on the side.*

### INGREDIENTS TO MAKE 1 CUP

* *1 cup tightly packed fresh coriander leaves with stems*
* *2 green chillies*
* *1 teaspoon lime juice*
* *½ cup chopped onion*
* *½ cup water*
* *salt to taste*

## METHOD

Grind all the ingredients together to a smooth chutney.

## FRIED OKRA STRIPS, *a rare delicacy.*

### INGREDIENTS TO MAKE 4 SERVINGS

* *20 tender baby okra*
* *1 cup rice flour*
* *1 teaspoon red chilli powder*
* *½ teaspoon turmeric powder*
* *½ teaspoon cumin powder*
* *½ teaspoon asafoetida powder*
* *½ teaspoon brown sugar*
* *2 cups oil for frying*
* *salt to taste*

### METHOD

Wash and wipe the okra dry with a kitchen towel.
   Slice off the stems. Cut each okra lengthwise in halves or quarters.
   In a bowl, mix the dry ingredients.
   Heat the oil in a wok on medium heat.
   Take 8 okra lengths, roll them in the dry mix till they are well coated.
   Drop the spice-coated pieces in the hot oil.
   Fry, turning over frequently, till they are crisp and brown.
   Remove with slotted spoon and drain in a paper-lined colander.

Serve with hot soup, soft beverages, tea, coffee or chilled beer.

## The Phone Call and Tiffin Meeting at the Ramakrishna Lunch Home in Madras

I graduated with a master's degree in Human Geography from the University of Madras in the year 1952, and the same year I joined Queen Mary's College as a junior faculty member. It was my good fortune that there was a vacancy in my own college, but the competition for that one vacancy was tough. I went with trepidation to the Madras Public Service Commission interview where fifteen other qualified aspirants had been invited. This was my first job interview. I was both nervous and anxious about the outcome of the interview. But my father's advice in his letter to me was, 'Just be yourself. If one door closes, there will be others that open.'

The interviewing board consisted of an all-male committee of eight members, three of whom were geographers from other universities; the five others were administrators and government officials from Madras, as I learnt later. The five non-geographers set the tone for the interview, and when the oldest of them, the one with a shaggy walrus moustache and navy-blue jacket adorned with an impressive and colourful collection of medals, bellowed as I walked in, tripping over the carpet, 'Come in, young lady, sit down, relax and tell us about yourself. We are not here to disembowel you...' I felt less intimidated. The remaining half-hour in the company of these august men was spent in pleasant conversation. It did not matter that not much of it had to do with what I thought I was there for, but I left them feeling good. I did not have to prove myself.

I was delighted when ten days later I received a letter of appointment, and my former teachers were happy to welcome me as a colleague. My teaching duties were heavy, as I taught two courses to students in the first and second year intermediate classes, and one course for each of the three-year Bachelor of Science and Bachelor of Arts students.

Within a few weeks of joining the department, I was invited to fill a vacancy in the staff committee of the college dramatics association and the debating society—I had been an active student member of both societies, and this was a welcome diversion and therapeutic in many ways for me. My enjoyment of acting and playwriting started as a school student and continued through my college days.

When I wanted to unwind, I went home to Tanjore over the weekend. And my father, as always, would be awaiting my arrival with eager anticipation to listen to my stories of college life, prodding me for my observations and more details of the student community, my friends, the staff and college events.

Queen Mary's College was established for the higher education of women, and though I found many of my fellow students meek and mild, the all-women teaching faculty was spirited and independent. I realized early on that here was an anomaly. In an otherwise conservative society such as I found in Madras, these women held liberal views, whether in social behaviour or politics, and that was refreshing. I enjoyed my three years as lecturer in Queen Mary's.

While I thought of myself as an educated, independent woman, the stark reality was that I continued to depend financially on my father. I must add that the state pay scale was miserable, and my starting salary was less than hundred rupees per month, which was a pittance compared to my living expenses even as a student in the same institution.

I was allotted a room in the Beach House, one of the staff quarters on the college campus facing the Marina, and that was home to me till I resigned my lecturership in 1955 when I married Chamu.

It was early August 1955, and with my position as the dramatic association secretary on the faculty of Queen Mary's College, I was up to my neck with supervising rehearsals for an evening's program of music, dance and plays in Tamil, Hindi and English, scheduled for the last Friday of the month. The chief guest on that occasion was the Chief

Minister of Madras, K. Kamaraj, and it was a matter of pride for the college that he had chosen to grace the occasion within the first year of assuming office. Needless to say, the college staff were in a tizzy.

A few days before the event, at about 6.00 p.m. when I was at the rehearsals, the college office sent word that there was a phone call for me. The staff quarters were not provided with pay-phones and all incoming calls were monitored through the college administrative office. This was the pre-mobile phone era. I requested the college office to pass on the telephone number of the caller to me, which they did. But I totally forgot to return the call. There was too much happening!

Ten days later, I was paged again by the office; again, a telephone call from the same number. I took the call this time. The deep voice greeting me with, 'Hello? Am I speaking with Rukmini? I am Chamu Srinivas, a friend of Sankho, my colleague at the M.S. University in Baroda, and his wife Ira Choudhary, and am in town for a few days,'

*Ira and Sankho*

drew me into a pleasant and interesting conversation, at the end of which Srinivas and I decided to meet the following day. The college office also handed me a letter from Sankho received two days earlier! Sankho had introduced his friend Chamu in the letter: 'Although a pipe-smoking brown Englishman from Oxford, he is an interesting person. Get him talking about Mysore, his home town, and you'll get him emotional.' I understood this when I met Chamu.

Ira told me recently, 'Rukka, I was not playing Cupid. This was pure and simple desi matchmaking.'

To introduce Sankho and Ira, I need to go back to the summer of 1953 in Tanjore, when I was home from college. Very early one morning, in the front porch of our home, I found my father chatting over a tumbler of coffee with Dr Paramasivam, a close friend of our family. Dr P, as we often referred to him, left in a hurry. That was a brief visit, I thought. We were used to unexpected visits from him, but he always stayed on to have tiffin. Soon after he left, Appa informed Amma that friends of Dr P, a Professor Sankho Choudhary and his wife Ira, were visiting Tanjore, and as Mrs Paramasivam was away in Madras, Dr P requested that I spend the day with them.

Dr Paramasivam was the chief archaeological chemist at the Brihadeeswara temple in Tanjore. He and his team were working on a project of exposing the splendour of the eleventh-century frescoes of the Chola period in the garbhagudi (sanctum sanctorum) by carefully and laboriously peeling off a superimposed layer of thirteenth-century paintings. The week he arrived from Madras in 1950 to start his new project at the Tanjore temple, he was introduced to my father by the principal of the local Serfoji College, and our families became good friends. From then on, Paramasivam Mama (honorific term for uncle) was a frequent visitor to our home, and because of his special status at the temple, we were admitted to view the astonishingly beautiful frescoes while the work of restoration was on.

That morning's meeting with Professor Sankho Choudhary and his wife Ira was truly under unexpected circumstances. Sankho, an acclaimed sculptor in the Fine Arts Department at the Maharaja Sayajirao University in Baroda, and his wife Ira, an accomplished potter, were on holiday in Ootacamund in the Nilgiris, and continued their tour of south India visiting temples not as pilgrims but as students and devotees of aesthetics. Moving from the visual feast at the Meenakshi Amman (Sundareswarar) Temple at Madurai, their next stop was at the Uchhi Pillaiyar temple built in the seventh century AD in Rockfort, Trichy. Both the fort and the temple complex built on the rocky outcrop are landmark tourist attractions of Trichy.

While on their way up to the temple, some urchins drew Ira's attention to some dirt on her saree. She stepped back into the temple pond to wash off the dirt, and in a trice, her handbag with all its contents was gone.

The station master at the Trichy junction understood their predicament. On Sankho's suggestion, he sent a telegram to Dr Paramasivam and paid for two tickets to Tanjore, besides loaning the distraught couple a few rupees! A few hours later, Sankho and Ira were in Tanjore.

Sankho and Ira connected instantaneously with my parents and with all of us. A joyous couple, Sankho with his hearty guffaw and Ira with her easy social grace, left an indelible mark on all of us.

My mother felt she was back with friends in Bombay. Her guests, in turn, were pleased that Amma could communicate with them in Hindi, and in short, we were all comfortable with each other. They were keen to go to Chittanavasal, the beautiful ninth-century Jain cave temple in Pudukottai district. I accepted their invitation to Pudukkottai and asked my sister Sarasa if she too would join. But she had a meeting with the local Guild of Service Committee, so Ira, Sankho and I left by bus the following day. I was amused to see the two lying on their backs for the better part of the day, admiring the frescoes on the ceiling of the temple. We got to know a bit about each other during that trip to Chittanavasal.

My parents invited Sankho and Ira the following evening to high tea, a special tiffin in lieu of dinner, as they were leaving for Madras by the night train. Amma made rava idlis and paal polis, which they enjoyed. Post-dinner, we had an evening of music and dance where we all sang, Ira and Sankho too. All this happened in 1953, two years earlier, and we had lost touch with each other.

Cut to two years later in August of 1955; a stranger, M.N. Srinivas, a good friend of Sankho and Ira, turned up at the staff quarters. When

*Sankho and Chamu in the eighties in Baroda*

I responded to the knock on my door, I saw a crouching figure with a head of greying hair, bent towards the ground, fingers tying his shoelace. 'Sorry about that,' and he smiled apologetically.

'Come in, Mr Srinivas.' He stepped in, somewhat abashed. In an attempt to ease the situation, I offered tea.

'I'll take a rain check on that,' he replied, adding, 'Call me Chamu, please.'

The accommodation I'd been allotted at the staff quarters was a fairly spacious and sparingly-furnished single room, with enclosed verandahs on two sides. I used one of the verandahs as a study. 'A nice airy and well-lit study,' was the comment. Chamu was interested in the courses I taught as a lecturer in the Department of Geography, and picking up a volume, he smiled, 'So, you use my colleague and friend Darryl Ford's book…is it for the undergraduate level.' We talked about my department, a little about my schooling, and so on. Nothing in particular, actually.

Nearing lunchtime, when I was wondering what I should offer Chamu for lunch, he said, 'My friend Ramachar has generously loaned me his car and driver for the next two days. May I take you out to lunch today? I am not familiar with the city, so you get to choose the place.' I did not know much about eating out in Madras, so I suggested the Ramakrishna Lunch Home, a vegetarian restaurant in Parry's Corner. I had been there a couple of times with college friends.

I realized on the first day that Chamu did not talk much about himself. In fact, I did most of the talking over tiffin of masala dosai, gulab jamun and coffee at the Ramakrishna Lunch Home, and it was mostly about my work and my family. As we drove back to Queen Mary's College, he told me a little about himself, his mother and his family in Mysore. I learnt that he had resigned from a lecturership in Oxford to start the Department of Sociology in the M.S. University in Baroda, and was still getting used to the change. We browsed in a bookstore on Mount Road, and stopped at P. Orr and Sons, the famous 'time' outlet, where he got a chain fixed to his pocket watch. Back in the car, he said, 'How thoughtless of me, I should have bought you a wristwatch.' He must have noticed I was not wearing one. 'Would you like to wear mine?' The Smith's man's wristwatch was his first gift to me. Dropping me back to college, he said he was free the following day, and if I was inclined to go out, he would like very much to spend time in Mahabalipuram. And we did. This was my first experience of the shore temples, and the day went by ever so fast.

Chamu was relaxed the second day, telling me more about his brothers and sisters. I got the feeling he wanted me to know his background and there should be no surprises for me. I, on the other hand, was attracted to his deep voice, his simplicity and his sense of the absurd.

Chamu was to leave for Baroda the following morning, and when I remarked how quickly those two days had gone by, he surprised me with, 'I will be back in Madras a few weeks later to finalize the arrangements for the International Anthropological Conference to be held here later this year, between 5 and 7 November.'

I received an invitation to the conference and enjoyed meeting scholars from around the world. I also got to spend more time with Chamu when he was in Madras in November. The day after the

*In Mahabalipuram shore temple*

conference ended, he expressed a desire to meet my parents and the rest of my family. When, in response, I told him that I had also wanted to invite him to Tanjore, he simply said, 'I read your mind and it should not surprise you to know that I feel the same way you do.' And we left for Tanjore.

My parents were very welcoming. The day went by without any questions asked nor answers expected. It was just one of those pleasant family gatherings. By the time we left that night for Madras, my parents knew that I had come with Chamu to introduce him to my family as someone special in my life. And my parents were happy for me. That he was a member of the Shrivaishnavite sect, an Iyengar, and I, an Iyer of the Shaivite sect, made no difference to them. And as Chamu told me later, he liked the interaction between me and my parents, particularly with my father and amongst us sisters.

Chamu wanted me to meet his family, too, and we left for Mysore to spend a couple of days with his mother, sisters, brothers, nieces and nephews. I felt comfortable with Chamu and was not nervous about meeting his family, who were very welcoming. There was a painted portrait of his parents in the main kalyana koodam, the main hall. I had learnt from Chamu that his father had passed away when he was in his teens. Parthasarathy, Pachu to family and friends, who was the eldest son, stepped in as the head of the household to discuss his younger brother's forthcoming marriage.

Chamu's mother was excited that her son had brought home his future bride. The evening we arrived from Madras, she took me to her favourite Srinivasa 'gudi', which translates to temple in Kannada. The following day, she and I shopped for wedding sarees and a few essential gold ornaments. I did not grow up in a family that placed any importance on jewellery, and she was pleasantly surprised at my refusal to buy expensive heavy gold ornaments. But it was fun shopping with her.

On that first visit to Mysore, I met the celebrated author R.K. Narayan, Kunjappa to family and friends, and he insisted Chamu and I visit his mother and have evening tiffin with them. The previous evening, Chamu had presented me with a copy of *Swami and Friends*, Narayan's maiden novel. I must confess I had not heard of R.K. Narayan, the acclaimed writer and novelist, till I visited Mysore. I had grown up with Thomas Hardy and Somerset Maugham.

We had delicious rava upma and coffee with Narayan's mother and his two sisters-in-law. Kunjappa was delighted that Chamu was marrying one of his 'jathwalis', a girl from his Iyer sect! From the moment we met, there was some chemistry between me and Kunjappa. I had the feeling I knew him from before. Chamu claimed that Kunjappa saw in me the likeness of Rajam, the dear wife he had lost. Kunjappa frequently said, 'Rajam was also tall and slim like you, Rukka. My meeting her was under very unusual and unorthodox circumstances. I was visiting relatives in Coimbatore, and at the public water tap in the street, my eyes fell upon this tall, young, slim girl who came every day with a "kodam" (water pot) to fill it with water from the street tap in front of my window, and go her way. One morning, I dared to ask her what her name was. I went home to Mysore and announced to my mother I had found Rajam, whom I wished to marry.'

'That was indeed quick and unconventional,' I remarked.

'Well, very much like Chamu,' said Kunjappa, and he laughed that inimitable laugh, throwing back his head just a little. Little did I know that we would spend much time together the following year in Berkeley, California.

On my return to Madras, to college, and Chamu's return to Baroda, my father sent me a Hindu newspaper cutting that read: 'This year's recipient of the coveted Rivers Memorial Medal awarded by the RAI, the Royal Anthropological Institute of Great Britain and Ireland, is Dr M.N. Srinivas, Professor and Head of the Department of Sociology in the Maharaja Sayajirao University, Baroda.'

'Did you know of this?' my father asked excitedly.

'I did not have the faintest clue,' was my honest response.

I give below the recipe for the creamy, rich milk dessert that Amma made the evening Sankho and Ira had tiffin with us in our Rajappa Nagar home.

PAAL POLI, *made on special occasions, it is quick and easy to prepare. I remember Amma made this delicious tiffin for us in Poona even without the excuse of a special occasion.*

### INGREDIENTS FOR 5 SERVINGS

* *1 can sweetened condensed milk*
* *1½ cups milk*
* *¼ teaspoon cardamom powder*
* *a few strands of saffron*
* *2 tablespoons sugar (optional)*
* *2 tablespoons raisins*
* *1 cup maida (white flour)*
* *¼ teaspoon salt*
* *1 tablespoon ghee*
* *¾ cup ghee and ¾ cup oil mixed to prepare the shortening for frying*
* *12 cloves*

### METHOD

Empty the condensed milk into a deep heavy pan. Add the milk, cardamom powder, saffron and sugar, if you are using it. Stir to mix well.

Heat the milk over a medium fire, stirring frequently, and when it comes to a boil, lower the heat. Toss in the raisins. Keep stirring once in a while to prevent a skin forming. Cook to a thin sauce consistency.

Turn off the heat. Keep stirring occasionally to prevent a film forming.

In a bowl, sift the flour and salt together. Add the ghee and mix. Sprinkle a little water at a time and knead to a stiff dough.

Transfer the dough to a work-table, knead and roll with your fingers to a rope. Divide the 'rope' into 12 equal parts, and roll each into a tight ball. Keep covered.

Heat the shortening in a wok on medium heat.

Take two balls of dough at a time and roll each into a thin disc (as thin as you can without tearing).

Fold each disc into half and fold again to form a triangle. Press a clove in the middle of the curved edge.

To test if the shortening is ready for the frying process, drop a pinch of the dough into the hot shortening; if ready, the dough will sink and, with a sizzle, immediately rise to the surface. Lower the heat.

Slide in the two triangles and fry for one minute, turning them over a couple of times. Drain well and drop them gently into the aromatic milk. Press gently to submerge.

Roll out and make two more triangles, pierce with the cloves and fry as before.

While the second batch is frying, remove the paal poli (the fried triangles) soaking in the flavoured milk and arrange on a serving dish.

Drain the second batch and submerge in the milk.

Continue rolling, shaping the triangles, frying and submerging with the remaining balls of dough. Control the stove temperature by raising and lowering it as necessary.

When all the paal polis are arranged in the serving dish, pour the rest of the milk over them.

Serve at room temperature.

*The Wedding in Tanjore*

Chamu and I decided to get married by the first week of December. He had told me, when we visited his family in Mysore, that he had already accepted an invitation to the USA. He had to leave in August 1956, adding that he had several professional commitments before then, and wasn't sure if he could take even a week off. I suddenly realized that I should tender my resignation to the college soon after I returned to Madras from our visit to Mysore. I was hesitant to broach the matter with the head of my department, as I knew the college would, most likely, not be able to find a substitute lecturer immediately to fill my position. But to my surprise, she was very supportive, thanked me for my concern for the students, and suggested I leave for Tanjore without delay. 'The rest of us in the department will take care of the students,' she assured me. Her understanding of my situation made me feel guilty and relieved at the same time.

My resignation from Queen Mary's College was accepted immediately, and I left for Tanjore to spend some time with my family before my marriage.

Chamu suggested to my parents that late November would be a good time for our wedding date. Just ten days to arrange and organize a wedding! For Chamu and me, it seemed doable. Neither of us were in favour of a big splash, a lavish wedding ceremony, spending money that my parents could ill afford. Two sisters younger to Sarasa were yet to complete their university education, and three of them were still in grade school. My father's response to our request for a wedding in less than two weeks was, 'Okay, Rukka, if you want it that way, let's do it.' But when Dr Chitappa heard of this, he said, 'Anna (Tamil for elder brother), I don't think that is possible. There are innumerable tasks ahead, even though Rukka says she wants a simple wedding.' And finally, he was the one who made all the arrangements for the function.

Chamu and I decided that we would get married in a simple wedding ritual to be performed on the terrace of my parents' home in Rajappa Nagar in Tanjore. He made a list of the basic essentials in a Hindu marriage ritual, and we cut out all the frills and saved time and money. The wedding was fixed for 21 November, after a few letters exchanged between my father and Chamu's eldest brother Pachu, who believed in astrology. He came up with the date after consulting his astrologer friend, Shri Gopalachar, in Mysore. My father went along. As far as I know, Appa was never influenced by astrology, superstition and the like. 'If the date is convenient to you, Chamu, his mother, and your mother, that is all that matters,' he said to me.

Chamu and I kept the details, including the date of our marriage, known only to a few close friends and immediate

*Wedding invitation*

relatives. He told me that his family of seven adults—his mother, brothers, sisters and four nieces and nephews—would come by car, which, he said, the children would enjoy.

I think there were about thirty of my parents' relatives who attended our wedding, including my uncles, aunts and their children. My Annam Athai arrived ten days before the wedding, and took charge of the two cooks who were specially engaged for cooking all the meals during the wedding. She supervised the making of the wedding sweets and savouries: sweet gunjaladdu, each the size of a tennis ball shaped by hand, with myriads of sugar-coated beads of fried gram flour; Mysore pak, crumbly beehive squares rich with ghee and sugar; juicy jalebis, my father's choice for the occasion, shimmering with an orange glaze; sweet, toasted semolina laddus studded with cashews and raisins; and savouries that only the natives of Tamil Nadu are skilled in preparing, like the kai murukku, each the size of a dinner plate, of eight to ten concentric rings of slender twisted lengths of rice flour dough fashioned by hand and fried. It is truly a work of art that comes only with practice. Annam Athai also insisted that two paruppu thengais be made: one of cashews and the other of manoharam, sweetened thenkozhal (fried rice noodles dipped in jaggery syrup). A paruppu thengai is a cone-shaped confection, taking its shape from the metal cone into which the ingredients are poured and pressed into a thick syrup. These again are the hallmark of south Indian sweets made on auspicious occasions.

Some relatives could not make it, and one of those was my Poonamalee Athai whom I truly missed. She was ever so kind to me when I was a student in Queen Mary's College. I had grown fond of her and I would have liked Chamu to meet her.

One relative, my Shirkali Periappa, my father's elderly cousin, appeared, uninvited, on the day of the wedding. I knew him as Shirkali Periappa since he lived in the village of Shirkali and was older to my father. I had met him a couple of times over the years in Tanjore when I visited home from college. He was informed of my marriage by the family priest, who was to officiate at the function, and his curiosity to 'see the Shrivaishnavite

*Rukka and Chamu's wedding*

*Rukka and Chamu's wedding*

groom' brought him to our home that day. It appears, in my father's extended family, I was the first to marry outside my Shaivite sect, and he made no secret of it when he told Dr Chitappa that my father 'was not just diluting but corrupting the ancestry by agreeing to this union'.

As I said, Dr Chitappa took charge of nearly all the wedding arrangements—the priests, the cooks, including the special cooks who made the sweets, the 'pandal' (celebratory awning) makers, the delivery of provisions, vegetables, fruits, flowers and milk. My mother insisted that I go with her to Kumbakonam, the centre for silk, to choose a few wedding sarees, and between Amma and Chamu's mother, I had quite a few.

I did not want my parents to spend on jewellery for me, but Amma insisted that I accept a pair of 'thodu', a pair of south Indian traditional diamond earrings. She also gave me what she had worn for decades—a pair of pearl bangles, a pair of black bead bangles set in a gold casing and a black-and-gold bead chain—all of which she had worn from her Poona days. I treasure these special gifts from Amma. She was greatly influenced by the Poona culture where the black bead chain is the mangal sutra, the auspicious chain signifying the state of being married.

Chamu's one request, on behalf of his mother who was a practising Shrivaishnavite, was for a Shrivaishnavite cook to prepare her food when she was in Tanjore. So for the three days that she was my parents' guest in Tanjore, an Iyengar cook was engaged solely for preparing food for Chamu's mother. She was touched by this gesture.

My marriage to Chamu was a quiet event, which took place on

the terrace of my parents' home in Tanjore. The ritual 'of giving away the bride', the kanyadanam, was performed by my Bombay Chitappa and his wife, my Bombay Chitti. This ritual is normally the privilege and duty of the father of the bride, with his wife endorsing him, but I understood why my father requested my uncle to stand in on his behalf. It was difficult for him to let go of me in spite of his affection for Chamu. My father and I shared something special.

My mother, as I have known her, was not one who visited temples on a regular basis, but on this day of my marriage, she wanted Chamu and me to visit the Sri Rama temple in Thillaivilagam. Sri Rama was her preferred deity. Chamu's mother was pleased with this arrangement, so his family and I spent the latter part of the day at the temple and when we returned, we found a wedding reception awaiting us. My sisters had organized an evening of music and dance, with my elder sister Kamala playing the violin, my sisters Sarasa and Leelu on the sitar and tabla, and my two teenaged younger sisters Malathi (Malu) and Sarala (Challu) dancing for us. It was truly a memorable grand finale to a day filled with pleasure. Gita, my youngest sister, around four years of age then, turned out to be the favourite in Chamu's family. That evening, Chamu and I left for Madras on our way to Baroda. My uncles and all the members of Chamu's family saw us off at the Tanjore railway station. My father hugged and said farewell to me at home. I left with mixed feelings. My uncles jokingly remarked that I had kept our honeymoon destination a secret. The fact was that Chamu had to get back to his duties at his university within four days of our wedding! The honeymoon had to wait till we were in Berkeley ten months later.

Two days prior to my wedding, my parents' guests were treated to elaborate breakfasts, lunches, evening tiffin and dinners.

The sweet served for the wedding lunch was jalebis with milk basundi or rabadi. Both were my father's favourites. In Jubbulpore, the halwai would come home to make jalebis and rabadi (creamy rich milk sweet) when my parents hosted a dinner party.

# JUICY JALEBIS, *crisp, saffron-coloured swirls of piped fried batter in a rich golden syrup.*

## INGREDIENTS TO MAKE 12 JALEBIS

- 1 cup white flour
- 1 teaspoon rice flour
- 1 teaspoon gram flour (besan)
- ½ teaspoon yogurt
- ½ teaspoon sugar
- 2 drops yellow food colour
- ghee for frying

## INGREDIENTS FOR THE SYRUP

- 1 cup sugar
- 1 teaspoon rose essence
- a few saffron threads

## METHOD

Sieve flours together in a bowl. Add yogurt, sugar and 1 tablespoon of water. Mix.

Dissolve food colour in ¾ cup of water. Pour into flour mix and whisk well, removing all lumps. Cover and set aside for 10 minutes.

### To Make the Sugar Syrup

Dissolve sugar in ¾ cup water in a deep pan and simmer for 5 minutes. The syrup should be just sticky. Stir in the saffron and rose essence. Remove from heat and set aside.

### To Make the Jalebis

Pour enough ghee in a shallow pan to a depth of 1 inch. Heat the ghee on medium heat.

Stir the jalebi batter and fill half of a single, small-hole nozzle bag with it.

Squeeze out the batter in concentric rings into the ghee, starting from the outer ring inwards. The jalebi should be about 1½ inches wide.

Deep fry the jalebis, turning them over, to a golden-brown. Lift, drain and drop gently into the warm syrup. Remove from syrup and serve.

Best served immediately.

# RABADI (BASUNDI)

## INGREDIENTS TO MAKE 6 SERVINGS

* *4 cups whole milk*
* *1 cup condensed milk*
* *3 tablespoons sugar*
* *½ teaspoon cardamom powder*
* *¼ cup unsalted pistachio nuts, chopped*
* *¼ cup blanched almonds, chopped*
* *a few saffron threads*

## METHOD

In a heavy-bottomed pan, bring the milk to a boil on medium heat. Stir occasionally to prevent burning at the bottom.

Stir in the condensed milk. Add the sugar and keep stirring and cooking till the milk thickens. Scrape the sides and bottom of the pan frequently while stirring. Scatter the saffron threads and cardamom powder and stir to mix well. Remove pan from stove when the milk turns to a thick sauce. Toss in pistachios and almonds.

Serve hot, at room temperature or cold. Puris with rabadi is a yummy combination.

# Apachi Amma, Akki Roti and Mango Seekarane

Chamu's mother—Alamelamma was her formal name—was in her sixties when I met her in 1955. She had a presence about her, gently and benignly commanding, yet not threatening to me as a daughter-in-law. She was light-complexioned, frail and slightly built. She had sharp, alert deep-set eyes, a dominant aquiline nose with a slight curve like a hawk's beak, and wavy grey hair that framed her face. Her expansive-pierced earlobes were adorned with large diamond earrings. Equally impressive was the long, thin, vertical vermilion caste mark on her broad forehead. She dressed in a nine-yard silk saree worn the traditional south Indian Shrivaishnavite-style.

She was an orthodox Shrivaishnavite Brahmin, observing all the rules of her Brahminical sect. However, she was very open-minded; friends, regardless of age, caste, class, religious affiliation and food preferences, came to spend time with her and to eat delicious vegetarian meals and tiffin at her home. Endowed with abundant practical wisdom and organizational skills, even in her seventies, she supervised the smooth running of her household of eight adults and five grandchildren, not including the cook Seshadri and domestic help Madamma, and the number only increased during the summer vacation, when we spent time with her at her Mysore residence.

When Chamu and I married in 1955, his family lived in the modest two-storeyed three-bedroom home on Venkatakrishnaiya Road, built by his parents. What is etched in my memory of the home, when

*Chamu with Apachi Amma*

I entered the very first morning in early November 1955 to be introduced to and meet Chamu's family, is the sheltered patio in the middle section of the house, with a slender pomegranate tree laden with fruit. On one side was a stone bench, on which Chamu's eldest brother Pachu sat, enjoying freshly brewed hot coffee in a metal lota (tall metal glass). The patio connected the living room to the dining and kitchen area, beyond which was a stone well. Chamu's mother told me with pride that the pomegranate tree, the seedless 'Kabuli' variety, was planted by the deceased father of her children. This is how she referred to her husband. There was no front garden, and the steps from the house led out onto the street. This family home may not have been able to accommodate the expanding family when her adult children got married and had children of their own, but it was a treasure trove of happy memories, especially for Chamu's mother. She told me of how Chamu's father worked along with the masons to build the family house, that she had never known him to raise his voice, and as she said, 'He would never hurt a fly.' That said a great deal about the gentleman that he was. The morning Chamu and I arrived, she first ushered me to the small puja alcove, the domestic shrine and altar, and showed me Chamu's father's photo, which shared sacred space with many icons of deities, and asked me to take his blessings. Over time, it became obvious that the family had to shift, and reluctantly, Chamu's mother agreed to sell her home, and till the family moved into another home of their own, they lived in rented houses. Sadly, she passed away before the new house was ready for the family to move in.

The sprawling single-storeyed home, that Chamu's younger sister Thanga built in the new suburb of Jayalakshmipuram, was set in a spacious corner plot; corner sites had a premium in the real estate market. It was similar to a farmhouse, with a cattle shed for the milch cows and a set of rooms at the rear end for the domestic maid and her family. Comfortable and well built, the house, surrounded by trees, shrubs, vines and potted plants, was one you could not miss in that locality. The side door of the house facing east led to a well-laid-out garden of tulasi plants (sacred basil) and jasmine shrubs. With the passing of Chamu's mother, Thanga assumed the responsibility of managing the home. Thanga was a professor in the Psychology Department at Manasa Gangotri, the postgraduate wing of the Mysore University. When Apachi Amma passed away, the cook and other domestic help trained by her continued to stay with the family, else Thanga would have found it difficult to manage the home and her responsibilities at the university.

It would be unfair to describe Thanga as just a professor. She was not only an enthusiastic gardener, she was a botanist by training, with a deep interest in all manner of flora; I would call her a walking encyclopaedia on plants. She collected exotic plants, the most impressive of which were her orchids and rare varieties of hybrid hibiscus and bromeliads. When it came to collecting plants, even her friends were on guard when Thanga visited them and they spotted her in their garden!

As a gift for her new house, Chamu and I bought her several plants, and later, every time we returned from abroad, her request would be for packets of seeds of flowering plants and vegetables. A gift that she cherished most was the fragrant gardenia shrub that Chamu gave her on her 50th birthday. The family house came to be identified as the Archad Maney (Archad, as in, the local pronunciation of orchid, and Maney, meaning house in Kannada)! The name evolved this way—among her neighbours and the Mysore tongawallahs, the letters 'O' and 'A' were interchangeable, and again, 'C' and 'H' in the word 'orchid' did not translate to the sound of 'K' but as in the word 'church', with which they were familiar. When, on one occasion, I took a tonga back home from the market in Mysore, and to make the location clearer, I stupidly said Orchid House, the tongawallah corrected me with, '*Archad Maney hogu bekka* (Do you want to go to the Archad Maney)?' and he took me straight home. Thanga also had a kind of mini-orchard surrounding the home, with coconut, guava, gooseberry, sapota (chikku) and lemon trees. So what's in a name?—Orchard or Orchid made no difference.

Between 1955, when Chamu and I were married, and 1970, when my mother-in-law passed away, we spent a few weeks every summer that we were in India with her. My firstborn Lakshmi, who was in elementary school, remembers her Patti, grandmother, better than her younger sister Tulasi, who was still in playschool. Alas, the grand lady passed away in her home in Mysore in 1970 when we four were in Palo Alto for the year. I later heard from Thanga that Apachi Amma did not wish that Chamu be informed of her brief illness before she passed away, lest he rushed back home. I believe she told Thanga, 'He is there to write an important book and should not be disturbed.' In more ways than one, *The Remembered Village* had a difficult and traumatic conception and birth that year.

Chamu's mother was affectionately called Apachi Amma, the 'mother of treats', by her grandchildren. True to the name, she had several containers of home-made sweets and savoury snacks in a special rosewood cupboard, referred to as the 'madi almirah', the ritually pure cupboard in her pantry which was out of bounds for all of us. Between three and four o'clock every afternoon the savouries and sweets from the 'madi almirah' would be served in the 'kalyana koodam', the central hall with a cathedral ceiling, where all of us gathered.

Chamu and I with our two daughters would spend the first few weeks of the summer vacation with my parents and sisters in Tanjore, and the remaining month with Chamu's family in Mysore. The pre-monsoon showers, typical of the season in Mysore, were a welcome change from the dry summer heat in Tanjore, and reluctantly, by early June, we left for sweaty Delhi, which, in a sense, was worse than the searing heat of Tanjore. Chamu's married younger sister Padma, a paediatrician, and her husband, a surgeon, and their two young girls would join us from Chinglepet. The six weeks every summer were a precious time, especially for my daughters and their cousins who met once a year.

In Mysore, on any given day during the summer vacation, we were, at a conservative estimate, ten adults and nine children, one family of four generations under one roof. Apachi Amma saw to our needs, particularly in the realm of food. Every meal, whether it was breakfast, lunch, afternoon tiffin or dinner, was elaborate. Pachu, her eldest son, minutely planned the structure of every meal and tiffin with a kind of obsession. He made the four weeks one long delicious gastronomic vacation, when Apachi Amma supervised the cooking of her childrens' and grandchildrens' favourite dishes.

Among Chamu's favourites were akki roti, savoury crisp, rice flour flatbreads, and mango seekarane, fresh mango dessert with raisins and cashews. Apachi Amma frequently made both for tiffin every summer we were in Mysore. Several baskets of the best Raspuri and Badami varieties of mangoes were carefully 'bedded' in hay and left to ripen in the spacious ugrana, store room, sharing space with sacks of rice, pulses, lentils, condiments and spices. With the ripening of the mangoes and the home-grown jackfruit, also a summer fruit, the entire house would smell rich and fruity, and frequently, ripe fruit accompanied by a glass of cow's milk was the preferred breakfast for the children. The making of seekarane was elaborate; several dozen mangoes were peeled, sliced and crushed to make a thick juicy pulp, which was stirred into flowery saffron and cardamom flavoured cow's milk, and enriched with plump and crunchy raisins and cashew nut pieces fried in ghee.

Rice flour is the main ingredient for many of the snacks and tiffin made in south Indian homes, and the flour was not available in grocery stores as it is today. In most homes, several pounds of rice would be washed, drained, sun-dried and milled into flour in a domestic quern. So it was in the Mysore home, too.

The ebony-black, shiny jackwood platter, in which Apachi Amma mixed the sifted rice flour with pungent green chillies, sweet-smelling dill, milky shredded coconut and smoky cumin for the akki roti, smelt like a herbaceous garden. With decades of use, the smooth, black, shiny platter smelt spicy and delicious and had acquired a character of its own. The rest of the making of akki roti would be left to the cook Seshadri. It was that special touch of hers with the right proportion of fresh herbs to the rice flour that made it so tasty every time. There is a telling maxim in Tamil that was oft repeated by my Annam Athai: 'Kai nannaa irundaa shamayal nichiyamma ruchiyaa irukkum,' which translates to 'if the hand is good the food is bound to be tasty!' Seshadri had a 'good hand' too, but he was temperamental and frequently needed an ego boost, which only Apachi Amma could handle with her fund of patience and her empathy for others. As she would often say in Kannada, 'Seshadri is stirring the kitchen pot because of a lack of education.'

Cooking food, even with the help of a cook, whether it be lunch, dinner or tiffin for a family of twenty, on a daily basis, is no easy task. But the women I have known were blessed with 'good hands' and an abundance of patience, their main concern being to keep their family well-fed and happy. Apachi Amma's kitchen was the stage for her activities and she was in total command. Not everyone was allowed entry into her kitchen, which she kept ritually 'pure'.

She would sit with us while we enjoyed the hot, straight-off-the-wok akki roti and mango seekarane to go with it. Making seekarane on a warm summer afternoon was an exercise in testing one's patience. And she suffered her grandsons' tricks with a knowing indulgent smile; after biting through and sucking out most of the pulp of one ripe mango, they would beg for another fruit, saying, 'That one was very sour, Apachi Amma. I want a sweet one.'

She also experimented with making seekarane from her favourite fruit, sitaphal (custard apple), although it was a time-consuming job, gently rubbing the seeds embedded in the pulp with a flat wooden spatula, separating the seeds from the pulp and passing it through a special sieve. But the slightly granular texture of the sitaphal made for an interesting dessert. And today, a few ice cream factories pride themselves in making sitaphal and chikku ice cream.

AKKI ROTI, *rice flour flatbread cooked in a wok—the roti served in the shape of a 'dome'—is unusual in appearance and tastes fabulous. I have modified the original recipe by adding chopped dill and onion.*

## INGREDIENTS TO MAKE 6 ROTIS

- *2 cups rice flour*
- *1 teaspoon cumin seeds*
- *3 green chillies, chopped fine*
- *1 cup loosely packed fresh dill, chopped*
- *¼ cup loosely packed fresh coriander, chopped*
- *½ cup shelled peas, blanched, or ½ cup shelled Indian beans (papdi lilva, avarekai, available frozen in Indian grocery stores abroad)*
- *1 medium onion, cut in half and sliced thin (optional)*
- *¾ cup shredded coconut, frozen or fresh*
- *1 teaspoon salt; more if needed*
- *½ cup oil*
- *¼ cup ghee*
- *water to mix the batter*

## METHOD TO MIX THE DOUGH

In a large bowl, mix all the ingredients except, the water, oil and ghee.

Add water, 2 tablespoons at a time, and mix to a soft dough.

Divide into 6 portions, roll into balls and set aside, covered, in a bowl.

## METHOD TO MAKE THE AKKI ROTI

Grease the inside of a medium—size wok with ½ teaspoon oil.

Place one ball of dough in the centre of the greased wok, and wetting your fingers in a bowl of cold water, work the ball from the centre outwards pressing over the greased surface of the wok, pushing and spreading it evenly with your fingers (the thinner you spread the layer, the crisper the roti). Make a few holes with a finger through the dough you have spread.

Drizzle a drop of oil in each hole and around the edges. Cover and cook on medium heat till the underside browns (about 2 to 3 minutes).

Check, removing lid after a couple of minutes.

Lift the cooked roti from the wok with a metal spatula, gently easing the edges. Transfer to a platter. Do not flip over and cook. The roti takes the shape of the wok.

Serve hot or at room temperature, with a dollop of freshly churned butter or a drizzle of ghee, and chutney or pickle.

I serve wedges of akki roti as appetizers frequently, with a dip or salsa, for a summer beer party.

**MANGO SEEKARANE,** *the colour of yellow gold, rich, smooth and fruity, it is a quick and easy way to make dessert. The addition of milk to mango lessens the heat generated by eating mangoes. For a richer version, fold in half a cup of almond ice cream or half a cup of cream.*

### INGREDIENTS FOR 6 SERVINGS

* 5 cups whole milk, boiled and reduced to half and cooled. I now use part canned condensed milk and part whole milk
* a pinch of saffron threads soaked in 1 teaspoon milk
* 2 cups sugar; less if you are using condensed milk
* 1 teaspoon cardamom powder
* 3 cups fresh or canned mango pulp. If you are using canned sweetened pulp, you may omit the sugar or reduce the quantity
* 1 cup ripe mango, peeled and diced (optional)
* 3 teaspoons ghee
* 2 tablespoons golden raisins
* 2 tablespoons raw cashew nut pieces

### METHOD

Empty cooled milk into a large bowl; add condensed milk, if you are using it.
Stir in the ground saffron, cardamom powder and sugar, if you are using it.
Add mango pulp and pieces. Mix.
Taste for sweetness and add sugar if needed.
Warm up the ghee in a small saucepan on medium heat.
Add raisins and cashew nut pieces.
Stir and fry till the raisins plump up and the cashew nuts are golden-brown.
Add to contents of bowl.
Chill and serve.

I add ½ cup honey instead of sugar and a few rose petals from my garden, for the taste and aroma of ambrosia. You could substitute cashew nuts with ¼ cup blanched almonds ground with 2 tablespoons milk.

**MANGO SHRIKHAND,** *creamy, saffron-flavoured, golden mango mousse is a favourite with my family. Canned mango slices and pulp make it possible to have a 'summer' dessert throughout the year.*

*Mango shrikhand and puris are the favoured combination for an Indian summer party. (I would like to try making mango shrikhand with whipping cream; that would be deadly and not quite the real McCoy!).*

### INGREDIENTS TO MAKE 6 SERVINGS

- *4 cups plain full-cream yogurt; you could substitute with 1 packet of Philadelphia cream cheese and 4 tablespoons sour cream*
- *2 cups sugar (adjust to your taste)*
- *1 teaspoon cardamom powder*
- *3 cups unsweetened mango pulp (canned or fresh). Adjust the quantity of sugar if the pulp is sweetened*
- *a pinch of saffron strands soaked in 1 teaspoon warm milk*

### METHOD

Empty the yogurt into a large strainer resting on a pan. Collect the whey. It will take 2 hours for all the whey to drain. Save the whey, refrigerate and use in soups, or make a delicious drink with a pinch of salt, ½ teaspoon crushed ginger, 2 teaspoons honey and a squeeze of lime.

Transfer the yogurt solids from the strainer into a large glass bowl.

Add the sugar and whisk with a wooden spoon to break the solids. You could do this in a food processor. Fold in the cardamom powder, saffron with the milk, and mango pulp.

Chill and serve.

Try mixing gulkand, a fragrant preserve of rose petals, into the shrikhand. Gulkand is available in the Indian grocery stores.

When cream cheese along with sour cream is substituted for yogurt, the preparation time is shortened by 2 hours, the time taken for the draining of the whey in the yogurt.

*Kamalu's Avarekai Adai*

Chamu's cousin Kamalu lived in her own cosy home, adjoining her mother's bungalow, in the suburb of Malleswaram in Bangalore. Her two adult sons lived with her. On our annual summer visit to Mysore, where Chamu's mother lived, we two would stop for the day to spend time with Kamalu. On arrival at the Bangalore Cantonment Station in early May, a cool drizzle, typical of the Bangalore weather this time of the year, greeted us; what a welcome change from the enervating heat and dust of the north Indian plains. Driving down tree-lined avenues, hearing the crescendo call of the Indian koels (*Eudynamys scolopacea*) and the mating call of the lineated barbets (*Megalaima lineata*), which I associated with the monsoon rains, I felt really blessed.

Kamalu, on seeing us at her gate, stepped out into the rain-drenched garden wrapped in a shawl, and welcomed us with a warning, 'This is treacherous weather. You will fall sick with cold, cough and flu, so take out your woollies.'

The fragrance of freshly brewed coffee greeted us as we entered her home, and even before we unpacked the gifts we had brought her, she produced steaming hot filter coffee in tall metal tumblers. Why was Kamalu's coffee so special? Was it the Mysore coffee beans, roasted to perfection and ground fresh every day, that preserved and enhanced the aroma? Did the water in Bangalore make a difference to the taste of the coffee? Was the secret hidden in the south Indian filter, which allowed the water to percolate drop by drop to draw out the essence?

Blowing on the dancing froth and warming my fingers on the tumbler, I enjoyed every last drop.

Kamalu never approved of our plan to leave for Mysore the same night. 'Why can't you stay a few days here? You have become a stranger to us, Chamu.' Her tone was one of hurt. Chamu tried to appease her by promising to return in a couple of weeks.

Kamalu was an epicure. Her meals were well planned and tasty. She put herself out, cooking breakfast, lunch and tiffin on the one day we stayed with her. Our efforts to explain to her that it was impossible to eat three heavy meals in the space of twelve hours fell on deaf ears. She knew one of Chamu's favourite tiffin dishes was avarekai adai, rice flour flatbread studded with local beans, and his preferred dessert was gasagase payasa, a nutty flavoured milk pudding with a paste of ground almonds and poppy seeds stirred in. Avarekai is a bean with a particularly rich and oily fragrance. Bangaloreans, Mysoreans and the people of Tamil Nadu love the flavour of this rich bean, but for many northerners it is an acquired smell. Kamalu cooked on a firewood stove, which she kept alive by frequently blowing through a tubular metal blower. She made several crisp, aromatic, griddle-cooked flatbreads, which she served straight off the hot griddle with butter and home-made sweet and sour lemon pickle. Chamu's comments after enjoying Kamalu's adai was, 'This is food for wrestlers! I must go for a run or at least for a l-o-n-g walk.'

Kamulu's recipe for avarekai adai was a well-guarded secret. Never before had I tasted that kind of adai nor have I met another person who makes it that well. However, I had tasted her avarekai adai several times to be able to deconstruct it, and Chamu's approving comments on the occasions I've made it made me feel good. But it did make a difference that the adai I made on a gas stove lacked the smoky smell of firewood.

# AVAREKAI ADAI, *delicious, crisp, aromatic, griddle-cooked flatbread.*

## INGREDIENTS TO MAKE 5-6 ADAIS

* 1 cup raw rice
* ¼ cup tur dal (yellow split pea)
* ⅛ cup chana dal (chickpea)
* 2 red chillies, more if you want a spicier adai
* 1 cup shredded coconut, fresh or frozen
* ½ cup avarekai, shelled beans soaked in hot water for 5 minutes and strained (frozen papdi lilva is available in Indian grocery stores)
* 10 curry leaves, torn in pieces
* ½ teaspoon asafoetida powder
* ½ cup oil
* ½ cup ghee (clarified butter)
* salt to taste

## METHOD

Wash and rinse the rice and dals together. Drain. Repeat till the water is not cloudy. Soak in cold water for 4 hours. Drain in a colander.

In a food processor, coarsely grind the rice and dals with the chillies, adding just enough water for the ground mix to hold together. Empty into a bowl, scraping the sides of the food processor.

Add the shredded coconut, shelled beans, curry leaves, asafoetida and salt and mix. Divide into 5 or 6 equal portions, roll into rough balls, and put back in the bowl.

Grease a flat wrought iron griddle with 1 teaspoon oil.

Take 1 ball of the mix and place it in the middle of the greased griddle.

Wet your fingers and pat the ball from the centre outwards to the edges, forming a disc roughly ¼ inch thick. Make a hole in the centre with your finger or a spoon.

Pour ½ teaspoon oil in the hole and drizzle 1 teaspoon oil around the edges.

Heat the griddle on medium heat, cover and cook for about 3 to 4 minutes till the underside is brown.

Ease the edges with a metal spatula and flip over and cook, uncovered, drizzling another ½ teaspoon oil in the central hole and around the edges.

Cook, brown and serve hot, with ghee and a sweet and sour pickle on the side. When patted thin, the adai cooks faster and is crunchy.

Cool the griddle under cold running water before you grease it and pat the next ball of mixture; else, the batter will start cooking before you can pat it to the desired thickness.

**GASAGASE PAYASA,** *creamy and nutty in flavour, this almond-poppy seed milk drink was often served as a nightcap in Chamu's mother's home in Mysore. This payasa is believed to give restful, uninterrupted sleep.*

## INGREDIENTS TO MAKE 4 SERVINGS

* *1 teaspoon rice grains*
* *1 tablespoon white poppy seeds*
* *½ cup grated jaggery or brown sugar; more for a sweeter drink*
* *2 cups water, plus more water for grinding*
* *½ cup blanched almonds*
* *2 tablespoons shredded coconut, fresh or frozen*
* *2 cups hot milk*
* *a trace of nutmeg powder*

## METHOD

Soak the rice in a bowl with 3 tablespoons water, and set aside for 30 minutes.

In a deep pan. dissolve the jaggery in 2 cups water, and boil to a thin syrup. Strain through a cheese cloth into a bowl, and set aside.

Roast the poppy seeds in a pan on medium heat till they change colour to a light brown and you smell the nutty aroma, taking care not to burn the poppy seeds.

Drain the water from the bowl of rice. Empty the rice into a blender and grind to a fine paste, adding a little water.

Add the roasted poppy seeds, coconut, almonds and ½ cup water to the ground rice in the blender. Grind to a smooth paste.

Empty the ground paste into a deep pot. Wash the blender, adding ¼ cup water, and add to the contents in the pot.

Bring to a boil on medium heat, stirring continuously. Cook for about 2–3 minutes.

Add the jaggery syrup to the pot. Bring to one boil. Turn off the stove.

Stir in the nutmeg powder and hot milk.

Serve hot.

In the year 1951, four years before our marriage, Chamu joined the Maharaja Sayaji Rao University in Baroda at the invitation of the vice-chancellor Dr Hansa Mehta. He had resigned from his academic position at the Institute for Social Anthropology in Oxford to accept Dr Mehta's offer as the professor to start the Department of Social Anthropology. Her support made Chamu leave a stable position in the Institute in Oxford and move to Baroda, a university town of repute in the western Indian state of Gujarat, the erstwhile princely state of the ruling House of the Gaekwads. Baroda is also referred to as Sanskari Nagar, the cultural city.

Two couples whom Chamu befriended in Baroda remained his friends for life. I have already mentioned Sankho Choudhary, an inspired sculptor in the Fine Arts Department of the University of Baroda, who was the younger brother of Chamu's friend Sachin Choudhary, the founder editor of the prestigious *Economic Weekly* in Bombay. Sankho's wife Ira is a gifted potter. Chamu enjoyed spending time with the fun-loving couple. (The day I spent with Ira and Sankho in 1953 in Tanjore was a fortuitous meeting for me.)

Sankho and Ira introduced Chamu to their dear friends Nanubhai and Savita Amin. The two couples and Chamu bonded and formed an intimate group.

When Chamu and I were married in 1955, the Choudharys and the Amins were my family in Baroda. Any time of the day was chai time, with delicious samosas, pakodas and other snacks, at the Choudhary home, with many students who felt free to walk in. Our relationship was easy and cordial and I have several fond memories of those years.

Nanubhai Amin was a man of many parts. Trained as an engineer, he was an innovator industrialist with a social conscience, who contributed in no small measure to the development of the state of Gujarat. A patron of the arts, a passionate gardener, an innovative cook, an avid reader, a tireless and enthusiastic tourist, and above all, a believer in change for the betterment of humanity, he was tireless in exhorting people to help themselves and not to look to the government for all assistance.

Savita, his spouse, was his natural complement. While she shared many of his interests, she was an enlightened educator and food entrepreneur.

Savita and Nanubhai were discerning and sensitive hosts, and Chamu and I frequently enjoyed their hospitality at their home in Baroda. A widely travelled cosmopolitan and

*Savita and Nanubhai*

adventurous foodie, Nanubhai would often pay for his gastronomic adventures. Though he enjoyed the novelty of the exotic, frequently he looked to simple vegetarian fare to cleanse his system. 'I have yet to nurse a stomach upset after eating south Indian vegetarian food even if it be in a remote village in south India,' he would say.

Nanubhai's well laid-out kitchen garden boasted of a wide variety of vegetables and herbs. He grew asparagus and celery, thyme and rosemary as successfully as he did fenugreek greens, spinach, tomatoes, okra, aubergine, chillies and coriander. His daily constitutional around his garden and hothouse decided the menu for the day. Some days, the wicker baskets would be full of small, purple, tender aubergines, a handful of cluster beans, a few vine-ripened tomatoes, a head or two of cabbage, a few green chillies, stems of curry leaves and sprigs of coriander, and on other days, a large snow-white cauliflower, freshly dug potatoes with the mud still clinging to them, and tender stems of aromatic dill.

I remember one leisurely Sunday morning when Nanubhai harvested over a dozen seedless Dacca lemons, and I helped him make sweet lemon pickle. With a couple of leftover lemons, I made lemon rice and a ginger-lemon drink. We had an elaborate lunch that Sunday with a mixed vegetable sambar, spicy tomato rasam and south Indian carrot kosambari, a fresh, clean-tasting salad. Nanubhai liked the taste of the sambar I cooked. I followed one of my mother's recipes calling for freshly ground spices with shredded coconut, and gave him the recipe for the sambar masala. Writing about sambar brings to mind a lively yet passionate discussion one evening at Savita's dinner table, when one of our European friends, a famed hostess of lavish parties in Baroda, argued naïvely that in comparison with Western food, cooking Indian food was 'easy', since all one had to do was 'add curry powder'. She could be pardoned for she was only voicing her cook's opinion. Months later, to introduce our genteel friend to the plurality of curry powder and the innumerable spice blends that make the Indian cuisine unique, I cooked, with the able assistance of Savita's cook Manu, four different varieties of sambar, each with a different combination of vegetables, spices and herbs. It was a kind of gastronomic symposium that weekend, with Savita demonstrating three varieties of garam masala, including the famous Kolhapuri masala powder from Maharashtra, and dhanshak masala which is a contribution from the Parsee cuisine. Needless to add, our European friend was left humbled and apologized profusely. She could be excused for her naivete. The Indian cuisine *is* complex and layered in its tastes.

Every Indian cook has his or her own recipe when it comes to making curry powder, garam masala powder, or for that matter, any spice blend, to add that unique taste and flavour to vegetables, pulses and grains or meat, fish and fowl.

Nanubhai often requested me to teach his cook Manu authentic south Indian vegetarian delicacies for tiffin, mostly for breakfast. Idli, dosai, vegetable rava upma and appam was what Nanubhai had in mind, besides the vatha kuzhambu with the ven pongal that he first tasted in our home in Baroda. Vatha kuzhambu is a gastronomic gem of Tamil cuisine, where sun-dried or fresh vegetables are cooked in an aromatic tamarind sauce. This spicy, tangy gravy pairs ideally with a bland-tasting dish like ven pongal or rice khichadi. In exchange, Manu showed me the secrets to cook traditional Gujarati Farsan (snacks)—khaman dhokla, steamed savoury chickpea flour cubes; thepla, herb-enriched flatbread; and handvo, a rice and lentil bake with vegetables.

## MANU'S KHAMAN DHOKLA, soft and spongy, mildly flavoured, steamed savoury, chickpea flour cakes. I have modified his recipe by including garlic and ginger.

### INGREDIENTS TO MAKE THE BATTER FOR 20-25 PIECES

* 1 teaspoon oil
* 1 cup chickpea flour
* ¼ teaspoon red chilli powder
* ¼ teaspoon turmeric powder
* ¾ teaspoon brown sugar
* 1 tablespoon fine semolina or cream of wheat
* ½ teaspoon citric acid crystals
* 1 green chilli
* 1 garlic clove
* ½ inch fresh ginger
* ¾ cup plus 1 teaspoon water
* 1 heaped teaspoon Eno's Fruit Salt
* salt to taste

### METHOD TO MIX THE BATTER AND STEAM

Drizzle 1 teaspoon oil and grease the bottom and sides of a 9-inch rimmed dish to go inside the steamer pan. Set aside.

Grind the green chilli, ginger and garlic clove into a fine paste and set aside.

Sift the flour, red chilli powder, turmeric powder, salt and sugar into a bowl. Add semolina, citric acid crystals and chilli-ginger-garlic paste and mix.

Pour ¼ cup water to the flour and mix, breaking all lumps to form a smooth batter. Add salt to taste. Add the rest of the water, 1 tablespoon at a time, and mix to a pancake batter.

Pour water to a depth of 1 inch in the steamer pan, and on medium heat, warm up the water.

Add the Eno's Fruit Salt to the batter, stir immediately, and whip it up to a creamy, frothy batter. Pour immediately into the greased dish, place it on a stand inside the steamer, and cook covered for 4 to 6 minutes, raising the heat to medium-high.

Remove lid and check by inserting a toothpick, which should come out clean.

Lift and remove the inside dish. Invert it on a larger platter, and tap to let the steamed cake drop on to the platter.

Wait for a minute to cool, and with the edge of a knife dipped in cold water, score the steamed cake into 1-inch squares. Transfer to a serving platter.

INGREDIENTS FOR THE GARNISH AND THE TEMPERING

* ¼ cup grated coconut, fresh or frozen
* ¼ cup loosely packed fresh coriander, chopped
* 1 teaspoon oil
* ½ teaspoon brown mustard seeds
* ½ teaspoon black sesame seeds
* 2 green chillies, slit lengthwise
* 3 tablespoons water
* ½ teaspoon sugar
* 1 teaspoon lime juice

Garnish the squares with shredded coconut and fresh coriander, chopped.

Heat 1 teaspoon oil in a small wok or saucepan on medium heat. Add the mustard seeds, and as they start popping, add the sesame seeds and green chillies. Stir once. Turn the stove off.

Add water, sugar and lime juice to the seasoned oil, stir well and, with the herbs and spices, spoon over the layer of coriander and coconut. Cover the entire surface uniformly.

Serve warm or at room temperature, with mint chutney on the side.

Dhoklas can be made a day in advance, refrigerated, and steamed again, or reheated for about 30 seconds in a microwave.

## EASY MINT CHUTNEY, INDIAN PESTO

Grind in a blender, 1 cup tightly packed fresh mint leaves, 2 green chillies, ¼ teaspoon salt, ¼ teaspoon sugar, adding ½ cup of water. Grind smooth. Empty into a bowl and stir in 1 teaspoon lime juice.

# METHI THEPLA, *a signature flatbread from Gujarat. The slightly sweet and savoury, soft tortilla keeps well for several days, and comes in handy for a meal or snack. Theplas make good travel snacks. In the last decade, my travels between Boston and Bangalore have increased, and my favourite 'in-transit' snack is thepla and lime pickle packed in my hand luggage.*

## INGREDIENTS TO MAKE 12 THEPLAS

* 2½ cups wholewheat flour, divided
* 1 teaspoon red chilli powder
* ½ teaspoon turmeric powder
* ½ cup fresh fenugreek leaves, methi, chopped (I sometimes use dried fenugreek leaves, kasuri methi, from a package)
* ¼ cup fresh coriander leaves, chopped
* ½ teaspoon brown sugar
* ½ teaspoon sesame seeds
* ¾ cup plain yogurt
* ¾ cup oil, divided
* water, if needed, to mix dough
* salt to taste

## METHOD

In a large bowl, mix 2 cups flour and all the ingredients, except the water and oil.

Add water, if needed, and knead to a soft dough. Add salt to taste.

Drizzle 2 tablespoons oil and knead. Cover and set aside for 10 minutes.

Divide into 12 portions, roll into balls, and replace in the bowl. Keep covered.

Dust a work-board with a little flour, if needed, and with a rolling pin, roll each ball into a 6-inch disc. Roll 2 discs at a time.

Warm up a griddle on medium heat. Cook one disc at a time, brushing a little oil on both sides and till brown spots appear. Flip over and cook both sides.

Continue the process and cook the remaining balls of dough.

# KHATTA HANDVO, *traditional Gujarati, savoury, lentil-vegetable cake.*

## INGREDIENTS TO MAKE 8 SERVINGS

* 2 cups rice
* 1 cup tur dal

- ¼ cup moong dal
- ¼ cup chana dal
- ¼ cup urad dal
- ¾ cup sour yogurt
- 3 cups mixed vegetables (grated carrots, chopped spinach, shelled peas, finely chopped fresh coriander, and grated bottle gourd) squeezing out the water
- 3 tablespoons oil
- 1 tablespoon sugar
- ½ tablespoon lemon juice
- 1 teaspoon Eno's Fruit Salt, or 1 teaspoon baking soda
- 1 teaspoon chilli powder
- 3 teaspoons ginger-chilli paste (grind 2 green chillies and 1-inch fresh ginger piece together)
- salt to taste

## INGREDIENTS FOR THE TEMPERING

- 3 tablespoons oil
- 1½ teaspoons brown mustard seeds
- 1½ teaspoons black sesame seeds
- 1 teaspoon ajwain (carom) seeds
- ½ teaspoon asafoetida powder

## METHOD

Wash and rinse the rice and dals together. Drain. Repeat till the water is not cloudy. Soak for 4 hours. Drain. Grind to a smooth 'cake' batter, adding enough water.

Transfer to a deep bowl, stir in the yogurt, and leave, covered, for 8 hours or overnight to ferment.

Fold in the vegetables. Add the oil, sugar, lemon juice, Eno's Fruit Salt or baking soda, turmeric powder, chilli powder, ginger-chilli paste and salt. Mix well.

Set the oven to 400°F. Grease a large baking dish and pour the batter in, but do not set to bake as yet.

Warm up 3 tablespoons oil in a wok on medium heat.

Add the mustard seeds, and when they start popping and spluttering, turn the heat off, and add the sesame and carom seeds and asafoetida powder. Stir and spoon out the aromatic oil, evenly with the seeds, over the surface of the batter.

Bake for 40 minutes or till a brown crust forms.

Test with a skewer, which should come out clean.

Leave to cool.

Cut into wedges or cubes, and serve with a chutney and yogurt.

# A Metate Comes in Handy in Berkeley

In the year 1956, a year after we were married, Chamu and I left for the USA, where he was to spend a year as a Rockefeller fellow in the Department of Anthropology at Berkeley in the University of California. I looked forward with excitement to my first trip overseas.

Though my parents were happy for me to experience new places and people and my father eagerly anticipated receiving interesting letters, and Chamu's mother was quite used to her son travelling widely on work and was quietly proud of him, both she and my parents were concerned that we would be away for more than a year and in a country several weeks away by sea.

That summer, we spent a few extra weeks with my parents in Tanjore and with Chamu's family in Mysore before leaving for Bombay, where we embarked on the Polish liner, the *Batory*, for Southampton in England, where we had planned to stop briefly and visit London, Oxford, Cambridge and Manchester, and by mid-November, set sail for New York. Annam Athai came to see me in Tanjore and was unhappy that Chamu and I were going far away and would not be celebrating our first Deepavali, Thalai Deepavali in Tamil, after marriage, in my parents' home, as was the practice for newly-wed couples in our community. During the first year of being married, it is customary for the newly-married couple to be invited by the bride's parents to most of the feasts, festivals, social and religious functions in the family. I believe it was also a way for the bride's kin to get to know the new member of the family, the son-in-law.

Deepavali is one such special occasion when the recently married daughter of the house and her husband are invited. Marriage is considered the ultimate blissful state for a girl and, as I see it, in a patriarchal society, much is made of the male partner. To show appreciation and respect for him particularly, and affection for both their daughter and her spouse, the bride's parents invite the couple to their home, and the celebrations are on a grand scale with lavish gifts showered on them. The expense on celebrations and gifts can prove ruinous financially for the bride's parents in many middle class families. Besides the gifts of new clothes for the entire family, the daughter can look forward to new jewellery and silver household articles, and gifts to the son-in-law, which may include a watch, camera, radio, car and immovable property in the form of a house site and house. I have heard of such gifts being exchanged among my relatives. I would like to think that all this is changing with the educated woman's perception of herself in society and in the marriage relationship. My parents, in this as in many other matters, attached no importance to 'outdated' traditional customs, as my father often said. But my Annam Athai did believe in observing all the customs and traditions of the south Indian Brahmin community, and was sorely disappointed to learn that Chamu and I would not be joining my family in the Deepavali celebrations. She came to Tanjore to meet us with a small stainless steel container of badam halwa, almond fudge, she made for both of us. I was touched—almonds were expensive and Athai's budget for her family expenses normally left no room to splurge.

Chamu and I sailed on 19 October 1956 from Bombay on the *Batory*, also christened 'The Lucky Ship'; I realized why 'lucky' after we reached Gibraltar. This was my first experience of travelling by ship, and I was sick as a dog. Chamu, a good sailor, found it difficult to understand why I was on my back and in our cabin for most of the twenty-odd days that it took to dock in Southampton.

Leaving Bombay, we sailed north across the Arabian Sea to Karachi in Pakistan, where the ship docked for a few hours. There was not enough time to go ashore, but from the deck, I looked out onto the port city

*On the Batory to Southampton*

where my father was posted some thirty-five years earlier, during the early years of his service, and where my eldest sister Kamala was born. This was during the pre-partition era when Karachi was a port city in India.

The *Batory* next docked at Aden in Yemen, and many of our fellow passengers bought packets of coffee beans and fresh dates from hawkers who crowded the wharf. Chamu bought some too. One vignette, a sad one that stands out in my memory, is of a group of very young boys, all younger than ten years of age, who, for the mindless sport of the passengers on the ship, would dive and pick up the coins flung into the quayside. 'Here you are...' and a fistful of coins would be flung into the water. Many of the swarthy, loincloth-clad youngsters sucked up the coins with their mouths in the shallow waters, and this was a feat much admired by all assembled on the deck. I felt sorry for the frail, skinny, sunburnt lads.

Leaving Aden, we sailed up the Red Sea, and halfway through, the atmosphere on the ship turned tense. Submarines were spotted in the Mediterranean Sea. Groups of adults with sombre and worried expressions listened to the latest news, huddled around the one radio set on the ship. Chamu would frequently come down to our cabin to check in on me and to give me the latest news. He informed me that our ship was being escorted by a couple of convoy ships, and that the political atmosphere was uncertain and a war may break out. Fortunately for us, ours was the last ship to cross the Suez Canal before it was closed in November, when the Egyptian President Nasser nationalized the canal, precipitating a political crisis. Israel invaded Egypt, and Great Britain and France sent armed forces to capture the canal. The United Nations' intervention forced an armistice, and the canal was reopened in April 1957. Once we neared Gibraltar on the western edge of the Mediterranen Sea, glasses clinked, toasts were drunk to the *Batory*, the 'Lucky' ship that had weathered many a wartime adventure on the high seas. The captain of the ship addressed the passengers and held a prayer meeting just before reaching Gibraltar, which would be the last port of call before disembarking at Southampton.

The *Batory* docked in Gibraltar for a few hours. Stepping into the bazaar at Gibraltar was like being back home in India. Touts from Muslim and Sindhi shops surrounded us as we disembarked. They nudged us, vying with each other to herd us into their shops, which sold all manner of cheap textiles and bric-a-brac. Chamu and I went on a quick tour of the bazaar and its alleys, and I felt even more at home hearing people speak Hindi.

I had not eaten much during our voyage, subsisting on apples and crackers, partly because I was seasick, added to which was the nauseating smell of somewhat stale non-vegetarian food permeating the air in the dining room. I avoided stepping into the dining room after my experience the first couple of days. The thought of food on the *Batory* made me puke.

In Gibraltar, Chamu and I had a lunch of well-cooked vegetable biryani, cucumber raita and papad, served on a thali (a metal dining plate), in a small 'dhaba'-like joint in one of the back alleys. Before returning to the ship, we also bought some freshly cooked dry phulkas (griddle-cooked wheat flour flatbread) and a small jar of pickle for the rest of the journey. The pickle helped cut the nausea. Talk about the magic of familiar food!

Within a few hours of sailing up north of the Iberian peninsula and heading for the Bay of Biscay, I felt the ship rocking even more than before. It was a stormy crossing, and finally, as we were sailing past the Isle of Wight in the south of England, Chamu assured me that we would soon be docking in Southampton. I couldn't wait to step on terra firma. From the porthole, I could see the Isle of Wight and the 'needles', the sharp pinnacles and chalk cliffs, towering towards the sky.

Miss Anderson, my geography teacher in the sixth standard in Christ Church School in Jubbulpore, came alive.

My maiden voyage by sea seemed longer than the twenty-odd days it took.

Normally, a week later, it would have been time for the return journey of the *Batory* from Southampton to Bombay. But this was a special year, and for the moment, future sailings through the canal were cancelled, thanks to the Suez camal crisis.

Before disembarking at Southampton, Chamu bought me a beautiful ivory-inlaid jewellery chest as a momento from the *Batory* shop, he was attracted more to the unusual shape of the box rather than its function; set on a narrow base, it grew upwards and outwards with a 'dome' set atop the curvature of the 'roof'. This was the second personal gift from Chamu; the first was the Smith's wristwatch in Madras before we were married. Sadly, I have lost the watch, but I do have the ivory-inlay box.

From Southampton, we took the boat train to London. Chamu and I spent just over a week travelling in England. That was indeed a hectic week when Chamu wanted to pack in so much, to introduce me to his friends and colleagues in Oxford, Cambridge and Manchester and to the sights and sounds of England. It was indeed a memorable week. We were booked to sail for New York by the *Queen Elizabeth*, and if I remember right, we sailed on 16 November, Chamu's birthday. I gave him a surprise gift of a cherrywood pipe, which I picked up in Oxford and which he kept long after he stopped smoking. In London, we rented rooms in Hampstead overlooking the Heath, and met Chamu's youngest sister Padma and her fiancé, both of whom were doctors. Together, we had lunch at a popular joint frequented by Indian students—I think it was at the Alfatha, which served north Indian fare, vegetarian and non-vegetarian. Chamu noticed that I missed Indian vegetarian food. I ordered parathas (griddle-cooked wheat flour flatbread), dal (spicy lentils cooked soft in a gravy), and aloo-gobi sabzi (dry, sautéed potato and cauliflower vegetable). The food, as I remember, was not great. But what I did enjoy in London was eating Welsh rarebit in a pub near Jack Straw's Castle in Hampstead. It was delicious and scalding

hot! Padma was amused at my trying to get at the stream of melting cheese cascading from the toast with my tongue out; it smelt so buttery and cheesy, real sharp English cheddar, a bechamel sauce with sharp mustard, and no Worcestershire sauce. One other delightful memory is of strolling with Chamu through Soho, shelling and munching warm roasted chestnuts sold on wheelbarrows. I had my first taste of dessert wine in a bar in Soho. That was simple, unadulterated fun.

In Oxford, I met Chamu's former landlady when he was a student in the 1940s. I heard, not from Chamu but from one of his Indian friends, that Mrs Jones' affection for Chamu was stifling, adding, 'In her efforts to keep a good Indian young man from going astray, she made it very clear that some of his English friends and graduate students were not welcome in her home. Tactfully, Chamu had to change lodgings.' But we did visit Mrs Jones in 1956 and we spent the day with her. Mrs Jones was at a loss to cook an all vegetarian meal for me. She explained that 'Chamu had no problem with eggs'. While I was with her for just the day, I demonstrated a rice-cheese bake with tomatoes, green bell peppers and mushrooms, with paprika and fresh mint. She was delighted with this 'no fuss' dish, as she categorized it.

My father was a teetotaller but his Poona friend, whom I knew as Bashyam Uncle, served wine and hard liquor at all his dinner parties, and as a young girl, I was drawn to the pleasant aroma of the Chianti Bashyam Uncle served. I remember his stately wife Mani Auntie, like a figure carved out of ebony, had decorated their sunlit front verandah with empty Chianti bottles in their straw baskets, and from each of which grew a money plant, a vine with thick fleshy leaves or a fern. I also remember my mother admiring her for her hydroponics gardening skills, cultivating all manner of plants in bottles and trays of water. At the most, I had inhaled the sweet and fruity aroma in the empty Chianti bottles. Soho and Chamu in London introduced me to the enjoyment of a drink.

Writing about wine brings to mind my father's first letter to me after I left India in 1956, and which I received on settling down in our home in Berkeley. My father asked, 'Rukka, have you had the opportunity to taste wine?' He was not critical, he was curious. I remember his physician advising him to sip a tot of Drakshasava to give him good sleep at night. Drakshasava was like liquor to him. My father suffered from asthma attacks, when he would lie awake for several hours at night. I remember once, on a visit to Tanjore from Delhi, I gave him a bottle of brandy and suggested he take a sip before his bedtime. I am not sure he even opened the bottle!

London, Oxford, Cambridge and Manchester, to meet with Chamu's friends and anthropologist colleagues, was fun but hectic.

Friends drove us to the Cotswolds, which had been the favourite holiday retreat for Chamu and two of his close friends when they were students in Oxford in the late 1940s. What I do remember of the Cotswolds now, after fifty-seven years, besides the beautiful church and the yew trees, is the fragrance of the lavender even before I saw the purple fields for miles on either side of the road. I had heard of lavender honey but not of lavender buds used to flavour chocolates. In Boston I finally got to taste lavender honey which is indeed a sophisticated spread. The rolling Cotswold countryside reminded Chamu of the Mysore-Bangalore region where he grew up. I loved what I saw of England. We travelled the length of the beautiful country by car in a matter of some hours! What a difference to the long train journeys extending for days in India. The whirlwind visit to England went by like a beautiful, refreshing breeze, and soon, it was time to set sail for New York.

The *Queen Elizabeth*, on which we travelled from Southampton to New York, was a luxury liner and I did not feel as sick as I did on the *Batory*. The transatlantic crossing was also a short voyage of just over five days, and in addition, there was no fear of an imminent war.

On the *Queen Elizabeth*, there was a wide choice of food I could eat for breakfast; oats, eggless muffins, croissants, soft and hard breads, a spread of European cheeses, marmalade and jams, fruit juice and cut fruit. I chose to have a heavy breakfast and skip lunch, as the daily menu had few vegetarian options except for a salad. For lunch and dinner, it was a choice of soup, either cream of potato soup, the classic red beet borscht, chicken or mulligatawny (anglicized version of mulagu tanni), which in our home we called mulagu rasam, a thin watery soup which we normally mixed with rice and ate as a second course during a meal. (I would highly recommend mulagu rasam as a hot drink to ease cold and sore throat.) I was assured by our table waiter that the soups were 'vegetarian', and only chicken broth was used, not beef! I tried, but finally gave up the fight of explaining what is truly vegetarian. For dinner, I opted for a vegetable au gratin; what I did not know then was that the cheese was made using rennin from the stomach membrane of a calf. Thankfully, today, some of the best-known cheeses are made with the use of certain fungi and are totally vegetarian. Even the boiled rice on the menu, and I could not understand why, for the life of me, was not spared the chicken broth! Boiled rice with lamb or chicken curry was rated very high by all the diners. When I asked for a serving of plain yogurt, our waiter responded with, 'Sorry ma'am, we only serve European food.' That settled it. Chamu persuaded me to not educate the kitchen staff. Today, a breakfast menu in Europe and the USA includes plain yogurt, non-fat yogurt, and a variety of fruit yogurt besides Greek yogurt.

Chamu, though a vegetarian by upbringing and choice, unlike me, did not fuss at the table. Having lived in England during the war years, when a vegetarian ration card was almost impossible to come by, he would eat the rice mixed with the so-called 'vegetable' soup 'not for taste but for sustenance', as he explained with a wry smile. He tolerated eggs at breakfast, frequently poached; 'fried eggs smell of bacon fat in which they are cooked,' he would say. His preference was for vegetarian food, but in a social setting, he would not draw attention to himself by starving, which I did on many an occasion. Mrs Jones, his landlady in Oxford whom I met in 1956 during our brief vist to Oxford, told me that after much delay, he was allotted a 'vegetarian' ration card, which meant he could buy butter, a luxury in wartime England. 'Chamu survived on bread, butter and a small salad on many days,' she added.

The relaxed atmosphere on the *Queen Elizabeth* was a contrast to the tense gloom and melancholy on the *Batory*. Fun and enjoyment marked all the five-odd days it took to cross the Atlantic. The passengers were mostly American tourists returning from a holiday in England. The swimming pool and the bar was where you would find them, day and night. The first two days, mine was literally a 'nodding' acquaintance with the ones I ran into. When, later, they overheard Chamu and me talk in English, they were surprised and more friendly, saying 'Gee! We did not realize you spoke English!' With the exception of a middle-aged engineer, who introduced himself as Sam who had visited Bombay, I met no one who even knew where India was. Lizzie, a painter from New York, befriended me and introduced me to her friends, with, 'Meet Rooka, an Indian from India!' A woman in a saree was a novelty for many, and two of the wives insisted on being 'wrapped' in sarees for the evening dance. There was great excitement as the two with four of their friends gathered that evening in my cabin. Much time was spent on discussing Indian fabric and their choice of saree for the evening. They found all of them gorgeous. The midnight-blue south Indian silk saree with a gold woven lace border and a black Benarasi with small gold polka dots were the final choice. They stood stiff as ramrods as I dressed each one of them, and feared the sarees would unravel when they 'strode' into the dance hall, which to our surprise and relief did not happen. As the evening wore on, they drank in all the praise from the dance floor and posed for photos throughout the evening. In turn, the following day, they offered to dress me in an evening gown, explaining how simple it would be to 'slip it on'. I politely declined, and till date, I have not succumbed to the 'ease' of wearing Western clothes. I continue to shuffle in my saree even during the deep winter in Boston.

Chamu and I got to know a few of the passengers on our wing of the cabins, and when they learnt that 21 November, the day we would dock in New York, was also our first wedding anniversary, they got together at our table for dinner, popped champagne, and sang to us to the loud accompaniment of the piano. They had as much fun as Chamu and I did. They plied us with questions about how and where we met, what kind of wedding we had, when we planned to have a family, and many more personal questions. Chamu was embarrassed when he was asked to give a speech, and we left that night for our cabin with dozens of calling cards! Many of them wanted to keep in touch. In fact, Bob Clarke, who was in the merchant navy, did turn up a few months later at the Anthropology Department in Berkeley.

The day, 21 November, in New York greeted us with a grey sky, chilly blustery weather and a dockworkers' strike. The Rockefeller representatives who met us were apologetic and hoped our sojourn of two days in NY—before our onward journey to Berkeley—would be pleasant. I had not heard of a 'Thanksgiving' national celebration, and I learned more about the significance of the day and the politics thereof over the week. I now remember what upset me most were the 'dressed turkeys' in the bay windows of upscale restaurants: they looked cruelly dismembered and unaesthetic to me. I could not fathom how birds could be exhibited in this fashion, although I had read of 'shooting' parties in India when the poor partridge was dressed for the table.

Manhattan was truly a 'one of a kind' experience even though we were there for just two days. Chamu and I stayed away from the touristy spots. Instead, we visited a friend in Greenwich Village, and wandered through Times Square, stumbling upon the original Broadway production of the musical *The Pyjama Game*, starring John Raitt. I loved the energy of this musical romance. I have seen folk dramas of Hindu mythologies staged as musicals in Tanjore, but this was my first experience of a western musical extravaganza. Our first wedding anniversary was just the way I would have wanted it to be. We spent time together doing fun things of exploring the city. While watching *The Pyjama Game*, Chamu slipped a beribboned box of Black Magic chocolates into my hands, and said, 'This is what girls are courted with. You tell me which is your favourite and I'll tell you mine.' As I now remember, there were twelve flavours and I remember most of them: Montelimar, Chocolate Almond, Hazel Clusters, Orange Cream, Truffle and Nougat, Butterscotch, Caramel, Coffee Cream, Strawberry and Marzipan; I don't recollect the two others. Well, my favourite that day was ALL of them.

While I enjoyed the sights and sounds of New York, I missed Indian vegetarian food. I was tired of soups, salads and bagels. At the hotel where we spent two comfortable nights, a friendly soul directed us to an Indian restaurant, I think it was The Woodlands, I'm not sure, but the traditional and authentic south Indian dinner was delicious and had the flavour of home-cooked food. We were served on metal 'thalis', big round plates with a rim. While the menu included the usual—potato roast, French beans curry with shredded coconut, the south Indian delicacy of avial (mixed vegetables cooked in a subtle fresh-smelling and delicious coconut yogurt sauce), tomato rasam (a light soup), appalam (toasted lentil wafers), yogurt and gulab jamun for dessert—what I remember even today is the signature south Indian 'shundakkai vatha kuzhambu' served with hot steamed rice and ghee (clarified butter). It is a tough call to describe the 'vatha kuzhambu'. Suffice it to say, shundakkai (*Solanum torvum*), also known as the Turkey berry, a slightly bitter berry, is a preferred vegetable, either fresh or dried, dunked into the 'vatha kuzhambu', a spicy, tart and flavourful tamarind gravy. The meal delineates the well-thought-out, epicurean, south Indian vegetarian menu at the Indian restaurant in New York.

I was truly not prepared for this feast. When we returned to our hotel, I learned that the good samaritan who had directed us to the fabulous meal had checked out. I couldn't thank him enough.

*With R.K. Narayan and Chamu*
*at Peralta Avenue, Berkeley*

After our whirlwind romance with New York, we continued to the west coast by railroad, stopping for three days in Chicago to meet and spend time with Chamu's academic friends in the Department of Anthropology: Professors Robert Redfield, Milton Singer, Sol Tax and Fred Eggan, among others. Celebrated writer, R.K. Narayan—Kunjappa to family and friends—was also spending that weekend in Chicago. He had told us, when we met him during my first visit to Mysore in November 1955, before Chamu and I were married, that he would also be spending the following year in the USA, also as a Rockefeller Fellow, like Chamu. But bumping into each other in Chicago was indeed a pleasant surprise for all three of us. He was there in the Anthropology Department at the evening reception for Chamu, and even before I saw him, I recognized his voice from behind me. A fairly thin, not very masculine voice, with a definite south Indian accent, happily called out, 'Ennamma,' in Tamil, which translates to an endearing, 'What Rukka, very nice to see you, and where is Chamu?' Kunjappa was in his uniform of light grey flannels, a couple of sizes too big for his small frame, a white open-collared full-sleeve shirt, tieless, and a checked brown light jacket. He was carrying a small, dark brown briefcase. He told me later that the briefcase, containing his passport, a few travellers' cheques, a few dollar bills, his small address diary and his spectacles, was his constant companion and he was lost without it. What he did not tell me then was that it contained a small packet of scented areca nut, which was his daily fix. As he came closer, he smelt strongly of the familiar aroma of cardamom-scented supari (betel-nut, areca nut), which Chamu was also addicted to. Though to all outward appearances Kunjappa looked calm and in control, I realized later, when we spent time together in Berkeley, that he was a nervous person who worried about small details. He wove his way through the group of anthropologists, patted me gently on the back with an enquiring, 'Yeppadi irukey? Yeppo vandel?' ('How are you? When did you both arrive?'). 'How long are you in Chicago?' he asked. We found Chamu at the far end of the conference room in what seemed to be a serious discussion with a group of young graduate students. Chamu was pleased to see Kunjappa, and since a few introductions were in order, I left them to join a group of women, wives of Chicago anthropologists. Later that evening, Chamu informed me that Kunjappa, too, was headed west the following day to spend the year in La Jolla near San Diego, in southern California, where he planned to complete writing his iconic novel *The Guide*. But we were in for a pleasant surprise. Kunjappa announced over dinner the same evening after the reception that he had changed his mind and postponed his departure. 'I am a footloose person, Chamu, and have decided to travel by train with you and Rukka to Berkeley.' If I remember right, it was the 'California Zephyr', and Chamu and I shared what was called a 'roomette', a sort of self-contained, very comfortable coupé. Sitting in the vista dome of the train travelling through the scenic Feather River Canyon, I was spellbound by the breathtaking visual feast, the panorama of the ever-changing American landscape spread out before me. Flat plains of waving corn, interrupted only by silos, gave way to stark mesas and bluffs, rising to snowcapped mountains and descending to fertile valleys and orchards, cheek by jowl with the Pacific Ocean. Truly a work of art. To think that we travelled in England from Southampton to Manchester in the matter of some hours, and to contrast it with crossing from New York to Berkeley in three days was amazing! That brought home to me the sheer size of the USA.

The train came to a halt and I heard Chamu call out, 'Come on Rukka, we are in Berkeley.' I was somewhat confused. Where was the station building and the platform? The railroad ran parallel to and within a few feet of the road. I was looking for a covered imposing station building, like the ones in India and in England. It just seemed like a level crossing that we were alighting at. David Mandelbaum, professor and chair of the Department of Anthropology in Berkeley, along with his wife Ruth were waiting for Chamu and me. Ruth looked stunningly beautiful and was very friendly to me and Chamu, though a bit distant towards Kunjappa for they were not expecting him! David Mandelbaum looked much older than his age; he was just forty-five when I met him.

Neither David nor Ruth was prepared for a third person— Kunjappa. The American couple was a little surprised to find a mild-mannered, bespectacled, middle-aged man alight along with us. Chamu introduced Narayan to them. David had, of course, heard of R.K. Narayan, the famous writer, and broke into a wide welcoming smile. The Mandelbaums helped with our luggage, and we left for our hotel on the university campus

Chamu was keen to settle in as soon as possible so he could start writing. He left the searching for a house to me. You must remember this was in the pre-Internet days and there was no Craigslist to help me! Ruth, the good Jewish mother that she was, took me under her wing. She had contacted a realtor and lined up a few houses for me to see the very day we arrived in Berkeley. As luck would have it, I liked the very first independent house we saw on Peralta Avenue. A well-maintained lawn, with baskets of pink and purple fuchsias hanging from intricately designed metal posts, led us to a well-kept house which was clearly the pride of its owners. I had made up my mind. This was the house for Chamu and me, a fully furnished two-bedroom house in a non-academic, quiet neighbourhood. Chamu and I were clear we wanted to spend the year living among middle-class Americans, and not all academics.

When I went the following day to check out the house, I met the elderly landlady, Mrs Zimmermann, who was waiting on the porch. She took me round the house and explained where everything was. She showed me the basement with a washer and lawnmower. The washer was truly a Victorian antique. It had no spinning mechanism to wring the clothes; instead, there were two parallel cylindrical bars, and Mrs Zimmermann demonstrated how

*Chamu in Berkeley*

to feed the piece of wet clothing between the two bars and turn the handle to wring them. The clothing came out flattened. It was much like a pasta press to flatten out a ball of dough into pasta sheets. She apologized she did not have a drier and added, 'Clothes are better dried in the sun.' That resonated with a middle-class Indian woman like me! Anyway, I had fun with her washer and wringing the clothes with the parallel bars! Today, it would be a valuable period piece, no doubt, found in a museum. And Chamu mowed the front and back lawns to his heart's content, appreciating the exercise in his activity. There was also a compost pit behind the garage to hold the lawn trimmings. I added all my vegetable trimmings to the accumulated pile Chamu made. I must mention the metal incinerator in most of the homes. We burnt all our paper and dry leaves in large metal barrels. This was banned some years later to control the air pollution in the city. Again, I don't remember carrying groceries in plastic bags. While some stores had brown paper bags, a few encouraged customers to use cloth bags. It was very much like shopping back home in India. The age and convenience of plastic followed soon after.

When Mrs Zimmermann wished me luck in my new home and

bade me 'goodbye', she choked; she was clearly upset to leave her own home. She had to suddenly put her house in the market for rent as she had lost her dear husband the week before, and her children wanted her to move to the east coast where they lived. She was leaving the house in running condition and was taking only her personal belongings with her. I felt sad for her, but Kunjappa remarked, 'You have lucked out, Rukka; this is a great find.' Ruth was pleased that I took a quick decision.

Beautiful period furniture adorned the house; the beds, the tallboy, the armoire, the twelve-seater dining table and the living room furniture were exquisite old treasures. Lithographs of New York and San Francisco cities over the decades decorated the walls. Ruth admired the old silverware and the porcelain crockery. Mrs Zimmermann was a meticulous and efficient homemaker judging from her house. Before she left, I had promised her I would try and maintain her high standard, and added, 'I love your house.' She was pleased that a university professor was to rent her home, albeit sad to leave after several decades of a happy life with her husband.

The kitchen was not very spacious but airy and well-lit, looking out on to a back porch beyond which was a well-manicured lawn with two apricot trees laden with fruit; the first time I saw fresh apricots! The back wall beyond the lawn abutted on to a school park. Against the back wall, facing the lawn, was a row of healthy hydrangeas.

Mrs Zimmermann had left behind her kitchen pots and pans, which I put away in the basement. Ruth understood and appreciated my 'kosher' upbringing. Though I had not been raised by orthodox parents, I preferred not to use utensils in which non-vegetarian food had been cooked. Ruth helped me buy essential kitchenware. I also bought bedlinen and towels.

Shopping in America was a discovery unto itself. Walking into Sears, I was dumbstruck by the size of the store and the abundance of goods in the various departments. Everything in the USA was BIG in size; the streets were wide, the stores were like little cities, the portions of food served in the restaurants were 'enough to feed a family', as Narayan often remarked. He would add with a wicked smile, 'And if you can't finish what you have ordered, Rukka, get it packed for your lunch tomorrow!'

I requested Ruth for help in finding a place for Narayan to stay for the year. That proved not as easy as you would have thought. Kunjappa had a problem with every place that was shown to him. He could not make up his mind between a furnished house, an unfurnished one, an apartment and a room in a hotel! He liked the location of the one-bedroom furnished cottage we saw the very first day. It was within walking distance of the house I had settled in, and that was an attraction to him. But with, 'Rukka, I don't want to be responsible for all the stuff in the house,' he ruled it out. When Ruth suggested an apartment and offered to furnish the place for him, he countered the offer with, 'How will I get rid of all the furniture and other stuff when I leave?' Ruth lost patience after a couple of days, and understandably so. She had a family of three young kids, which left her very little time to herself.

Kunjappa finally decided to rent a room in Carlton Hotel on Telegraph Avenue, in the neighbourhood of the university and within walking distance of restaurants. It wasn't a great place, as Kunjappa declared after he moved in, and added, 'But it is an interesting place. I wait to see the drama unfold during the weekends and holidays, when many of the older residents of the hotel, who are mostly above seventy years of age, some in wheelchairs, wait in the hotel lobby eagerly anticipating the arrival of relatives and friends. Many of them are very frail and lonely. I have material for another novel, Chamu. I will call it "Waiting".' The book was never written.

While he looked forward to settling down without the bother of running a home, and was eager to start writing his novel *The Guide*, he was unhappy that Carlton Hotel was not within walking distance of our home on Peralta Avenue, and since we had no intention of buying a car, in which event we could have ferried him back and forth, he wondered how often he would be able to meet Chamu and me in our home, and spend an extended period of the day with us. I thought I had a solution to his problem when I suggested that he take a cab and come over during the weekend and spend a night or two with us. 'Kunjappa, we are all set. We even have a spare bedroom for you!' But no, he wanted to see us every day, if possible, and not just during weekends. The resourceful person that he was, he soon found a graduate student in the Economics Department who kindly offered to drive Kunjappa to Peralta every day on his way home in the late afternoon, since he lived in our neighbourhood. Kunjappa proudly told me this little story of his success, and when I said, quoting him, 'You have lucked out, Kunjappa,' he felt it was not his 'luck' but his tireless effort that solved the problem. And he did spend many an evening with us; wonderful evenings for me. In fact, for the better part of that year, I was privy to the twists and turns of what Madame Fate had in store for Raju and Rosie in the story of *The Guide*. One evening, he entered our porch with a grave question, 'Rukka...tell me; should I kill Rosie now, in which case there will be no story to follow and what will I do with Raju? The two have become so dependent on each other.'

Kunjappa was a great storyteller whose tales unfolded minute to minute. He spent an entire evening over pakodas and coffee narrating Raju's dilemma of 'living up' to the image of a wise man and a spiritual leader among his local followers.

He also found Chamu and me to be 'good' listeners, and used me as a sounding board.

He published a hilarious and very telling short book, *My Dateless Diary*, about his stay in the USA that year.

Chamu and I enjoyed our stay in our home on Peralta Avenue in the beautiful university town of Berkeley, although it took me a while to get used to more cars and fewer people on the streets. The only sound I heard was that of a car driving by. I wistfully remembered the call of the street vendors back home in India, the barking and baying of street dogs, the familiar sights of tongas (horse-drawn carriages), the crows, the cows, the vultures, and strangely, I missed all the noise.

Berkeley was beautiful. On a clear day from our house, we could see the bay, and by night, the twinkling lights across it. Our neighbours on Peralta Avenue were friendly and helpful. Robert Muir, a retired engineer, and his beautiful wife May, an elderly couple from Scotland, had followed their son to Berkeley. The week after we moved in, May came by to greet us with a bowl of chocolate pecan pleffernusse. She told us she baked these very special German cookies for Christmas every year. They looked like white, sugary snowballs and smelt of cloves and cinnamon. When Chamu tried unsuccessfully to bite into one, May suggested that he dunk one in tea and enjoy it. Frequently, they would drop in for a beer before dinner. They felt closer to us than they did to their American neighbours. Suddenly one morning, a week before Christmas, Mrs Muir's son informed us that Bob had died of a heart failure a few hours earlier. Though we had known him for just a few weeks, he had been good company and was a helpful person. A couple of days after we moved into our new home, a chubby, middle-aged, friendly man had rung the doorbell, introduced himself as our neighbour Bob, and said, 'Feel free to ask for help. You know... I mean small electrical, plumbing and the like... I may be able to fix it.' That was very kind of him to offer help, as both Chamu and I were totally useless when it came to house repairs. We could change a light bulb, at the most!

I felt sorry for May who, from what she had told me, had been happily married for fifty-five years to her childhood sweetheart.

When Kunjappa heard of the tragedy, he asked us, in all seriousness, 'What is this, Chamu? People are falling like nine pins! Would Rukka like to move out of this neighbourhood?' I laughed off his suggestion for I enjoyed living on Peralta Avenue.

Our neighbours on the other side, the Heisels, were a young couple with a four-year-old girl Kristie and a two-year-old boy Stephen. The mother Nancy was a homemaker and Mr Heisel worked in San Francisco, I think. Weekends for them were barbecue evenings in their backyard, and the smell of barbecued hotdogs pervaded the air. I don't think I ever got used to the smoky smell of meat cooked on embers, a smell that filled the air almost every evening between five and seven o'clock, mostly during the summer. I tried to counter that smell with the pleasant fragrance of agarbatti (incense sticks) that I lit every evening at home during the same time.

Life that year in Berkeley was pretty predictable. Chamu and I settled down in our new home in a matter of a few days. Chamu, feeling deep guilt, repeatedly said, 'I have enjoyed a long holiday since September, and now, I must settle down to work.' Most days, he would write sitting under the apricot trees in our backyard.

My life underwent a sea change after marriage. From being a full-time working woman before I was married, this year was a kind of 'sabbatical' for me. Curiously, I did not miss my university and my colleagues. I was immersed in being a spouse and in running a home, experimenting with cooking (I missed home-cooked food during several weeks of travel and eating in restaurants), entertaining Chamu's colleagues, our friends, and travelling within and outside California. In a sense, I was still in touch with academia, since most of Chamu's friends were anthropologists, linguists, economists and the like, and there was always academic gossip, which Kunjappa was privy to since he spent many an evening with us and was introduced by Chamu to many of his friends. Kunjappa often remarked, 'I say, Chamu, there are a million stories waiting to be written—the intrigues within a department, and it is fascinating to hear the wives, who just by hanging around the sets, knew of all the plots. You know, this woman, I think she is the secretary of the department, is a fountainhead of salacious news about graduate students and professors!' Kunjappa was a keen observer, a good listener and spoke little; he was, in fact, an anthropologist trained in the field.

What I did miss though was talking to my family, my parents and, in particular, my father. I was unable to talk to my father on the telephone. For one thing, those were the days when international calls to India had to be booked through a telephone operator and added to this the time difference between India and the USA led to many inconveniences. Also, my father did not have a phone connection at home in Tanjore, but his friendly neighbour did. I remember the one call that I did book on my birthday to talk to my parents was to this neighbour, but the irony of it was that the call came through when my parents, nay, all of India would have been fast asleep. The only way my father and I kept in touch was through letters, long letters, each of which was an essay in itself. His one regret was that I did not write to him frequently enough.

Our other neighbour on Peralta, the Heisels, after their dinner at precisely six o'clock, would walk over for a chat with us on most evenings. That is when, very often, I would be in the kitchen cooking dinner for Chamu and me and Kunjappa who would join us. We were the first Indian couple they had met, and they were curious to know more about us and our country. Many middle-class Americans in the USA were surprised that we spoke English fluently; one of their leading questions was, 'Did you go to school in England?' This often led me to give them a brief history of India as a colony of the British, about our struggle for independence, about Mahatma Gandhi and so on.

Nancy was very active in her church, and requested me to give an informal talk, one Sunday in January, about my country. Where do I begin? I thought. Since it was January and my thoughts were back home celebrating Pongal, or Sankranthi, with my parents in Tanjore, I described the significance of the south Indian harvest festival, which resonated with them and the good folks in the church educated me on their Thanksgiving feast. Later that year, I invited my neighbours and a few couples down the street for the Indian festival of Diwali. I made some sweets like Mysore pak and rice payasam, and also vegetable bajjis, which they enjoyed. They got into the spirit of the joyful day, and the women were eager to wear sarees. I had fun dressing them, and they joined me in lighting candles in the front and back porch. Today, the White House celebrates the festival of Diwali.

As I have said, Kunjappa was a frequent visitor to our home. One evening, he turned up with a

*Rukka, Chamu and Biligiri in Berkeley*

young Indian doctoral student, Biligiri, from the Linguistics Department. Biligiri, who was also from Mysore and had finished his undergraduate studies from Mysore University, had heard that M.N. Srinivas (Chamu) was spending the year in Berkeley and had expressed a desire to meet him.

After the initial meeting, Biligiri frequently accompanied Kunjappa to our home in Peralta Avenue. Like Chamu and me, they were both vegetarians and found it frustrating to eat out. It was a time when vegetarianism was not understood even in the bigger cities of the USA.

Kunjappa had this story to tell us. The week he arrived in Berkeley, he was invited to dinner by a young American scholar. They went to Shakey's Pizzeria. The host ordered a pizza with pepperoni topping, and Narayan liked the look of the slices of cherry tomatoes. But these tomatoes tasted different, he thought. The young student explained what pepperoni was, and when he realized that Narayan was a strict vegetarian, he helpfully removed the bright red discs from one side of the pizza and re-offered it to Narayan, who manfully took a few bites. He called me later that evening and requested a bowl of rice mixed with yogurt as 'cleansing' food, as he put it.

On the advice from friends to study the labels on every can and package in the grocery store, Kunjappa became an avid student of food labels; grocery shopping turned out to be an adventure and a serious study of the ingredients on food labels. He would caution me against buying certain baked goods because the shortening used was lard, and when he spotted a label that read 'vegetarian vegetable' on a soup can, he picked up a few of those.

After scouting around a bit, I found that the Co-op in Berkeley, Draegers in Menlo Park and China Town in San Francisco stocked more food that vegetarians like me could eat. Chamu and I made frequent trips on the F train from Berkeley to China Town in San Francisco, where, to my delight, many of the vegetables that I was familiar with, like the white pumpkin, bitter gourd, colacasia tubers, ridged gourd, Japanese yellow pumpkin, green chillies and fresh coriander, were available. My first lesson in alternative American English names for some vegetables I was familiar with was on the streets and in the markets of China Town in San Francisco. What I knew in India as lady' finger is called okra, fresh coriander is cilantro, white pumpkin is winter melon, bitter gourd is bitter melon, aubergine is eggplant, a variety of double beans is fava beans, and so on.

I did not bring with me any of the spices or even spice powders that I needed from India. I had assumed that in the USA, like in England, I would be able to get most of the commonly used Indian spices. I was disappointed. But it never occurred to me to pack any spice powders. Did all Indians bring with them the spices and spice powders? I wondered. Chamu and I did a bit of research and found that the Greek stores in San Francisco carried most of the spices I needed, which I ground in small quantities. We also frequented the Armenian and Greek stores on Market Street in San Francisco for slabs of tamarind pulp, coriander seeds, cumin seeds, whole red dried chillies, spices like cloves, cardamom, bay leaves and saffron, and Chamu's favourite sweets, Turkish halwa and baklava, both of which he said closely resembled the sweets made by the well-known Indra Bhavan sweet stall in Mysore.

David Mandelbaum had done field work in the Nilgiris in south India. He and his wife Ruth were familiar with our dietary restrictions and the problems we faced with the local food available. Ruth took charge and familiarized me with Co-op and Natural Food Store in Berkeley. I was thrilled to find many of the ingredients that I needed and were integral to my cooking. Rice flour, garabonzo flour, basmati rice, some of the lentils and legumes, and fresh coconut were available, and I stocked up on these.

On weekends, without fail, Kunjappa and Biligiri would come home for a late afternoon tiffin and stayed on to a simple dinner. Kunjappa was happy to eat rice mixed with curds, with a side dish of a vegetable, and pickle. The menu for tiffin was dictated by Kunjappa, who wanted ulundu vadai (deep-fried, spicy, split blackbean batter doughnuts) and Biligiri requested bread upma. To satisfy Chamu's sweet tooth, I made cobri mithai frequently. The three men were very particular about filter coffee. Chamu did a bit of research on coffee, and after a few weeks of trying different grinds, we settled for Caffe Magdalia D'oro espresso which seemed closest to the strong Mysore brew we were accustomed to in India. Like us, Kunjappa had also brought a metal coffee filter with him from Mysore!

Biligiri would come early to help me with all the preparation work for the tiffin. Making bread upma and cobri mithai was not a problem. Making ulundu vadai was a challenge. I did not have the equipment to grind the dal into creamy batter. Ruth offered to loan me her electric blender. I was not comfortable with that for more than one reason; she would have had to buy a second one for her kitchen, and besides, I had never used an electric grinder to grind batter! I was used to a large granite mortar and pestle back home in India. Only as a last resort would I grind in an electric blender.

While Biligiri and I would be working away in the kitchen, Kunjappa would walk in every now and then and gently ask, 'Rukka, have you also planned on curd rice for dinner?' The good south Indian Brahmin that he was, no meal was complete and satisfying without curd rice (thayir chaadam) and pickle. And yes, he was also addicted, like Chamu, to 'vasaney paaku', a flavourful blend of broken pieces of areca nut or betel nut mixed with ground cardamom, nutmeg and mace, that is chewed on as a mouth freshener after meals. Kunjappa had brought his home-made stock from Mysore, and so had Chamu, whose sister Seethu, an expert at making vasaney paaku, had lovingly made it for him with the addition of 'diamond' sugar crystals, hulled melon seeds, saffron and grated cobri (dessicated coconut), mixed together with a teaspoon of hot ghee (clarified butter) rubbed in.

Once, when I had casually mentioned to David that I would have liked a stone grinder for grinding fresh spice powders instead of an electric blender, he suggested, with a twinkle in his eyes, that I visit the Anthropology Department museum, adding that I could borrow whatever I needed. I wondered what he meant till I came face-to-face with a spectacular array of exhibits displaying indigenous cooking equipment, mostly of stone and wood, used by Native American tribes. I took my time at the museum examining the numerous exhibits, and decided to borrow a metate—a flat-stone grinder, a two-feet-long rectangular block of granite, which came with a twelve-inch-long cylindrical granite roller—used by Native American Indian women to grind corn. Nowadays in Boston, I use the granite mortar and pestle that Mexicans use for making guacamole. My daughters are still hopeful that I'll start using the food processor some day.

The metate exhibit no, site location, period and date found its place of pride on my kitchen counter, and David was amused that a museum piece, an American Indian flat-stone corn grinder was finally being put to use by an Indian woman from India. From then on, I ground all my fresh masalas for mixed vegetable sambar (a lentil-based flavourful south Indian stew), chilli-garlic chutney and the batter for ulundu vadai on the metate. I grew very fond of it as it did a great job.

*Metate, a flat-stone grinder*

That year, Chamu and I hosted a Christmas cocktail party in our home for the faculty and doctoral students of the Anthropology Department. Biligiri helped to make ulundu vadai, moong dal pakodas and mint chutney on that occasion, and told me decades later, when I met him in Bangalore in 1993, that my kitchen in Berkeley was his 'training ground' in Indian vegetarian cooking. Our guests that evening felt amply rewarded for the loan of the metate.

The last week of our stay in Berkeley, when I went to return the metate to the Anthropology museum, both Kunjappa and Biligiri accompanied me. They were as grateful as I was for the loan of the very special kitchen equipment. Chamu and I left Berkeley for India in October 1957, and Kunjappa left to spend some weeks in New York before returning to Mysore. Biligiri stayed on to complete his graduate studies, and bade Chamu and me a touching farewell at the railroad station. I remember he gave me a beautiful card with a photograph of the Berkeley hills, with an inscription that said 'Till we meet again', and surprisingly, we did meet in Bangalore in 1993 at my daughter's wedding, when he arrived as a member of the bridegroom's party! And we picked up the conversation where we had left it in Berkeley thirty-six years earlier.

Chamu and I went back to New York by train to board the *Ile De France,* the art deco, outstanding, transatlantic liner, that would sail to Southampton since we had planned on spending a month in England to perform his younger sister Padma's wedding in London. She married Dr H. Srinivasan, a surgeon, whom we had met briefly on our way to the USA the previous year. It was a traditional south Indian wedding, and Chamu and I had very little time to make all the arrangements, but we were lucky in being introduced to Dr Shekar, a surgeon, who helped young Indians by performing the role of a Hindu priest! Dr Shekar arranged for everything, from the traditional garlands of jasmine flowers to lunch at India House. The wedding rituals were performed at the home of leading British social anthropologist F.G. Bailey in London.

Chamu and I revisited our friends in Cambridge, Oxford and Manchester, and managed to visit a few of the touristy spots, like Stonehenge and Stratford-upon-Avon. I was thrilled that we could see *The Tempest* at the Royal Shakespeare Memorial Theatre. After a hectic and wonderful stay in England, we sailed for Bombay by a P&O liner; the Suez Canal had reopened, and the voyage was uneventful on our return trip to India.

This time around, Chamu's friend Emrys Peters, professor of Social Anthropology in Manchester, and his wife Stella, with whom we stayed, encouraged me to use their kitchen, so I cooked, and Stella learned, some simple Indian dishes, mostly tiffin dishes which, as I explained to her, could be enjoyed any time of the day and could even fill in for breakfast, lunch or dinner. As I recollect, I taught her to cook upma with vegetables (soft, savoury semolina couscous), chapatties (wheat flour griddle-cooked flatbread), cheese-stuffed chapatties, a couple of south Indian salads with tomato, cucumber and watercress, and almond halwa (ground almond fudge).

ULUNDU VADAI, *deep-fried, soft, spongy doughnuts of split blackbean batter with aromatic fresh herbs and spices. Today, the making of vadai is made simple with a vadai maker, a cylindrical extruder, much like a doughnut maker, which pushes the batter in uniform rounds with a central hole.*

## INGREDIENTS TO MAKE ABOUT 30 VADAIS

- 2 cups urad dal, soaked in water for 2 hours and drained
- 1 teaspoon salt
- 2 green chillies, chopped fine
- 6 black peppercorns, powdered coarse
- 8 curry leaves, torn in pieces
- ¼ teaspoon asafoetida powder
- ¼ cup small pieces of fresh coconut (my mother's description was 'tooth-size')
- 1 teaspoon fresh ginger, grated
- 1 flat tablespoon flax seeds (optional)
- ¼ cup water, plus 2 tablespoons
- 2 cups oil for frying

## METHOD TO MAKE THE BATTER AND FRY THE VADAIS

Grind the dal in a food processor to a thick, smooth, creamy batter of dropping consistency, adding ¼ cup water. Stop frequently, push down from the sides of the blender with a spatula, and grind, adding a little more water if needed. Empty the batter into a bowl.

Add the salt, green chillies, black peppercorns, curry leaves, asafoetida, coconut, ginger, and flax seeds, if you are using them. Mix briskly. Divide into 30 equal portions and set aside on a platter.

In a wok or fryer on medium heat, warm up the oil but not to smoking point.

Wet your fingers, pick up one portion, place it on a plastic sheet, flatten slightly with your fingers, and make a hole in the middle with your index finger. Make 6 doughnuts at a time on the plastic sheet. Pick each one and slide into the hot oil, frying 6 in one batch.

As you slide in each one, it will initially sink to the bottom, and in a few seconds, rise to the surface, swelling up. Gently separate them if they stick to each other. Fry to a golden-brown, turning over with a slotted spoon.

Remove and drain on a paper towel. Check one to see if the inside has cooked by pulling the sides apart. Well-fried vadais will be crisp and brown on the outside and soft and spongy within.

Serve hot with creamy onion coconut chutney.

Ulundu vadai disappears faster than you can make them!

## ONION COCONUT CHUTNEY

### INGREDIENTS TO MAKE 1 CUP

- 3 teaspoons oil, divided
- 1 teaspoon chana dal
- 1 teaspoon urad dal
- 1 red dry Kashmiri or Byadagi chilli, less spicy and adds more colour
- 1 small onion, chopped coarse
- 2 green chillies, chopped coarse
- ½ cup shredded coconut, fresh or frozen
- ½ teaspoon salt
- 1 tablespoon lemon juice
- ½ cup water

### INGREDIENTS FOR THE TEMPERING

- ½ teaspoon brown mustard seeds
- 10 curry leaves, torn in pieces

### METHOD

In a small wok or heavy-bottomed saucepan on medium heat, warm up 1 teaspoon oil, but not to smoking point.

Lower heat, add chana and urad dals, and stir-fry till they turn a light golden-brown.

Remove the wok from the stove and add red chilli, stir twice and empty into the blender.

Put the wok back on the stove on medium heat with 1 teaspoon oil.

Stir in the onions and sauté till translucent. Stir in the green chillies. Turn off stove.

Add the sautéed onions, chillies and coconut to the blender.

Add salt, lemon juice and half the quantity of water, and grind to a smooth consistency. Empty into a bowl. Wash out the blender with the rest of the water and pour into the bowl. Mix the chutney.

Heat 1 teaspoon oil in the same wok, and add the mustard seeds. When they start popping, turn off the stove and stir in the curry leaves.

Empty the contents of the wok into the ground coconut chutney.

Stir and serve with ulundu vadai.

I use a thicker version of this chutney as a base spread, like a pesto, for tomato and cucumber sandwiches.

## BREAD UPMA, *quick, easy and innovative use of bread that is not very fresh.*

### INGREDIENTS TO MAKE 4 SERVINGS

* *2 medium loaves of bread. (Day-old white bread works well)*
* *3 tablespoons oil*
* *2 medium onions*
* *4 green chillies*
* *1 teaspoon mustard seeds*
* *1 teaspoon chana dal*
* *1 teaspoon urad dal*
* *10 curry leaves, torn in pieces*
* *1 teaspoon lime juice*
* *½ cup water*
* *½ cup coriander leaves, chopped*
* *½ cup grated carrots (optional)*
* *salt to taste*

### METHOD

Slice and cut bread into ½-inch cubes. Empty into a bowl. Set aside.

Chop onions coarsely. Slit green chillies lengthwise and chop fine. Set both aside.

Warm up the oil in a wok or heavy pan on medium heat.

Add mustard seeds, and as they splutter and pop, add chana and urad dal, and stir till they turn lightly brown.

Add onions and sauté till translucent.

Stir in the green chillies and curry leaves.

Add the bread pieces and sprinkle salt.

Toss them around to coat well with the onion and herb oil.

Stir and roast till the bread turns light brown.

Stir the lime juice into the water and sprinkle evenly over the pieces of bread to moisten. Toss frequently and cook for about 5 minutes.

Sprinkle coriander and toss.

Transfer to serving bowl and garnish with grated carrots, if you are using them.

Serve warm or at room temperature.

## MOONG DAL PAKODAS, *mottled yellow and green, these crisp, knobbly lentil-batter fries are a party favourite.*

### INGREDIENTS TO MAKE 6 SERVINGS

- *1 cup yellow moong dal*
- *½ cup methi (fenugreek) leaves, chopped coarse. I often use dried kasuri methi from a packet.*
- *2 tablespoons fresh coriander leaves with tender stems, finely chopped*
- *2 green chillies, slit lengthwise and finely chopped*
- *¼ teaspoon asafoetida powder (optional)*
- *½ teaspoon salt*
- *⅛ teaspoon baking powder*
- *2 cups oil for frying*

*I sometimes use watercress or fresh mint instead of methi leaves.*

### METHOD

Wash and rinse the moong dal till the water is clear. Soak in 3 cups water for 2 hours.

Drain dal and empty into blender.

Add water, 2 tablespoons at a time, and grind to a coarse batter of dropping consistency, stopping frequently to push down towards the blades with a spatula.

Empty batter into bowl.

Add all the ingredients, except baking powder and oil. Mix.

Heat oil in a wok or fryer on medium-high heat but not to smoking point. Lower heat to medium.

Whisk in the baking powder into the batter. Take 1 teaspoon of the batter and slide it into the hot oil with another spoon.

Fry one till it is light brown, turning it over with a slotted spoon. Drain and taste for salt.

Slide in about 8 or 10, but do not crowd the oil in the wok.

Fry, turning them over, till they change colour to a golden-brown.

Drain and serve hot or at room temperature.

Moong dal pakodas, though fried, are light and easy to digest.

## COBRI MITHAI, *Chamu's favourite chewy, caramelized coconut toffee speckled with poppy seeds.*

### INGREDIENTS TO MAKE 20–25 PIECES

* *1 teaspoon unsalted butter*
* *2 cups grated jaggery or light-brown sugar*
* *1 cup water*
* *2 cups shredded coconut, fresh or frozen*
* *1 teaspoon cardamom powder*
* *3 tablespoons white poppy seeds, lightly toasted*
* *½ cup cashew nuts, broken and toasted*
* *2 tablespoons ghee*
* *a scant pinch of salt*

### METHOD

Grease a 9-inch square baking dish with butter and set aside.

Dissolve the jaggery in a bowl with the water. Strain through a cheese cloth. Squeeze out all the jaggery water, and in a wok or heavy saucepan on medium heat, cook the jaggery water to a thin syrup, stirring continuously.

Add the coconut and salt, stir and cook to a rolling ball, scraping the sides and bottom, taking care to see that it does not get burnt.

Add the cardamom powder, poppy seeds and cashew nuts. Continue to stir with a circular motion, scraping the sides till the contents are sticky to the touch.

Add the ghee, mix and stir till it is incorporated into the toffee.

Pour the hot sticky mass into the greased baking dish.

Score into small squares when still warm. Leave to cool, and store in an airtight container.

# BADAM HALWA, *soft, ground almond fudge, a no-fuss recipe from a friend. I prefer the halwa a little runny.*

## INGREDIENTS TO MAKE 6 SERVINGS

* *30 almonds, blanched*
* *1 cup whole milk*
* *½ cup milk powder*
* *¾ cup sugar; ¼ cup more for sweeter halwa*
* *½ teaspoon cardamom*
* *2 tablespoons ghee*
* *a few threads of saffron*

## METHOD

In a blender, grind the blanched almonds with ½ cup milk. Empty into saucepan. Wash the blender with the remaining milk and add to saucepan.

Stir in the sugar, milk powder, ground cardamom and saffron. Mix well.

Cook on medium heat, stirring continuously till the mixture thickens, for about 15 minutes.

Add the ghee, stir and cook for 10 minutes.

Remove from stove and let it cool.

Either cut in squares or spoon out, and serve.

The time that Julian Pitt-Rivers and Chamu spent at the Institute for Social Anthropology in Oxford, England, overlapped in the late 1940s. In 1956, I met Julian and his wife Margo in Berkeley. Chamu and Julian were happy to renew their friendship, and we four spent many happy hours in our home on Peralta Avenue. Margo and I became good friends. She was an inspired baker and I enjoyed her scrumptious buttery scones with crushed nuts and her blueberry shortbread. And she salivated at the mention of garlic-coriander chutney sandwiches I made. She called them 'Rukka's pesto' sandwiches, and we frequently met for tea at one of our homes or outdoors for a picnic. The brilliant Californian sunshine beckoned and we two would set off for long drives, with a well-stocked picnic basket, to explore the beautiful California countryside.

I would leave Chamu to work on his manuscript and join Margo to explore the Berkeley hills. We went up to the Tilden Park frequently with sandwiches, scones and tea. One evening when Margo stopped by our home, I was making Mysore pak. She sniffed the air as she walked in the front door and was drawn to the kitchen, following the rich sweet smell. She watched me carefully as I finished making the deliciously sweet and crumbly fudge. 'I am dumbstruck seeing the frothing of the chickpea lava mix which cooks only with sugar and ghee,' she said, as she helped herself to more than one cube. She named it the 'wonder treat' and asked me for its recipe. I, in turn, was addicted to her buttery scones and she pampered me with dozens of blueberry scones and shortbread every time we met.

A few weeks later, she arrived with a sample of her maiden attempt at making Mysore pak! She also brought a small kitchen hammer and, somewhat abashed, asked, 'Rukka, how has my Mysore pak turned out a rock candy?'

In the December of 1956, the American Anthropological Association's (AAA's) meetings were to be held in La Jolla, near San Diego, on the southern California coast. Julian and Chamu planned to attend the meetings and Julian suggested that we make a short holiday of it. It was a two-day trip each way and he offered to drive all four of us down the scenic coastal highway 101.

Margo was a devout Catholic and was looking forward to visiting the Spanish monasteries and chapels en route to La Jolla. My neighbour in Berkeley, Mrs Muir, had suggested that we stop at Solvang, on the way, to taste a bit of Danish culture, most importantly, the buffet-style food, the 'smorgasbord', which I later found was heavily meat-based. What Mrs Muir did not know was that I was an uncompromising vegetarian who eschewed even eggs!

Margo and I were in charge of getting information on the restaurants along the way for the drive down to La Jolla, and for making arrangements for our stay. I knew finding food along the way would be difficult for me and Chamu, though our friends assured us that if nothing else, there would certainly be pizzerias off the highway. I would have been happy with a salad of greens and some garlic bread. But for how many days would I have to live on this diet? I didn't want a repeat of what had happened on the Polish ship, the *Batory*!

Not wanting to take a chance, Margo said she would bake scones and biscuits and I offered to make garlic-mint chutney sandwiches and cheese parathas (fresh wholewheat flatbreads stuffed with an assortment of cheese). But I ended up also making pea parathas (flatbreads with a cumin-flavoured green peas stuffing) and masala puris (deep-fried, spicy, airy, puffy breads). I also packed fruit, fresh yogurt and a few cartons of juice. When Julian and Margo came by to pick us up, they were astonished at the quantity of food I had packed for a two-day trip down the coast. Chamu said I had gone berserk. They teased me about my food insecurity, but I knew from my previous attempts at eating out that it was nearly impossible to get anything truly 'vegetarian', as I understood the term. Often, waiters would just remove shrimp and hard-boiled eggs from previously prepared salads and assure me that they were now vegetarian! I often wondered what my dear Annam Athai would have done under similar circumstances. Fortunately, my friends were understanding about my dietary restrictions and were often distressed by my inability to join in their gastronomic adventures at restaurants.

Frankly, if it hadn't been for the sandwiches I had packed for our trip, I would have had to munch fruit for lunch in Solvang. Julian and Margo enjoyed the frikadeller (meatballs). Chamu relished his aebleskivers, the traditional Danish pancake, which looked like soft tennis balls sprinkled with powdered sugar with a topping of strawberry jam. He cut open one 'tennis ball' and dug into the apple slices buried within. He seemed to enjoy them. But what interested me was the wrought iron seven-cup aebleskiver pan, similar to the 'kuzhi appam' pan in south India. Kuzhi appams can be mildly sweet with mashed bananas mixed in the batter. I have also tasted savoury ones, pungent, with green chillies. Kuzhi appams look like aebleskiver, but the resemblance stops there.

The first day of our trip was leisurely. We drove down the coast on a sunny day with intermittent winter showers, stopping every few hours to just wallow in the natural beauty of the coast and countryside, or to take in a dark and beautiful monastery or church and allow enough time for Margo to genuflect at every shrine. Our picnic baskets came in very handy. We stopped for the night at Millie's Motel not far from Pebble Beach.

On the second day, we drove down the cliff-side, past seemingly unending stands of California eucaplyptus with piles of tinder and layers of dry leaves. Chamu said in passing, 'Looks like the perfect place for an arsonist.' Julian laughed. I didn't give a thought to Chamu's remark. Soon, we left the eucalyptus groves and drove through exclusive residential estates, when flashing lights and highway patrol cars blocked our way. The Malibu hills were ablaze and smoke and flames fanned by strong winds were spreading for several miles around. We were ordered to turn around.

Julian briskly headed down a narrow road to a bridge across a fast-flowing stream and climbed up a steep hillside. Despite all our protests that none of us remembered this road, he charged ahead. After driving for about an hour up that road, which became narrower and narrower as it wound up the hillside and finally became a dirt path, Julian slammed the brakes and we came to a rude halt before a menacingly huge metal gate with a NO ENTRY sign. Powerful lights were turned on our car. It turned out we had arrived at some top-secret government facility! The eerie silence in the car spoke eloquently of our anxiety. Julian nonchalantly reversed downhill in the darkness of the night, with the only light coming from the glow of the burning hills in the distance. Margo clutched her rosary. I was petrified, since I was sitting on the side overlooking the steep cliffside and was convinced that the car would plunge over.

I was relieved when we made our way to the state highway again. It was past midnight. Exhausted and famished, we found our way to a small motel, I think between Ventura and Oxnard, where we spent the rest of the night. There were no restaurants and no stores open. We opened my picnic basket and enjoyed a quiet dinner of cheese parathas with garlic-mint chutney, fruit and yogurt. Margo had packed bottles of wine. Julian and Chamu were thankful for the 'picnic' which saved the day.

When we finally drove to the American Anthropological meetings, we were just some eight hours late! Many others who took the same route arrived even later. The AAA conference participants were seriously discussing the multiple facets of arson when we four arrived at the venue, travel-weary but certainly not famished, thanks again to the picnic baskets.

I recall here some of the recipes of the food I had packed that added so much flavour to an already interesting trip.

CHEESE PARATHA, *cheese-stuffed flavourful flatbread. For me, this is a good way to use leftover hard cheese mixed with aromatic spices. In cool weather, cheese parathas keep well at room temperature for two days, and refrigerated, they are good even for a week. Reheated and served with a salad, this is a wholesome meal. Cut into bite-size pieces, topped with onion rings or with a dip of your choice, they can be served as appetizers.*

## INGREDIENTS TO MAKE 6 PARATHAS

* 1½ cups wheat flour, divided (I use multigrain flour)
* ½ teaspoon salt
* 1 cup mixed shredded hard cheese (any leftover cheese is good)
* ½ teaspoon red chilli powder
* 2 cloves garlic, minced
* ½ teaspoon cumin seeds
* ½ cup freshly chopped fresh coriander, including tender stems
* ¼ cup melted ghee
* water to mix the dough

## METHOD

Sift 1 cup of the flour and salt into a bowl. Sprinkle water, 1 tablespoon at a time, mix and knead the flour to a soft dough. Set aside, covered with a moist kitchen towel, for 10 minutes.

Mix the shredded cheese with the chilli powder, garlic, cumin seeds and coriander in another bowl.

Remove the dough from the bowl, place it on a work-board and knead again for 5 minutes. Divide dough into 6 portions, roll into balls and set aside in the same bowl, covered with a moist kitchen towel.

Dust a thin layer of flour on the work-board, pick up one ball of dough and roll into a disc approximately 4 inches in diameter. Place roughly 2 tablespoons of the cheese mix in the centre of the disc, and bring the edges of the disc together. Pinch to seal.

Dust a rolling pin with flour and roll the cheese-stuffed ball into a disc ⅛-inch thick. If there is a tear, seal with a little dough, dust a little flour and complete rolling,

Roll 3 parathas at a time and keep them covered with a kitchen towel.

Warm up a griddle on medium heat. Cook each paratha on both sides till brown specks appear.

Transfer to a platter and brush both sides lightly with melted ghee.

Lower the heat, roll out 3 more and cook, raising the heat to medium.

PEA PARATHAS, *flatbread stuffed with delicious aromatic peas. The parathas can be made and refrigerated for 3 days. Warm up and serve with yogurt raita and pickle. This saves much time and energy at the end of a long working day.*

## INGREDIENTS TO MAKE THE FILLING FOR 10–12 PARATHAS

* *3 cups shelled peas, fresh or frozen*
* *½ cup grated coconut, fresh or frozen*
* *½ teaspoon ginger paste*
* *½ cup fresh coriander leaves, finely chopped*
* *½ teaspoon turmeric powder*
* *½ teaspoon red chilli powder*
* *½ teaspoon garam masala powder (available in Indian grocery stores)*
* *½ teaspoon whole cumin seeds*
* *1 teaspoon lime juice*
* *salt to taste*

### METHOD TO MAKE THE FILLING

Blanch peas. Drain and wipe with paper towels.

Empty into a large bowl, add all the other ingredients, and gently mash the peas coarsely, mixing all the ingredients together. Add salt to taste. Set aside, covered.

The pea filling should be moist, not wet.

## INGREDIENTS TO MAKE 10–12 PARATHAS

* *2 ½ cups multigrain flour, divided*
* *¼ teaspoon salt*
* *4 tablespoons oil*
* *½ cup oil and ½ cup ghee mixed, for the shortening*
* *water to mix dough*

### METHOD TO MAKE THE DOUGH

Sift 2 cups flour and salt into a bowl. Drizzle 4 tablespoons oil and rub it into the flour to form pea-size crumbs.

Sprinkle the water a little at a time, mix and knead to a soft dough. Cover the bowl with a kitchen towel and set aside for 10 minutes.

Remove the dough, place it on a work-board. Knead and roll it into a 'rope' with both palms. Cut the 'rope' in 10 or 12 equal portions. Roll each piece into a ball. Keep the balls of dough covered in the bowl.

## METHOD TO MAKE THE PARATHAS

Lightly sprinkle the work-board with a little flour. Place one ball of dough and roll out into a 3-inch tortilla.

Brush lightly with the shortening on the side facing you. Place 2 tablespoons of pea filling in the middle.

Gather the edges of the tortilla, pinch them together in the middle and seal them.

Dust more flour, if needed, and roll evenly into a ¼-inch thick paratha.

If there are tears while you are rolling, patch them up with a little dough.

Roll out 2 or 3 parathas at a time and keep them covered with a kitchen towel.

Heat a griddle on medium heat.

Brush the surface of the griddle with ⅛ teaspoon of the shortening.

Place one paratha on the warm griddle and cook one side for about 2 minutes till light brown specks appear on the bottom.

Brush the uncooked side with the shortening and flip the paratha over.

Cook for another 2 minutes and remove from griddle onto a platter. Cook all 3 parathas.

Lower the temperature of the stove and roll out the remaining parathas in batches of 3.

Cook them one by one.

For a quick and simple raita, grate a cucumber into a bowl. Stir in 2 cups of plain yogurt . Add salt.

Stir and serve with the parathas.

## MASALA PURIS, *soft, airy puffs of aromatic fried bread. Best served hot off the wok.*

### INGREDIENTS TO MAKE 20 PURIS

- *2 cups wholewheat flour, plus ½ cup for dusting*
- *½ teaspoon salt*
- *⅛ teaspoon turmeric powder*
- *⅛ teaspoon cumin powder*
- *2 green chillies*
- *½ cup fresh coriander leaves, including the tender stems, finely chopped*
- *2 tablespoons tomato puree*
- *2¼ cups oil, divided*

## METHOD

Sift 2 cups of flour, salt, turmeric and cumin powders in a bowl.

Grind the green chillies and coriander into a fine paste, adding 1 teaspoon of water. Add the ground paste and the tomato puree to the sifted flour and knead to a stiff dough.

Transfer the dough to the work-board. Sprinkle a little water, if needed, and knead again.

Put the dough back in the bowl and keep covered with a kitchen towel for 10 minutes.

Transfer the dough to the work-board, flatten with your fingers, pour 2 tablespoons of oil and work it into the dough. With your palms, roll into a 'rope'. Cut the 'rope' into 20 equal parts. Roll each part into a ball and set aside covered in a bowl.

Warm up 2 cups oil in a wok on medium heat.

Lightly dust the work-board with a little flour. Roll out one ball into a disc 4 inches across. Roll out 4 or 5 balls of dough. Test to see if the oil is ready by dropping a pinch of the dough into the oil. It should sink immediately, and within a few seconds, rise to the surface.

Slide the discs gently, 2 at a time, into the hot oil. They will soon rise, puffing up. Cook for 1 minute.

Slowly turn them over with a slotted spoon. Fry on both sides till they turn pinkish-brown in colour and are puffed up well. The second side should take 1 minute or less to cook.

Drain on a colander lined with paper towels. Do not stack them. They will get deflated.

Roll out the remaining balls of dough, a few at a time, and fry them.

For the puris to puff you should monitor the heat, which should be medium-high. If the oil is too hot, the puris will cook too soon and not puff up, and if it is not hot enough, the puris will take longer to cook and turn out flat and greasy. Secondly, as soon as you slide the puri into the oil, press it down gently with a slotted spoon to encourage it to puff up with air.

# GARLIC CHUTNEY SANDWICHES, *Margo called them pesto sandwiches. They were also an all-time favourite with my colleagues in the Geography Department of the Delhi School of Economics, where I was a lecturer from 1959 to 1972.*

I make the sandwiches without sour cream or butter for elderly friends and for those who don't eat dairy products.

## INGREDIENTS FOR 6 SLICES OF BREAD

- **2 green chillies, chopped coarsely**
- **½ cup tightly packed, fresh coriander leaves**
- **2 cloves fresh garlic**
- **½ teaspoon salt**
- **¼ teaspoon sugar**
- **½ cup sour cream (optional)**
- **½ cup butter at room temperature (optional)**
- **slices of bread of your choice**
- **3 tablespoons of olive oil when not using sour cream or butter**

## METHOD

Grind the first 3 ingredients to a smooth paste, adding salt and sugar. Mix the ground herb paste with sour cream and melted butter or oil, whichever you are using.

Take 2 slices of bread and brush one side of each slice with the garlic-coriander spread. Place the slices with the 'spread', facing each other. Press gently. Trim the edges. Cut diagonally into triangles.

I use the same chutney as a base for cucumber, lettuce, sprouts, tomato, avocado and watercress sandwiches.

*Happy Hour at Stanford University*

Early in 1958, a few months after we returned to Baroda from Berkeley, Dr V.K.R.V. Rao, well-known economist and, at the time the vice-chancellor of Delhi University, invited Chamu to start the Department of Social Anthropology in the Delhi School of Economics (DSE). In 1960, I, too, joined DSE as lecturer in the newly established Department of Geography. Within the space of six years, our daughters Lakshmi and Tulasi were born.

In 1964, Chamu was invited to spend a year at the Center for Advanced Study in the Behavioral Sciences (CASBS) in Palo Alto, California. Delhi University was kind enough to give me leave of absence from my department and my teaching commitments so we could spend the year together as a family.

I was relieved we were not travelling by ship this time around. The nightmare of sea travel was something I definitely wanted to avoid. We flew by the Pan American Airlines from Delhi to San Francisco via Europe. To ease the stress of the more than 20-hour flight, Chamu arranged for a break of a few days in Rome. Even so, travelling with two young children—one an energetic, curious child and the other an infant, though thankfully, a placid contented bundle—was tiring. Although in those days of international travel, children were well looked after by the stewardesses; colouring books, crayons, chewing gum and mint kept them engaged. The stewardesses were beautiful, and my older daughter Lakshmi instantaneously decided she wanted to be an 'air hostess on the Pan Am' wearing the 'blue wing badge' and 'stewardess cap'! That was her ambition as a child.

One of Chamu's former students in the Delhi School of Economics was a priest in training, and when he was selected to go to Rome, he came home and invited both Chamu and me to Rome. So, here we were, and the Father had made arrangements for an interview with the Pope in the Vatican garden. This was a rare opportunity for a face-to-face meeting with the religious head of several millions around the world; I couldn't believe it. Mary Nana, our childrens' nanny in Delhi, would have been in a state of ecstasy had she known of our interview. A devout church-going Catholic, she would have given her life to just have a 'darshan' of the Pope; and on the spot, it occurred to me to get two rosaries blessed by him for Mary. That was my gift to her; while Chamu's student, when he heard stories of Mary, bought some small mementoes of Rome for her. We enjoyed our stay in Rome and visited, among the sites of tourist interest, a memorial for Mussolini on the outskirts of Rome where he is said to have held his political meetings. It was a beautiful drive through the countryside, with viticulture farms on both sides of a narrow unpaved road, but I must warn you that the cab drivers in Rome are as notorious as Indian cab drivers, weaving through crowds at the risk of running over a few. This was in 1964. Fortunately Peter, our cab driver, brought us back to our 'pension' without a scratch.

In Rome again, it was an extended period of fasting for me. Pasta everywhere was made with egg in the dough, and the tomato sauce was meat-based. I couldn't wait to alight at San Francisco and start my kitchen in Menlo Park. Lakshmi could not understand how, after such a long flight, we could arrive in San Francisco a few hours earlier on the same day we had left Delhi. She asked her father, 'How can it be Saturday today also, when we left yesterday which was a Saturday?' Her little mind could not wrap itself around this big mistake.

Paul Hockings, a graduate student of the Anthropology Department in Berkeley, met our flight at the San Francisco airport. Paul has strayed into our lives one way or another since we first met. We settled in our new home in Menlo Park without further ado.

This time around, when I wanted to bring some spices and home-made spice powders from India, Chamu dissuaded me saying, 'I am sure you will find most things you will need.' He meant 'in the grocery stores'. But I did pack a small jar of my mother's home-made vadu manga pickle and about half a kilogram of her sambar powder, both of which my mother advised me to pack. I am happy I listened to her. Vadu manga pickle, which Amma made with home-grown baby mangoes, is to me one of the more sophisticated pickles. It calls for an elaborate preparation, when baby mangoes of a particular pickling variety are plucked tender with stems without being bruised, each one wiped with a clean dry cloth and smeared with fresh castor oil, and dunked in brine with turmeric powder and salt. After a few weeks of soaking, this pickle is ready, delicious as is, but some prefer it spicy with ground red chilli paste and ground mustard added; it is the perfect combination with curd rice. I am happy I listened to Amma, particularly in packing the pickle. I would like to believe it is a signature pickle of Tamil Nadu Iyers. But now, with changing food habits and the universality of food dishes, one can never be sure where the origin of each lies. And Chamu's mother packed a little puliyohare gojju, a spicy fudge-like blend common to the indigenous cuisines of the southern states of Tamil Nadu, Karnataka and Andhra Pradesh. This gojju (paste) is made by boiling tamarind juice and several ground spices till it thickens, and is the basic ingredient in mixing puliyohare, the delicious, tart mixed rice. Shrivaishnavites, the Iyengar community members, claim they make the best puliyohare gojju.

But there was a pleasant surprise awaiting me on arrival at our home in Menlo Park. The Bengali couple who vacated the house a week earlier had left a few kitchen pots and pans and a pantry full of spices, including 'panch phoren' the five-spice blend of Bengali cuisine, dals as also basmati rice! The thoughtful lady had even stocked the fridge with milk, yogurt and a few vegetables. She had been told an Indian family with young children was moving in the following week. There was a welcoming note on the kitchen table addressed to me, listing the grocery stores in the neighbourhood that she frequented, and that she hoped I would be able to use the leftovers from her pantry! Kunjappa would have said, 'You've lucked out again, Rukka.'

That very evening, I cooked a simple dal and rice dinner. I was starved for a vegetarian meal. Paul stayed on for dinner and took me shopping to J.C. Pennys for bedlinen and some things I needed for the children. Lakshmi had to start her new school a couple of days later, and the following Monday morning, Chamu began his routine of walking to the Center across the golf course adjoining Stanford University with Milton Konvitz, who was also a Fellow that year at the Center and who lived with his dear wife Mary on the same street a few houses away. Our initial acquaintance with Milton and Mary deepened into a friendship where we enjoyed each other's company and experiences. Milton, the son of a rabbi, would never refuse an invitation to share a meal with us at our home, 'Rukka, I know you keep a kosher kitchen, and Mary and I will join your table even at short notice!' Milton was a renowned scholar of Constitutional and Labour Law, Civil and Human Rights at Cornell University, but his scholarship sat ever so lightly on his slender shoulders. He knew about the Cochin Jews but was eager to learn more about them from Chamu. Both Mary and Milton were especially fond of our young daughters and would stop by even without an invitation to dine with us. They welcomed masala chai.

It was a ritual at the Center that the sixty Fellows with their families met every Friday evening. The Friday Happy Hour was followed by a potluck dinner contributed by the Fellows and their spouses. Getting to know the Fellows' families in a relaxed atmosphere was a good reason to attend. The potluck dinners forged many bonds of friendship for me.

I remember the first couple of Friday Night dinners, where there would be trays of food laid out in the open courtyard and, yet, I would come home famished; fish, beef, lamb, pork and chicken, roasted, stewed, braised and curried, along with bowls of soup and platters of salad greens, assorted fruit pies and ice cream filled the tables. Chamu, on the other hand, managed very well; he ingeniously put together his sandwich with a serving of salad greens and helped himself to a generous bowl of ice cream. For me, it was not a matter of taste alone; it took a while to tolerate the smell and sight of non-vegetarian food. The lesson I learned after a couple of potluck parties was to have dinner at home and enjoy the eggless fruit desserts at the Center.

Why I wasn't eating was what many of the women wanted to know. Some of them tried to help, 'I can get you the egg salad I've made,' said Joan. Ruth said she made the lightest crêpe suzettes and I should try one. 'No? I thought being vegetarian meant you did not eat meat and fish but eggs were okay.' 'Will you taste the soup? I made it myself. Oh! It has chicken stock.' 'What CAN you eat?' asked May and her husband Peter. Joan was concerned and asked helpfully if I would like to have a meal with boiled rice and curried peas which she had cooked herself with all fresh ingredients and Worcestershire sauce. 'I've added curry powder so you'll certainly like the taste.' What Joan did not realize was that anchovies were an important ingredient of Worcestershire sauce. They threw up their hands. I could not be saved.

Soon, my vegetarian leanings became a hotly debated topic among my friends. Many of the women thought a vegetarian diet was unbalanced and would result in health problems over the years, but a few were interested and requested me to talk on vegetarianism to their groups at the local churches. I agreed. This was the America of the mid-1960s when Indian vegetarian cooking was not the fad it is today.

For one of the Friday Night dinners the first month, I cooked vegetable rava bhath and carrot halwa—much appreciated by my American friends.

A few weeks later, three of the Fellows' spouses came to me with personal requests. Their teenaged sons and daughters, who had turned vegetarian, were 'living on peanut butter and jelly sandwiches'. 'My daughter Cherisse who could earlier boast of a beautiful figure is now obese,' said Marianne. Could I teach these kids to put together a simple, Indian vegetarian meal? Some time later, she suggested I send in vegetarian recipes to the *Sunset* magazine, which I did, and to my surprise, they were published. I was even more surprised with a cheque for a 'stuffed bell pepper' recipe I had submitted.

I started classes for six kids in my kitchen in Menlo Park—and thus began my foray into teaching Indian vegetarian cooking to non-Indians in America. We decided to meet on Saturday mornings. I introduced the children to a variety of Indian spices, herbs and vegetables, and kept the recipes simple at first. I organized trips to the Farmers' Market and to the orchards and farms in the Los Altos Hills neighbourhood for fresh vegetables and fruit. It was a revelation for them to see the variety of seasonal fruit, vegetables and herbs, and they were clearly excited plucking the apples, peaches and lemons and gathering eggplant, tomatoes, bell peppers and strawberries. We had fun together.

One of the mothers suggested I charge a fee for each class. That sounded preposterous to me. When I said the joy of teaching children and young adults the pleasure of cooking simple Indian vegetarian food is in itself a reward, they were touched and gifted me a beautiful casserole and multipurpose stainless steel skillet at the end of the four-to-ten weeks' class. It is hard to believe but I still have the skillet and I use it too!

The following month, the number of kids swelled to sixteen. My kitchen proved too small, so I had two sessions, Saturday and Sunday mornings, during the month of December in 1964 and again in the summer of 1965. The sixteen enthusiastic, serious teenage students were my first batch to experiment with Indian vegetarian 'home-style' cooking in the USA.

The 1960s was a period of great dissatisfaction with the social order of things, and young people were looking for ways and philosophies they believed would bring about a change for a 'better world'. Vegetarianism was one way of experiencing a different culture, philosophy and lifestyle. As my first class of pupils told me, 'You are what you eat.'

I started the group off on a simple recipe of assembling a raita with sliced onions and cucumber in yogurt, tempered with aromatic herbs, and moved on to mango lassi, canned mango pulp stirred in a tub of yogurt and flavoured with aromatic cardamom. Mango lassi was an instant favourite. And so was the magic of a puri, the flat disc of dough puffing up in hot oil. The youngsters learned to steam cook rice and cook a lentil curry with eggplant to go with the rice. Alan, who had turned eleven, the baby of the group, wanted to learn to brew masala chai and he liked his chai with honey.

I heard later that the group of sixteen not only enjoyed cooking but held vegetarian cooking classes for a nominal fee at the local Farmers' Market under the banner 'You are what you eat'. In this chapter, I give the more popular recipes among this group of youngsters.

Word spread in the Center about my cooking classes, and

when Chamu was invited again in 1970 to spend another year, the administrative office requested me to run a series of classes similar to the ones I had taught in 1964, but this time around, my hands were full with the activities of my young daughters, both in school and with their friends. Besides, I had also enrolled at Stanford University in two courses on secondary school education and to audit some classes.

What I did though during our stay in Palo Alto in 1970 was to organize informal classes, and not on a regular weekly schedule, for a few of my friends who wanted to learn to cook simple Indian vegetarian dishes. My neighbour Susan would call her friends and whoever was free would come over. Six of us would meet and cook in the spacious enclosed patio in our house on Amaranta. The house was set in a large lot, the front garden with holly bushes and in the backyard a cherry tree, several apricot trees, two almond trees, a magnificent fig tree, a plum tree, a persimmon tree and several artichoke plants. This was my introduction to enjoying artichokes and persimmon fruit. We cooked in this sunlit patio on a makeshift wood stove put together by the house owner, who was an environmentalist in the Stanford faculty. My friends would also come over to harvest the fruit to 'can' them; we also made dozens of pies for the Center's Friday Night Happy Hour dinner parties. I have never seen so many birds as I did in our orchard that year in Palo Alto. That winter, Lakshmi and I rescued many blue jays inebriated with gorging on holly berries and bashing into the glass doors and windows facing the front garden.

## CREAM OF WHEAT VEGETABLE BHATH, *this 'anytime' snack can substitute for a meal. Cooking time is less than half an hour. Keeps well in the fridge for three days.*

### INGREDIENTS TO MAKE 6 SERVINGS

- *4 tablespoons oil*
- *½ teaspoon black mustard seeds*
- *½ teaspoon chana dal*
- *½ teaspoon urad dal*
- *¼ cup cashew nut pieces*
- *1 large onion, chopped fine*
- *1 green chilli, chopped fine*
- *1-inch piece fresh ginger, chopped fine*
- *10 curry leaves, torn in pieces*
- *4 cups water*
- *1 teaspoon salt; more if needed*
- *¼ cup grated carrots*
- *¼ cup chopped French beans*
- *¼ cup shelled peas, fresh or frozen*
- *1 medium tomato, chopped fine*
- *2 cups semolina (sooji/rava/regular cream of wheat)*
- *1 flat tablespoon flax seeds (optional)*
- *½ cup fresh coriander leaves and tender stems, chopped*
- *juice of ½ lime*

## METHOD

In a heavy-bottomed pan or wok, heat the oil on medium heat.

Toss in the mustard seeds, and when they pop, add chana and urad dals and cashew nuts. Stir to a golden-brown.

Add onions, green chillies, ginger and curry leaves. Stir till onions turn translucent. Pour the water and bring it to a boil.

Add the salt, carrots, peas and beans. Cook for 2 minutes.

Add the tomatoes. Drizzle the semolina, half a cup at a time. Toss in the flax seeds, if you are using them. Give one quick stir to break up the lumps.

Reduce the heat to low and cook, covered, till all the water is absorbed and the semolina is cooked soft, removing lid from time to time and folding from the bottom up. This should take about 8 minutes. If the semolina is not moist and soft, sprinkle ½ cup water, fold and cook for another minute or two, breaking all lumps.

Turn off the stove. Cover and let rest for 2 minutes. Stir in the lime juice and coriander. Fluff up the vegetable bhath and serve with coconut chutney, red radish raita or plain yogurt.

Best served warm or at room temperature.

RED RADISH RAITA, *delicious and creamy yogurt salad. Visually appealing with streaks of pink and red, the raita is cooling and is served as a side dish for most Indian meals. Other vegetables which could be used are grated cucumber, thinly sliced onions, diced tomatoes, sautéed spinach or watercress, or boiled and roughly mashed potatoes.*

## INGREDIENTS TO MAKE APPROXIMATELY 3 CUPS

- *2 cups plain yogurt, whisked smooth*
- *1 cup coarsely grated red radish*
- *¼ teaspoon salt*
- *¼ cup water*
- *⅛ teaspoon roasted cumin, powdered fine*

## METHOD

Mix all the ingredients in a bowl. Chill and serve.

# HEALTHY MIXED GREENS-POTATO BAKE, *delicious and satisfying! A good way to use leftover greens.*

## INGREDIENTS TO MAKE 4 SERVINGS

* *2 large potatoes, washed and grated with skin, and immersed in a bowl of water*
* *1 medium onion, minced*
* *2 cloves garlic, chopped fine*
* *½ teaspoon red chilli powder*
* *¼ teaspoon turmeric powder*
* *1 cup finely chopped greens; watercress, spinach, turnip or beet tops, cabbage leaves and scallions, and any others in the combination you like*
* *2 tablespoons breadcrumbs*
* *3 tablespoons oats*
* *½ cup mixed shredded cheese; any leftover hard cheese is good*
* *water, if necessary, to mix and bind*
* *4 tablespoons melted butter*
* *salt to taste*

## METHOD

Turn oven to 300°F.

Grease a 9-inch x 6-inch baking dish with 1 tablespoon of butter, and set aside.

Squeeze all the water out of the grated potatoes and place in a bowl.

Add all the other ingredients, except the breadcrumbs, oats, cheese, butter and water. Mix to hold together. Sprinkle a little water, if needed, to hold.

Add salt to taste and mix.

Empty mix into greased baking dish and pat lightly to cover the bottom. Scatter breadcrumbs, oats and cheese evenly on top. Drizzle the remaining melted butter on top.

Bake for 15 to 20 minutes.

Turn the oven off, and leave the baking dish in the oven till a brown crust forms, or cook under broiler.

Score into pieces and serve warm.

# HEALTHY SPINACH MOMOS, *steamed rice flour wraps with an aromatic spinach filling.*

## INGREDIENTS TO MAKE 10–12 MOMOS

* *Buy a packet of rice flour wonton wraps*

## INGREDIENTS TO MAKE THE FILLING

* 3 cups chopped fresh spinach, (you could use 3 cups frozen spinach, thawed and the water squeezed out)
* ⅛ teaspoon turmeric powder
* ½ teaspoon cumin powder
* ½ teaspoon coriander powder
* ½ teaspoon red chilli powder
* 1 clove garlic, ground to a paste
* 2 tablespoons chopped fresh coriander
* 1 flat tablespoon flax seed, coarsely ground
* 2 tablespoons pine nuts
* a squeeze of lime
* 1 teaspoon oil
* salt to taste

## METHOD TO MAKE THE FILLING

In a wok or heavy pan, put all the ingredients, except the pine nuts and lime juice. Stir and cook till the spinach is cooked moist.

Stir in the pine nuts and lime juice and set aside.

## METHOD TO MAKE AND STEAM THE MOMOS

Dip two wonton wraps at a time in cold water. Remove immediately and pat with dry kitchen towel. Grease the top steamer plate with oil.

Fill each wrap with 1 tablespoon of the curried spinach, wet and seal the edges, and place in the greased top plate of the steamer.

Fill, seal and arrange all the wraps. Wraps should be sealed well, else they will open up while steaming.

Steam for 7–8 minutes.

Serve hot with a raita or chutney of your choice.

VEGETABLE CHAAT, *spicy potatoes, sprouts and mixed greens in yogurt sauce. What began as 'street food' in many Indian cities has been elevated to an appetizer in upscale hotel menus.*

## INGREDIENTS FOR 4 SERVINGS

* 1 large potato, peeled and cut into ¼-inch cubes, and boiled soft in salt water
* 1 large sweet potato, peeled and  cut into ¼-inch cubes and boiled soft in salt water. Take care to see they retain their shape and are not overcooked.

- 4 shallots or 1 onion, chopped fine
- 1 medium ripe firm tomato, chopped fine
- 1 cucumber, peeled and cut in ¼-inch cubes
- 1 cup mixed micro greens, alfalfa, flax, mustard and others
- 1 cup bean sprouts
- ¼ cup finely copped fresh coriander leaves with tender stems
- 2 teaspoons chaat masala (available in Indian grocery stores)
- 1 cup plain yogurt, whisked with the juice of half a lime and 1 teaspoon of sugar
- ½ cup roasted unsalted peanuts, coarsely crushed (optional)
- 2 generous handfuls of spicy potato chips, crushed coarsely with a rolling pin

## METHOD TO MAKE VEGETABLES CHAAT

In a large bowl, toss all the above, except the yogurt, peanuts and potato chips.
  Drizzle the yogurt evenly on top.
  Serve in bowls topped with peanuts and crushed potato chips.


# FRUIT CHAAT, *fruit salad with a distinct Indian flavour.*

## INGREDIENTS TO MAKE 4 SERVINGS

- 1 raw or semi-ripe mango, peeled and cut in ½ inch cubes
- 1 cup fresh orange segments, threads, membrane and seeds removed
- 1 cup bananas, cut in ½-inch discs
- Any seasonal fruit of your choice; strawberries, blueberries, raspberries, grapes, sliced peaches, apricots, apples, pineapple, watermelon and kiwi (the last three skinned), cut in bite-size pieces
- ½ cup dates, chopped
- ½ cup golden California raisins
- ½ cup of honey
- ½ cup mixed nuts (optional)
- 3 cups plain yogurt, whisked with ½ teaspoon salt and 1 tablespoon chaat masala (available in Indian grocery stores)

## METHOD TO MAKE FRUIT CHAAT

In a large bowl, mix all ingredients, except the nuts and yogurt.
  Chill for 1 hour and serve in individual bowls topped with yogurt and nuts.

**MASALA CHAI,** *a warm aromatic herbal tea, good with or without milk. It helps ward off a cold. Chai masala, the herbal powder, is available in Indian grocery stores but can't compare with the home-made mix.*

## INGREDIENTS TO MAKE 6 CUPS

* 3 cardamom pods
* 3 cloves
* 5 black peppercorns
* 1-inch piece cinnamon stick
* 5–6 cups water
* 5 teabags or 3 heaped teaspoons black Indian leaf tea (Orange Pekoe/Ceylon tea)
* ½-inch piece fresh ginger, crushed
* sugar as preferred, or honey
* milk as preferred

## METHOD

In a spice grinder, or mortar and pestle, grind the first 4 ingredients to a fine powder. Store this chai masala in a jar with a lid.

In a deep pan, bring the water to a boil.

Add teabags or leaves and bring to a second boil.

Lower heat, add 1 teaspoon of chai masala (dry spice powder) and ginger.

Turn off stove, cover pan and let it rest for two minutes.

Strain brewed tea into cups.

Warm up the milk and add to the brew in the cups.

Stir in sugar or honey.

Serve piping hot.

The number of teabags you use depends on how strong you want your masala chai. If you are brewing in a teapot, put the tea bags and masala in, pour the boiling water, cover with a tea cosy, and steep for 5 minutes for a strong cup. Add hot milk and sugar to taste.

I prefer honey or raw agave syrup as sweeteners.

## Of Birthdays and Snacks

In 1966, Chamu and I, with our two children, returned to Delhi from Palo Alto after a memorable 18-month stay. Chamu resumed his responsibilities as Chair of the Sociology Department in the Delhi School of Economics, and I went back to teaching in the Geography Department. We had retained our house on Cavalry Lane allotted by the university to Chamu. In fact, our cook Veluswamy, Rattan Lal, our young Nepali domestic help, and Mary Nana, our daughters' nanny, stayed and looked after the house and our daughters' canine pet Kittu while we were away. It was easy for me to get back to full-time teaching at the Delhi School of Economics.

Cavalry Lane on the Delhi University campus was a quiet tree-lined dead-end street with six bungalows for professors and their families. The trees were home to a variety of birds. A pair of white owls nested in the neem tree across from our bedroom. There was great excitement on our entire street

*Schoolgirls: Tulasi and Lakshmi*

*Birthday party in Cavalry Lane, Delhi*

one year when a peahen hatched her six chicks at the base of an old magnificent jacaranda tree opposite our front lawn.

Many of the children living on Cavalry Lane were of school-going age, and the annual calendar of the resident adults was punctuated by the children's birthdays. Birthdays that fell during the summer and winter vacations, when some of the families were away, were celebrated soon after they returned, so that no child missed the fun, food and special gifts. One year, we celebrated fourteen birthdays, as the Nepalese cook of one of my neighbours brought both her young girls from Nepal to Delhi to join the primary school on the campus, and another neighbour's resident gardener moved in his family of four kids from a village in Bihar.

A rotating committee of three women took charge of the party arrangements every year. Magic shows and fancy dress parties were popular, but the toughest decision was about the food.

The birthday cake was ordered from Wenger's, a well-known bakery and delicatessen in Connaught Place in New Delhi that still draws in crowds despite competition from fancy 'new age' bakeries and delicatessens. The fruit chaat came from the New Kamla Nagar Chaat Shop, a popular meeting place for young

*Birthday party in Cavalry Lane, Delhi*

university students, and the staff and their families in Kamla Nagar, a suburb of old Delhi adjoining the university. The proprietor of the chaat shop arrived with his assistant, and the chaat was 'custom-made' for each child. The green and yellow van would arrive well before the party, and the assistant would get busy putting up the banner. No sooner had the van arrived the children would rush to help arrange the tables and set out all the fruit, chutneys, spice blends, syrups, and plates and bowls. Chaat was the number one favourite with the children and they couldn't wait to order the combination of their preference. Would it be pineapple chunks, apple slices, grapes and banana discs with a dusting of black salt and a generous drizzle of sticky sugar syrup drenching the fruit, or would it be star fruit, sweet lime and orange segments, raisins and pomegranates with a sweet and sour yogurt dressing? The combination of fruit did vary with the seasons, and while some were happy getting the fruit they liked, others were disappointed. The proprietor would be heard consoling them, 'Beta (my child)...jamun fruit is not available now. That you will get only in the rainyseason. Try this other combination. I am sure you will like it.'

Mrs Das Gupta, who lived three houses down the road, came over to help me fry cauliflower pakodas, Indian tempura, an all-time savoury favourite with the children. My neighbour from Rajasthan sent mathris, crisp, buttery, flaky rounds of savoury dough. She contributed several dozens for every birthday party. Veluswami, our family cook, helped make the gaajar halwa, a sweet carrot confection, another favourite with most of the children.

# KNOBBLY CAULIFLOWER PAKODAS, *cauliflower florets dipped in creamy, yellow chickpea batter and fried; a good snack between meals, an inviting 'side dish' with dinner or lunch, a winner with drinks, and above all, a way to get children interested in eating vegetables.*

## INGREDIENTS TO MAKE ABOUT 50 FLORETS

- 1 large firm head of cauliflower, broken into medium-size florets washed and set aside in a bowl
- 3 cups chickpea flour (besan/gram flour)
- ½ cup rice flour
- ½ teaspoon turmeric powder
- 1 teaspoon red chilli powder
- 1 teaspoon carom seeds (ajwain), crushed
- ½ cup freshly chopped fresh coriander leaves and tender stems
- 1 large onion, minced
- water to mix the batter
- 2 ¼ cups oil, divided
- salt to taste

## METHOD TO MIX THE BATTER

Sieve together the gram and rice flour, turmeric and chilli powders and salt in a bowl.

Add the carom seeds. Heap the coriander leaves and onion on top, but do not mix.

Heat 4 tablespoons of oil in a wok or saucepan on medium-high heat, and when it starts to smoke, pour it over the minced onion and chopped coriander leaves. The aroma fills the air with a sizzle.

Mix flour with fingers to a pea-size crumble, incorporating the oil and herbs into the flour.

Sprinkle water 2 tablespoons at a time and mix, breaking up the lumps. Add enough water to mix to a creamy batter somewhat thinner than the one for pancakes.

## METHOD TO FRY THE PAKODAS

Heat 2 cups of oil in a heavy wok on medium-high heat. Reduce heat to medium.

Dip 6 florets at a time in the batter to coat them well, and gently drop them, one by one, into the oil. Do not crowd the wok.

Turn over frequently with a slotted spoon and fry to a golden-brown. Drain in a colander lined with paper towels.

Repeat the process and fry the remaining florets.

Serve hot.

Tomato ketchup is the favourite dip for children. My adult friends favour honey mustard or a wasabi dip.

## RAJASTHANI MATHRI, *crisp, spicy and crumbly discs.*

### INGREDIENTS TO MAKE THE DOUGH FOR 20-25 MATHRI

* *4½ cups white flour, divided*
* *salt to taste*
* *½ teaspoon baking powder*
* *½ teaspoon baking soda*
* *½ cup melted ghee, at room temperature*
* *water to mix dough*

### METHOD TO MAKE THE DOUGH

Sift 4 cups of the flour, salt, baking powder and baking soda into a bowl.

Add the melted ghee and work it into the flour to form a crumbly mix.

Sprinkle water, 1 tablespoon at a time, mix, transfer to the work-board and knead to a stiff dough. Do not overwork the dough.

Transfer the dough to a bowl, cover with a kitchen towel and set aside, while you make the filling.

### INGREDIENTS TO MAKE THE FILLING

* *1 cup besan, gram or chickpea flour*
* *1 teaspoon red chilli powder*
* *2 teaspoons ajwain seeds (carom), coarsely crushed*
* *4 tablespoons oil*
* *1½ cups oil mixed with 1½ cups melted ghee, the shortening for frying*
* *salt to taste*

### METHOD TO MAKE THE FILLING

Sift the flour, red chilli powder and salt together in a bowl. Combine the crushed ajwain seeds with the flour. Transfer to a wok.

Dry roast the flour on low heat till it turns dry and powdery. Take care to see that the bottom does not burn. Return flour to the bowl and, while it is still warm, add 4 tablespoons oil and mix well, pressing the fat into the flour. Set aside.

### METHOD TO MAKE THE MATHRI

Transfer the dough from the bowl to the work-board.

Knead the dough once again and roll it with your palms into a long 'rope'.

Divide the 'rope' into 20-25 equal portions, roll each portion into a ball and replace in the bowl.

Cover the bowl and refrigerate for 1 hour. Take out the bowl from the refrigerator.

Sprinkle the work-board with a little flour, and with a rolling pin, roll each ball of dough to a 2-inch disc. Roll 4 balls at a time, keeping the rest covered.

Place a little less than 1 tablespoon of the filling in the middle of each disc, bring the edges together in the middle and seal firmly.

Roll out to a 4-inch disc. Prick the surface with a fork to prevent puffing up while frying.

Heat the shortening in a wok on medium-high heat and gently slide in 3-4 discs at a time. They will sink to the bottom and rise in a minute. With a slotted spoon, turn often and fry to a light honey colour.

Remove with a slotted spoon before they turn brown. Drain. Lay them in a colander lined with paper towels. After 3-4 minutes, transfer the crisp mathries to a platter.

Continue with the rest of the dough the same way. When cool, store them in airtight containers.

They stay fresh for a week.

To vary the flavouring, add garlic powder or kasuri methi (dried fenugreek leaves) to the filling. Kasuri methi is available in Indian grocery stores.

GAAJAR HALWA, *ubiquitous in India, a striking, deep-orange dessert of grated carrots. A favourite at Indian parties is a bed of halwa dressed with a scoop of vanilla ice cream on special occasions. This is my mother's recipe.*

## INGREDIENTS TO MAKE 6 SERVINGS

- *4 cups grated carrots*
- *¼ cup dates, minced*
- *¼ cup dried figs, minced*
- *½ cup water*
- *4 cups whole milk*
- *1½ cups sugar*
- *2 teaspoons grated orange rind*
- *½ cup ghee (clarified butter)*
- *a few strands of saffron*
- *1 teaspoon cardamom powder*
- *4 tablespoons honey*

- *1 teaspoon rose water*
- *¼ cup blanched and toasted almond slivers*
- *10 toasted cashew nuts broken in pieces*

## METHOD

Cook the grated carrots in a heavy pot on medium heat, adding the minced dates, figs, water and milk.

Stir and cook till the milk is absorbed and the mass comes together in a ball. The raw smell of the carrots will disappear. Stirring continuously prevents burning at the bottom.

Add the sugar and orange rind and continue to stir and cook till sticky to the touch. Add the ghee, stir and cook till it is absorbed.

Fold in the saffron, cardamom powder, honey and rose water.

Empty into a serving dish and garnish with almonds and cashew nuts.

Serve warm at room temperature.

## Max Gluckman, Bombay Bonda and Shahi Tukda

Professor Max Gluckman, Chamu's social anthropologist colleague and friend from Manchester, UK, was visiting for a term in the 1960s at the Department of Sociology in the Delhi School of Economics. He had rooms in the university guesthouse but spent most evenings with us, and soon, was addicted to a sundowner of Indian rum and home-made snacks. 'Rukka, are we having those scrumptious potato balls and lotus roots for appetizers this evening? What a great way to eat potatoes!'

When we hosted Max to dinner at our home in Cavalry Lane, he knew the food would be vegetarian, but I worried that he was not getting enough of the protein-rich diet he was used to. And if I suggested we go out to dinner so he could get his fish, mutton or chicken, with a wave of his hand he would dismiss the idea, saying, 'I love your home-cooked vegetarian food, Rukka. I have as much energy now as before and frankly, in this weather and with the variety of vegetables you cook, I don't miss meat one bit.' And he continued, 'Tell me, what are we having for dinner?' To assuage my conscience about the lack of protein, I made steamed, savoury lentil kozhukattai, which looks like a pierogi. Max said it reminded him of a Chinese baozi. Max did enjoy spicy food, but once in a while if he bit into a green chilli, with eyes tearing and amidst sniffles, he reached out for the mango slices and shahi tukda which I had planned to serve for dessert.

Two discoveries of his in Delhi were that vegetarian food was most suited to the hot weather of the tropics, and the wonder of a

'phat-phatti', the four-seater rickshaw that took him across the length and breadth of Delhi. He found it the most affordable form of intra-city transport. Didn't he find the ride noisy and rocky? No, he loved it. He proudly informed his family and colleagues back home that he rode in it to Teen Murti Marg when he interviewed the then prime minister of India, Pandit Jawaharlal Nehru. He was hoping it would be introduced with some modifications as a form of both intra- and inter-city transport in the UK. Decades later, I was delighted to find 'auto-rickshaws' plying in Times Square in New York. Some years back, I read with pride and delight of a Midwesterner in the USA who brought back an Indian auto-rickshaw, which he was using as a family transport vehicle and was even renting it out. He translated Max's idea into reality, but in the USA. Nonetheless, I was proud that a Bajaj auto had made it.

# BOMBAY BONDA, *an all-time favourite, fried spicy potato balls coated with chickpea batter to soak up party beverages.*

## INGREDIENTS TO MAKE 8 BONDAS

- 2 large potatoes, boiled soft and peeled
- 1 large onion, chopped fine
- 2 scallions, bulb, stem and leaves, chopped fine
- 2 green chillies, finely chopped
- 1-inch piece fresh ginger, coarsely grated
- 10 curry leaves, torn in pieces
- ½ cup chopped coriander leaves with tender stems
- ¼ teaspoon turmeric powder
- ½ teaspoon red chilli powder (optional)
- ½ teaspoon fennel seeds, coarsely crushed
- ½ cup raw cashew nut pieces
- 1 teaspoon oil
- ½ teaspoon black mustard seeds
- juice of ½ lime
- salt to taste

## METHOD TO MAKE POTATO BALLS

In a large bowl, mix all the ingredients, except the oil and mustard seeds. Coarsely mash the potatoes, while retaining some chunks in the mix.

In a wok, heat the oil on medium heat and add mustard seeds.

When the seeds splutter and pop, turn off the stove. Add the tempered oil to the bowl of potatoes.

Add salt to taste and mix.

Divide the potato mix into 8 equal portions and roll each portion loosely into a ball. Set aside on a platter covered with a damp kitchen towel.

## INGREDIENTS TO MAKE THE BATTER FOR CRISPY SHELLS

- ¾ cup gram flour (besan/chickpea/garbonzo flour)
- ¼ cup rice flour
- ⅛ teaspoon turmeric powder
- ½ teaspoon sugar
- ½ teaspoon ajwain seeds (carom), crushed
- 1 green chilli, 1 clove garlic, ¼-inch piece fresh ginger, coarsely pounded together
- 3 tablespoons oil
- 2 cups oil for frying
- water to mix the batter
- salt to taste

## METHOD TO MAKE BATTER FOR SHELL AND BONDAS

In a large bowl, mix the gram and rice flour, salt, turmeric powder and sugar.

Add the ajwain seeds and herbs, but do not mix.

Heat 3 tablespoons of oil in a wok almost to smoking point. Turn the stove off.

Pour the hot oil over the ground herbs. You will hear a sizzle scenting the air with a herbal aroma.

Immediately start rubbing the warm oil into the flour with your fingers, to form a crumbly mix. You may want to pick up the flour a little at a time and rub it well with the herbs between the palms and fingers with a forward and backward movement. Let the flour fall back into the bowl.

Add water 2 tablespoons at a time and mix, breaking all lumps, to form a pancake batter (for a thinner batter, add a little more water and mix).

Heat 2 cups of oil in a wok or fryer on medium-high heat but not to smoking point. Lower the heat to medium.

Take 4 potato balls, dip and roll them in the batter, coating them well. Gently drop them, one by one, into the hot oil.

Fry to a golden-brown, turning over frequently. Separate them if they stick to one another.

Remove with a slotted spoon and drain in a colander or platter lined with paper towels.

Fry the remaining potato balls the same way.

They are best served hot. When cool, the shell tends to become soft and limp.

## LOTUS ROOT BAJJI, *crunchy discs of lotus root clothed in spicy batter and fried.*

### INGREDIENTS TO MAKE 5-6 SERVINGS

* **2 cups lotus root discs**
* **salt**

### METHOD

Wash and peel lotus root; slice into discs ⅛-inch thick, sprinkle ⅛ teaspoon salt, mix and set aside, while you prepare the batter as you would for potato bondas.

Dip and coat each disc with the batter and fry in hot oil, turning over frequently. Drain and serve hot.

SHAHI TUKDA, *also called double ka meetha, was a favourite at childrens' parties when I was growing up. The lowly bread pudding is elevated to a royal dessert, and hence, this treat is called shahi tukda, which translates to royal pieces. As I remember, in Poona in the 1930s and 40s, our breadman Anthony, who used to deliver western loaves of high-dome, crusty white bread to our family every evening at the stroke of 5.00 p.m., would ring his cycle bell and call out, 'Madam, kitne double roti mangtaa?' (How many loaves of bread do you need?') So, I've always believed that double ka meetha got its name from the loaves of western white bread baked with yeasty dough which rises to double its volume and which, I think, is the best bread for this treat. Decades later in Bangalore, our breadman George delivered the same kind of bread from Koshys, a landmark bakery in the cantonment area.*

My mother's friend Shabnam was from Hyderabad and this is her recipe for shahi tukda. Actually, Shabnam used up leftover day-old bread to put together this quick and easy, tasty dessert, dripping with the goodness of flavoured milk. Yummy with whipped cream or ice cream.

## INGREDIENTS TO MAKE 10 SERVINGS

- ❋ *10 slices white bread, preferably a couple of days old*
- ❋ *¾ cup melted butter or ghee*
- ❋ *1 can condensed milk*
- ❋ *2 cups whole milk, scalded*
- ❋ *2 tablespoons sugar*
- ❋ *1 tablespoon rose water*
- ❋ *1 teaspoon cardamom powder*
- ❋ *a pinch of saffron threads soaked in 1 teaspoon hot milk*
- ❋ *¼ cup slivers of almonds, blanched and toasted*
- ❋ *½ cup sweet baking coconut, shredded (optional)*
- ❋ *½ cup thick cream or ice cream*

## METHOD

Trim the edges of all the slices. Liberally lather butter on both sides of each slice. Cut each slice diagonally and set aside.

Roast both sides of each slice, one at a time, on a shallow pan on medium low heat. Roast crisp and to a honey colour. Arrange on a serving dish.

Add the condensed milk to the pan of scalded milk, and stir to mix. Stir in the rest of the ingredients, except the cream or ice cream.

Dip each slice of fried bread in the flavoured milk for 1 minute, remove and arrange on a serving dish. Pour the remaining milk over the arranged slices.

Serve 2 pieces per serving with 1 tablespoon of cream or ice cream for a decadent dessert.

I prefer chilled shahi tukda.

ULUNDU KOZHUKATTAI, *delicate, crescent-moon pillows of steamed rice dough stuffed with aromatic, ground split black gram. Initially, making the casing may be a daunting experience, but over time, you can become an expert. In the process of steaming, a few of the casings may crack or open up and the filling spill over, but this is part of the game.*

I paired the kozhukattai with lotus root bajjis, which were foreign to south Indians. I first tasted cooked lotus root in the 1940s in my friend Sushma Swarup's house in Jubbulpore. And now, in 2012 in Boston, my friend Michael Herzfeld, anthropologist at Harvard University, surprised me with a gift of lotus root pickle which he made! They are absolutely delicious, crunchy, spicy and Asian, with the strong nutty aroma of sesame oil.

## INGREDIENTS TO MAKE THE FILLING FOR 10 KOZHUKATTAIS

* *1 cup urad dal, rinsed twice, soaked for 3 hours, and drained*
* *2 tablespoons chana dal, rinsed twice and soaked with the urad dal, and drained*
* *3 green chillies*
* *¼ cup finely chopped coriander leaves and tender stems*
* *10 curry leaves, torn in halves*
* *¼ teaspoon asafoetida powder*
* *3 tablespoons shredded coconut, fresh or frozen (optional)*
* *1 tablespoon oil*
* *½ teaspoon black mustard seeds*
* *salt to taste*

## METHOD TO MAKE THE FILLING

Grind the two dals and green chillies coarsely, sprinkling just enough water to hold it together.

Add chopped coriander, curry leaves, asafoetida and salt. Mix gently.

Spread the batter on the inside plate of a steamer.

Steam and cook for 10 minutes.

Remove from steamer, and cool.

Break with a fork leaving no lumps. Add the coconut.

Heat oil in a small pan on medium heat.

Toss in the mustard seeds, and when they splutter and pop, turn off the stove.

Add the oil and seeds to the steamed mix and stir. Divide into 10 equal portions and set aside.

## INGREDIENTS TO MAKE THE CASING

* *1 cup water, plus 1 tablespoon*
* *1 tablespoon oil*
* *1 cup sifted rice flour*
* *a pinch of salt*
* *a bowl of cold water*

## METHOD TO COOK THE CASING

In a deep pan on medium-high heat, boil the water, adding salt.

Lower the heat to medium. Add the oil and drizzle the flour, ¼ cup at a time. Stir and cook, breaking lumps that may form.

Stir and cook till all the water is absorbed.

Empty ball of dough onto a work-board, and wetting your fingers in cold water, knead the warm dough to a smooth texture. Divide into 10 equal portions, roll into balls and set aside, covered, in a bowl.

## METHOD TO SHAPE AND STEAM THE KOZHUKATTAI

Take one ball of dough, wet your fingers in a bowl of water, knead and shape into a shallow round cup of even thickness, and ideally, very thin.

Place one portion of the filling in the middle, bring the edges together and seal well, either in the shape of a crescent moon or a round dumpling, gathering the edges on top. Continue to fill and make the dumplings. Pluck out excess dough from the top. If the dumplings are not sealed well, during the process of steaming, gaps and openings develop, and it is heartrending to find the filling messing up the outside of the casing, and instead of a definite shape, you find a formless lump of steamed dough and filling. But take heart, the making of a dumpling improves with practice.

Fill the bottom pan of a steamer with water to a depth of 1 inch and set it to boil on high heat.

Place the dumplings on a greased steamer tray and steam, covered tightly, for 5 minutes.

Turn off the stove and remove the lid. Remove each dumpling gently without breaking the casing. Transfer to serving platter.

Serve at room temperature with a sour and spicy pickle or chutney. Smells and tastes even better smeared with a drop of sesame oil.

*Padma's Khara Obbattu with Pineapple Gojju*

Chamu accepted Dr V.K.R.V. Rao's invitation to join him in making the idea of the Institute for Social and Economic Change in Bangalore a reality, and we left Delhi in the summer of 1972 with our daughters Lakshmi and Tulasi and their canine friend Kittu.

On our daily constitutional with Kittu, we walked past the imposing gates of the Jayanagar Nature Cure Clinic, in front of which a young mother and her teenage son sat statue-like on the steps. They were not begging for alms, nor did they appear to be waiting to go in. Every evening, without fail, they were there. I was curious and therefore talked to the mother one day. Her story was a soap opera of oft-repeated human tragedy; a contented even-paced life shattered with the sudden death of a husband killed in a traffic accident. Not being able to pay the monthly rent, she had to vacate the two rooms they were living in, and now, she sought shelter on the verandah of the hotel where she did some odd jobs. Her son was out of school. Her world had collapsed.

That night, Chamu contacted a friend who was a trustee of the Ashaktha Poshaka Sabha, a free home for the destitute and disabled, near the Sajjan Rao Circle. The friend arranged for the mother and son to be admitted to the home. The boy was admitted to a school nearby in Basavanagudi. The woman was very weak and malnourished. She needed to rest and recover. I went by the home a couple of times and found both mother and son had adjusted very well. Soon, I forgot about her and hardly had time to spare after I, too, joined the Institute.

More than two years went by, and one Sunday, there was a visitor. Padma, the woman we left at the home, was at the door. Her son had completed his senior school studies with a diploma in accounting, and was keen to pursue a college education out of town. She moved in with us.

Padma turned out to be an innovative cook. Her speciality was a silky, savoury crêpe stuffed with herbed ground lentils, khara obbattu, which none of my friends nor family had heard of. Years later, when Chamu and I were invited to a potluck dinner party, we introduced our friends to khara obbattu. The toast of that party was Padma, and it was no surprise that all the guests wanted the recipe.

Padma also introduced me to the two-day Groundnut Fair, the Kadalekai Parishe, a carnival held annually in the suburb of Basavanagudi. One of the oldest cultural events in the city of Bangalore, the carnival dates back to four centuries, when peasants and traders from the neighbouring villages would come with freshly harvested peanuts as offering to the deity of Basava in the famous Bull Temple. Literally, hillocks of groundnuts would be up for sale. Numerous stalls cropped up overnight; village crafts of wicker and raffia, clay and wooden toys, locally made sugar candies and more, attracted people from near and far. A giant ferris wheel and magician's tents added more attraction to the carnival.

The weeks following the Parishe, we had peanuts every day in one form or another; boiled, roasted with salt and chilli powder, peanut brittle with jaggery, and crunchy batter-fried peanuts, not to speak of peanut halwa.

## PADMA'S KHARA OBBATTU, *soft, delicate savoury crêpe with a fresh coconut, ground lentil and herb filling.*

When I make this delicacy, I stagger the process by first cooking the filling, which keeps well when refrigerated for 2 days. I bring the filling to room temperature and complete the process by mixing the dough for the wrap, and cooking the obbattu, which also stays fresh refrigerated for 2–3 days. When I have more time, I make the obbattus and refrigerate them. Before serving, I warm each one in a skillet with a drizzle of ghee.

## INGREDIENTS TO MAKE THE FILLING FOR 6 OBBATTUS

* 1 cup tur dal, washed and rinsed till the water is clear, soaked for 3 hours, and drained
* 1 tablespoon chana dal, rinsed and soaked with the tur dal, and drained
* ½ cup grated coconut, fresh or frozen
* ½ cup chopped coriander leaves with tender stems
* 3 green chillies
* juice of ½ lime
* salt to taste

## METHOD TO MAKE THE FILLING

Cook tur and chana dal together in 2 cups water till just soft and not overcooked.
Drain and set aside. Save the broth.

Grind the dals along with coconut, coriander, chillies, salt and lime juice to
a smooth consistency in a food processor, without adding any water.

Divide into 6 portions. Set aside, covered, in a bowl.

## INGREDIENTS TO MAKE THE COVERING

* ½ cup white flour
* ½ cup wholewheat flour
* 2 tablespoons fine semolina (sooji/rava/cream of wheat)
* ⅛ teaspoon turmeric powder
* ¾ cup oil
* ½ cup ghee to brush on the cooked obbattu
* water to mix to a soft dough; use the broth you have saved
* salt to taste

## METHOD TO MAKE THE COVERING

In a large shallow platter with a rim, mix white flour, wholewheat flour, semolina,
turmeric powder and salt.

Add the broth a little at a time, and with a circular motion of your hand, mix with
your fingers to a smooth loose dough, breaking up all the lumps.

Add ¼ cup oil and mix (the dough will be sticky at first).

Pat out the dough and spread it in the platter. Pour another ¼ cup oil over it and
let it rest, covered, for 15 minutes. Some of the oil will be absorbed. Divide the dough
in 6 portions.

## METHOD TO MAKE THE OBBATTU

Warm up a heavy flat griddle on low heat. Brush with a little oil.

Grease a 10-inch square, thick plastic sheet with ¼ teaspoon oil. Place a ball of
dough with a little of the oil on it. Pat it evenly with your fingers from the middle
outwards to a 3-inch disc.

Place one portion of the filling in the middle of the disc. Take the edges of the disc towards the middle and over the filling, covering it well.

Press evenly all around with your fingers to flatten the disc as thin as you can. If any tears develop, paste them over with a little dough, dip your fingers in the oil and continue to press. With practice, the discs will become thinner.

Lift the plastic sheet, invert it and place the disc on the griddle, taking care to see that the plastic does not come in contact with the warm griddle. Lift the plastic sheet, starting with the edge nearest you, while the crêpe drops onto the griddle.

Cook for 1–2 minutes till brown specks appear. Ease the edges and lift gently with a metal spatula, turn over and cook the other side for another 2 minutes. Transfer to a serving platter.

Brush with ghee (clarified butter), optional.

Best served hot or at room temperature.

Use a fresh sheet of plastic for every 3 obbattus. Traditionally in India, banana leaves are used to pat out the crêpes.

## PINEAPPLE GOJJU, *sweet, sour and spicy relish. When pineapples were in season, Padma made delicious tangy and spicy gojju, which makes for a tasty spread on toast.*

### INGREDIENTS TO MAKE ABOUT 1 ½ CUPS

* **2 cups coarsely crushed pineapple pieces with juice**
* **½ cup jaggery or brown sugar grated, adjust the quantity depending on the sweetness of the fruit**
* **10 curry leaves, torn in pieces**
* **1 teaspoon grated fresh ginger**
* **½ teaspoon red chilli powder**
* **¼ teaspoon dry roasted cumin, powdered**
* **½ teaspoon lime juice**
* **salt to taste**

To make gojju, put all the ingredients in a heavy wok or saucepan, and cook on low heat to a jam-like consistency.

# BANGALORE BONDA KADALEKAI, *crunchy, spicy, battered and fried peanuts.*

## INGREDIENTS TO MAKE 2 CUPS

* ½ cup rice flour
* 1 teaspoon red chilli powder
* ½ teaspoon asafoetida powder
* 1 tablespoon oil
* 2 cups shelled raw peanuts with skin
* ½ cup oil for shallow frying
* water to mix batter
* salt to taste

## METHOD

Mix rice flour, chilli powder, salt and asafoetida powder in a bowl.

Heat 1 tablespoon oil in a wok on medium heat and add to the flour mix. Turn off the heat.

With your fingers, work oil into the flour to form a crumble.

Drizzle enough water and mix to a thick batter.

Toss peanuts into batter. Mix, coating the peanuts well.

Heat the oil for frying in a wok on medium heat.

Drop a handful of 'battered' peanuts into the hot oil, stir-fry till light-brown. Remove with slotted spoon and drain on paper towel. Fry the rest in batches.

Cool and store in an airtight container.

*Paul Hockings and Potato Polee*

I have known Paul since 1964, when he was a graduate student in the Department of Anthropology in Berkeley, California. Chamu was to spend the year at the Center for Advanced Study in the Behavioral Sciences in Palo Alto, and Paul met us at the San Francisco airport and drove us to our home in Menlo Park. He offered to teach me to drive despite my telling him I had an international driver's licence. Driving in India is challenging, what with the chaos that governs the roads, with pedestrians, animals and a variety of vehicles sharing the space. But the driving rules in California are tougher, and I remember once hesitatingly coasting through a STOP signal, and Paul commenting worriedly, 'You've gotten away this time, Rukka. You are driving in California, not in Delhi.'

*Paul Hockings at Stonehenge*

Occasionally, my driving lessons would drag on till dinnertime, and Paul would accept my invitation to stay and have dinner with us, usually chapatties, dal, rasam or sambar, a salad or dry vegetable curry, steamed rice and yogurt. As I got to know him better, I found he was very interested in all things 'other'.

More than a decade later, I received a parcel in Bangalore from Paul, a couple of weeks before he arrived on his way to the Nilgiris to do fieldwork. The custom's clearance label read 'ENEMA KIT!' I was intrigued. On opening it, I found a compact plastic kit, a collapsible jar with tubes, two airlocks and step-by-step instructions in his handwriting on the use of the kit. He later gave me the company's wine-making instruction sheet when he met me in person. We had a good laugh, and this story has made the rounds among friends. Paul knew of my interest in home wine-making. Over the years, I have made several gallons of wine—red, white and rose—with his gift. And thereby hangs a tale of missed opportunities. Chamu's young friend, I think Raghu was his name, was employed with the United Breweries in Bangalore, and after tasting the rose wine at our home, he insisted he get the contents of one bottle tested for all that it takes to produce and market it. He got back to us excitedly, saying the colour, body and taste had passed the strictest of tests. I mentioned this to our friend G.V.K. Rao, who was then the chief secretary of Karnataka, and he encouraged me to start a women's cooperative promising to lend his official support. Although that story stops there, over the years I have shared my home-made wine, made with Paul's gift, with many friends.

Paul had a pad in Bangalore not far from our home and would visit us whenever he was in town. If he was not dining at Koshy's, a favourite restaurant for Bangaloreans and visitors alike, he would stay on for a glass of home-made wine, and sweet potato polees and instant dosai, neither of which needed elaborate preparation work.

# INSTANT MULTIGRAIN DOSAI, *healthy, crisp, light, delicious crêpes, easy and quick to cook.*

## INGREDIENTS TO MAKE THE BATTER FOR 15-20 DOSAIS

* *1 cup cream of wheat (rava/sooji/semolina)*
* *½ cup rice flour*
* *¼ cup wheat flour*
* *2 tablespoons urad flour*
* *3 tablespoons ragi (finger millet) flour*
* *1 teaspoon fenugreek flour (optional)*
* *1 large onion, minced*
* *2 green chillies, slit lengthwise and minced*
* *1 tablespoon minced fresh ginger*
* *½ cup freshly chopped coriander leaves with tender stems*
* *½ cup buttermilk*
* *1 teaspoon cumin seeds*
* *2 cups water; more, if needed, for a thinner batter*
* *salt to taste*

## INGREDIENTS FOR THE TEMPERING

* *2 teaspoons oil*
* *1 teaspoon mustard seeds*
* *½ cup oil to cook the dosai*

## METHOD TO MIX THE BATTER

Mix the ingredients for the batter in a large bowl.

Heat 2 teaspoons oil in a small wok on medium heat.

Add the mustard seeds, and when they pop, turn the heat off and empty the oil with the mustard seeds into the batter.

Add more water, if necessary, and mix to a fairly thin batter.

## METHOD TO MAKE DOSAI

Heat a flat wrought iron griddle, with a handle, on medium heat.

Brush it with ½ teaspoon oil.

Stir the batter with a ladle or cup and pour ½ cup on the hot griddle, and immediately lift and tilt it around slowly, spreading the batter evenly. If there are spaces in between, do not fill them.

Drizzle ½ teaspoon oil around the edges and in the spaces.

Cook for 1 minute, and as the edges turn brown, gently ease and flip over with a metal spatula, and cook for 1 more minute.

Ease the edges, lift and serve hot.

For a crisper dosai, drizzle ¼ teaspoon more oil after flipping it over, and cook for an extra half a minute.

A creamy coconut chutney or a spicy relish of tomatoes, apples and ginger are winning accompaniments.


# TOMATO, APPLE, GINGER CHUTNEY, *tart and spicy.*


## INGREDIENTS TO MAKE ABOUT 1 CUP

* ¼ cup oil, plus 1 tablespoon
* ½ teaspoon mustard seeds
* ½ teaspoon cumin seeds
* 12 curry leaves, torn in pieces
* 1 teaspoon grated fresh ginger
* 1 apple, any sour variety (Granny Smith or Cox Pippins works well), coarsely grated
* 1 large ripe tomato, chopped fine
* 1 teaspoon red chilli powder
* ½ teaspoon turmeric powder
* 1 teaspoon brown sugar or jaggery
* ¼ cup water
* salt to taste

## METHOD

Heat the oil in a wok on medium heat. Add the mustard seeds, and as they start popping, lower the heat. Toss in the cumin seeds, curry leaves, ginger, apple, tomato, red chilli powder and turmeric powder. Stir once. Cover and cook for 1 minute.

Remove lid, stir and cook for about 3 minutes, or till all the ingredients get incorporated and cooked.

Add the brown sugar, salt and water. Raise the heat to medium. Stir and cook till the chutney thickens and comes together. Stirring continuously prevents burning.

Cool and store refrigerated in an airtight jar. Will stay fresh for one week.

# SWEET POTATO POLEES, *soft and tender, these healthy stuffed sweetbreads are easy-to-make.*

The humble sweet potato is so versatile, it is amenable to any treatment. Cut the polees into wedges, top them with orange marmalade and sour cream for a special treat.

## INGREDIENTS TO MAKE THE FILLING FOR 8 POLEES

* *3 cups boiled or baked, and mashed sweet potatoes. Do not peel the skin, just scrub and wash sweet potatoes*
* *4 tablespoons water*
* *1 cup jaggery or brown sugar*
* *1 teaspoon cardamom powder*
* *½ cup shredded coconut, fresh or frozen*
* *1 teaspoon poppy seeds*
* *3 tablespoons ghee*
* *⅛ teaspoon nutmeg powder*
* *one pinch of saffron threads soaked in ½ teaspoon milk*

## METHOD TO MAKE THE FILLING

Stir jaggery in water and dissolve. Strain through cheese cloth to remove impurities.

Heat jaggery liquid in a wok on medium heat. Cook for 1 minute.

Add the mashed sweet potatoes, cardamom powder, coconut, poppy seeds and 3 tablespoons of ghee. Lower heat, stir and cook to a rolling ball, without burning the bottom.

Turn off the stove. Stir in saffron and nutmeg powder. Cool.

Divide roughly into 8 portions and set aside in a bowl.

## INGREDIENTS TO MAKE THE CASING

* *2 cups all-purpose flour, divided*
* *1 cup wholewheat flour*
* *½ teaspoon salt*
* *⅛ teaspoon turmeric powder*
* *4 tablespoons oil, divided*
* *½ cup ghee*
* *water to mix dough*

## METHOD TO MIX THE DOUGH FOR THE CASING

Sift together 1 cup white flour, wholewheat flour, salt and turmeric powder into a bowl.

Sprinkle water, a little at a time, and mix to a soft elastic dough. Transfer the dough to the work-table. Smear 2 tablespoons oil and punch a couple of times. Transfer the dough to the bowl.

Cover with a kitchen towel and let it rest for 10 minutes. Transfer the dough back to the work-table, knead a couple of times, and with your palms roll into a rope.

Divide the rope into 8 equal portions. Roll each portion into a ball and keep covered in the bowl.

## METHOD TO MAKE THE POLEE

Grease a 6x6-inch sheet of plastic with oil. I prefer to use banana leaves when I have them.

Place one ball of dough on it. Dip your fingers in oil and press the dough from the centre outwards to a 4-inch disc.

Place one portion of the sweet potato mix in the middle. Fold over the edges and seal.

Press with your fingers into a 6-inch disc as evenly as you can press it. You could also dust the work-board with a little flour and roll out with a rolling pin. If there is a tear, seal it with a little dough. Make 2 at a time.

Warm a heavy griddle on medium low heat. Grease it with ½ teaspoon ghee. Place the plastic sheet on the griddle with the disc facing it. As the disc rests on the hot griddle, lift the plastic sheet, leaving the disc behind to cook till light brown specks appear, about 2 minutes. Lifting the plastic sheet off the griddle, leaving the disc behind, takes practice.

Brush the top surface with ghee, ease the edges and turn over the polee with a metal spatula, and cook this side light brown.

Remove and serve hot.

For a crisper polee, brush more ghee and cook longer on medium low heat.

Use a fresh sheet of plastic for every 2 or 3 polees.

Sounds unorthodox but a sweet, sour and spicy lemon pickle or orange marmalade goes very well with polee.

Polee can be refrigerated for 3 days, and reheated in the oven or on a griddle.

## The Return of the Native and Ragi Dosai

One Friday afternoon in Bangalore, I think it was in June 1993, Chamu came home from the National Institute of Advanced Study where he was a Fellow, visibly excited. Mekhri, his childhood friend, now living in Karachi in Pakistan, was visiting us the following evening at four o'clock.

We discussed what I should cook for the afternoon tiffin, and I made plans to serve masala dosai, lentil-rice crêpe wrap with spicy aromatic potato curry tucked in, Mysore pak, beehive fudge of gram flour, and strong Mysore filter coffee. 'If Mekhri remains a true Mysorean, he would enjoy this tiffin,' said Chamu.

Making masala dosai needs advance preparation work of about one day. So, I immediately washed and soaked the rice and urad dal, ground for the batter, that night before we went to bed, and left it to ferment on the kitchen counter. On Saturday morning, the slightly sour aroma of fermented batter greeted me as I entered the kitchen.

The grand-nephew of Enayathullah Mekhri, a public-spirited freedom fighter from Bangalore after whom the Circle on Bellary Road in Bangalore is named, Chamu's classmate and friend, Mekhri grew up in Mysore. They were childhood buddies while they were both students in Maramalappa's High School in Mysore, and their friendship continued through their years in Maharaja's College, also in Mysore. They played cricket together on the same team. Mekhri continued to be a frequent visitor to the family home even after Chamu left to join Bombay University for higher studies. In 1949, post partition of the Indian subcontinent, Mekhri moved to Karachi in Pakistan on the insistence of his wife, who had relatives there. Chamu told me this was Mekhri's first visit to India since leaving for Karachi.

It was an emotional home-coming for Mekhri. When he entered our home on Benson Cross Road, he embraced Chamu, reverentially touched the floor, and said, 'This is my mathru bhumi, my homeland.' He drew up a chair, sat me down, and told me stories of his friendship with

Chamu, R.K. Narayan, Raja Ramanna, the scientist, T.S. Satyan, the photographer, Van Ingens, the taxidermist brothers, and other mutual friends in Mysore. Then he turned to me and asked, *'Rukmini, nimmige Kannada barutha?* Do you know Kannada? And more importantly, what's for tiffin?' adding, 'would it be too much of a trouble to make ragi

dosai with coconut chutney? I long for the taste of Mysore Badami mangoes. These are some food items I have not tasted in decades after leaving Mysore.' I was with a friend I had not met!

I told myself Mekhri is a 'true Mysorean'. Only a native would long for and appreciate the taste of ragi dosai and Badami mangoes, the pride of the state. Ragi dosai was Chamu's favourite too, and I frequently made them for weekend breakfast. The delicate, crisp, chocolate-brown finger millet crêpes are indigenous to the Mysore region.

It was fascinating to hear Mekhri and Chamu reminisce about their school days, their trips to Bangalore to watch the Ranji Trophy cricket matches, and their evening forays into the Bandipur jungles to watch wildlife, as I made each ragi dosai on the sizzling tava (griddle). He ate several of the hot dosais with creamy, smooth coconut chutney and ghee. 'Each dosai brings back more memories,' he said. He stayed late into the night, and left reluctantly, close to midnight. I packed a dozen cubes of Mysore pak in a stainless steel tiffin carrier for him to take. He looked fondly at the tiffin carrier and smiled wistfully. His mother would send his school lunch in a blue three-tiered enamel tiffin carrier, he said.

RAGI DOSAI, *healthy, crisp, finger millet flour crêpes. They are easy and quick to make, gluten-free, rich in iron and calcium and a good source of fibre. Roasted ragi flour makes excellent porridge. The ragi millet, both as a grain and flour, as well as the roasted porridge flour, are now available in grocery stores internationally. Rice and urad flour are also sold in Indian grocery stores.*

### INGREDIENTS TO MAKE 8–10 DOSAIS

- *1 cup ragi flour*
- *1 tablespoon rice flour*
- *1 tablespoon urad flour*
- *1 tablespoon fine sooji*

- 3 green chillies, slit lengthwise and chopped fine
- 1 inch piece unpeeled fresh ginger, minced
- 1 medium onion, quartered and sliced thin
- ½ cup loosely packed fresh coriander leaves with tender stems, chopped
- 1 teaspoon cumin seeds
- ¼ cup buttermilk
- water to mix the batter
- ½ cup oil to cook the dosai
- salt to taste

## METHOD TO MIX THE BATTER

Sift the ragi flour along with the rice and urad flour and salt into a bowl. Add the other ingredients, except the water and oil. Mix well with your fingers, breaking any lumps that may form.

Add enough water and mix well to a fairly thin batter.

## METHOD TO MAKE THE DOSAI

Warm up a heavy griddle on medium heat.

Brush the griddle with ½ teaspoon oil and test the griddle with a spray of water. The water should evaporate with a sizzle.

Pour ¼ cup of the batter in the middle of the griddle. Immediately lift and rotate the griddle to spread the batter like a pancake. This motion has to be quick before the batter has time to cook and set when it comes in contact with the warm griddle. This movement comes with practice.

Drizzle ½ teaspoon oil around the edges and in the spaces within the dosai. Cook for 2 minutes.

When the edges curl up, ease with a metal spatula, and flip over. Cook this side for 1 minute.

Best served hot, straight off the griddle. Pair with coconut chutney and ghee. A spicy, red chilli-garlic chutney is my preference.

## METHOD TO MAKE RED CHILLI-GARLIC CHUTNEY

Heat 1 tablespoon oil in a heavy pan on medium heat. Add 10 garlic cloves. Stir and roast them till they are soft but not brown. Lower the heat. Drain and empty roasted garlic into a blender. To the same oil add 4 dry red chillies. Turn off the heat and stir. Add to garlic in blender. Add salt to taste and a pinch of sugar. Blend coarse. Empty in serving bowl. I use the garlic chutney as a base spread for sandwiches. They are yummy.

*Pilgrimage and Tiffin*

I digress, but as I said, the scope of this book is not a full-fledged autobiographical account of my life. There are so many cherished vignettes involving tiffin, stories Dr Chitappa told me about my forefathers, offering fascinating peeks into their lives.

This anecdote handed down from one generation to the next about his great-granduncle Chandrasekharan, born in the 1880s, recreated for me a tiny part of the world my ancestors inhabited. My uncle reverentially referred to him as Chandru 'kollu taata'. In kinship terms, 'taata' means grandfather in Tamil and the preface of 'kollu', when added, means great-grandfather.

Chandru, son and heir to Ramaswamy, known in his village as Mirasdar Ramu, was the only surviving child of four children. Ramaswamy owned two villages in the fertile Cauvery delta in the Tanjore district of south India, and was one of the wealthiest and influential landowners for miles around. Heir to the vast property, Chandru was married to his mother's brother's daughter, his maternal cousin Vijayalakshmi, when he was not quite fourteen and still a student at the High School in Kumbakonam, the nearest big town. Vijayalakshmi had just turned ten. The 'coming of age' celebration for Vijayalakshmi was a public event, a dazzling spectacle with a procession, culminating in a feast to which many relatives and villagers were invited. And my uncle added, 'It was a public announcement, nothing was private and personal.'

A few years went by and the couple remained childless. Both sets of parents and close relatives were gripped with anxiety over the possible discontinuity of the lineage. The family astrologer was consulted, and on his advice, the couple went on a pilgrimage to Rameswaram to worship at the temple of Shiva, praying for a virtuous son like Rama. The temple is situated on an island off the southern tip of Cape Comorin in south India and across the Pamban bridge. The journey by train took several days.

This was the couple's first train journey. In fact, they had never spent a night outside their home in their village in Tanjore district, their travels confined to nearby villages to attend familial ceremonies during weddings, births and deaths. Much planning went into this hazardous trip. The head priest at the Rameswaram temple was known to them, and once they reached their destination, they would be taken care of.

Purity pollution rituals governed the everyday lives of the couple. Enough food to last them on the way was packed in banana leaves and wrapped in ritually pure silk cloth, 'madi thuni' in Tamil. Parched rice and bits of dried coconut, pori urundai, puffed rice jaggery confection, satmaavu, roasted rice flour with dessicated coconut and cardamom powder mixed with jaggery and ghee, sweet appams, shallow-fried coconut confections, banana halwa and bunches of home-grown bananas, along with a silver kooja, a water jug, purified with a few tulasi leaves, and a container of sacred water from the Ganges river, was their main luggage.

At every major junction along the way, when the train stopped to refuel and fill up on water, the young couple would rush out towards the steam engine, which was being replenished with water on the platform, have a quick headbath that amounted to wetting the body while fully clothed from head to toe, sprinkle a few drops of the sacred Ganges water on their head and body to change their status from 'polluted' to 'pure', and change into fresh clothes. These had been packed in a woollen bag, since wool and silk were non-polluting. They would wash the soiled clothes, dry them on the platform, and rush back to their seats clutching a bundle of semi-dried clothes, to eat the food they

had brought along with them. Racing against time, the all-important cleansing activity was frenetic but essential. No water would be drunk nor a bite eaten till the train stopped again at the next major junction, when the purifying exercise would be repeated.

On the couple's return, a 'thanksgiving' puja at the village temple was held, a prayer service arranged by Chandru's parents. Vijayalakshmi and Chandru had undertaken this arduous journey, and were honoured by well-wishers with the chief priest of the local temple officiating at a celebratory function. The garlanded couple was taken on a procession through the streets of the village with live clarionet music, accompanied by drums and women waving camphor lamps and trays of turmeric water in front of them, both to honour them and to ward off the evil eye. For decades to follow, a much talked about event was the elaborate commemorative lunch served to all the residents of both villages. When it came to status spending, Ramaswamy spent like a toddy-addled villager. This worried Chandru, who realized if he did not gain control of the management of the lands, the family would be bankrupt. There was a constant comparison of father and son among relatives and peasant clients.

In due time, the couple was blessed with eleven children, six sons who inherited hundreds of acres of wet paddy land in the fertile Tanjore delta, and five daughters whose weddings were landmark events in the village. A quarter of a century and eleven children—the family astrologer was vindicated.

It may sound farfetched but the food my ancestors ate is still popular and not just on train journeys.

Pori urundai, crunchy balls of puffed rice speckled with glazed caramelized jaggery similar to caramelized popcorn, were the favourite. These 'no-fat' treats are now sold in confectioners' stores in India and in Indian grocery stores in the USA. I was thrilled when my American friends voted the pori urundai as superior to caramel popcorn.

Here is my mother's recipe.

# PORI URUNDAI

### INGREDIENTS TO MAKE 15-20 PORI URUNDAIS

* *4½ cups puffed or parched rice*
* *¼ teaspoon salt*
* *3 tablespoons water*
* *1 cup jaggery or brown sugar*
* *½ teaspoon dried ginger powder*
* *1 teaspoon cardamom powder*
* *¼ cup nail-size bits of coconut, or ½ cup unsweetened, dessicated, shredded coconut*
* *½ cup mixed almonds and cashew nuts, coarsely chopped*
* *2 tablespoons honey (optional)*
* *1 tablespoon ghee or melted butter*
* *a bowl of water to wet fingers*

### METHOD

In a shallow large bowl, mix the puffed rice and salt. Set aside.

Empty the jaggery or brown sugar into another bowl. Pour enough hot water to submerge the jaggery. When jaggery is dissolved, pour through cheese cloth and strain for dirt and impurities.

Pour liquid jaggery into a wok and boil, on medium heat, to a 'rolling ball' consistency.

To test drop 1 teaspoon of the syrup in a saucer with 3 tablespoons water. Jelly-like, the jaggery should neither disintegrate nor harden.

Lower the heat to medium low. Add ginger powder, cardamom powder, coconut, nuts and honey. Give it one stir, cook for 1 minute, and pour over the puffed rice in the bowl.

Toss with a wooden spoon, coating the puffed rice with the syrup.

While the mix is still warm, wet your fingers in the bowl of water, pick up 1 tablespoon of the mix and shape into small balls, pressing with your fingers and in the palm of your hand. This comes with practice. Today, special gloves are donned to shape the hot mix into balls without the fear of scalding the palm!

Alternatively, empty the mix into a 9-inch square baking dish, press gently with the back of a spoon and flatten evenly. I prefer doing this.

Cut or break into pieces or slabs.

Cool and store in airtight containers.

**SOJJI APPAM,** *aromatic, sweet, fried confection of rice flour and coconut. The salty shell complements the sweet filling. Stays fresh for weeks.*

## INGREDIENTS TO MAKE THE FILLING FOR 15 APPAMS

- **3 cups shredded coconut, frozen or fresh**
- **2½ cups grated jaggery or brown sugar**
- **4 tablespoons ghee**
- **1 teaspoon cardamom powder**
- **¼ cup cashew nut pieces**

## METHOD TO MAKE THE FILLING

In a blender or food processor, grind coconut and jaggery to a coarse paste.

In a heavy wok on medium heat, cook the coconut paste to a sticky rolling consistency, stirring frequently. Take care to see that the bottom does not burn.

Add ghee and stir till it gets absorbed.

Turn off stove, mix in the nuts and cardamom powder. Divide into 15 portions and roll into balls. Set aside on a platter. They will harden a bit on cooling.

## INGREDIENTS TO MAKE THE OUTER SHELL

- **2 cups rice flour (I use 1 ½ cups rice flour and ½ cup all-purpose flour)**
- **½ teaspoon salt**
- **½ cup ghee or cold butter cut in cubes**
- **4 tablespoons milk**
- **½ cup water, if needed**
- **¼ cup poppy seeds (optional)**
- **1 cup oil and 1 cup ghee mixed, the shortening for frying appam**

## METHOD TO MAKE THE OUTER SHELL AND APPAM

In a deep bowl, mix flour and salt.

Add ghee or butter and mix to a crumbly pea texture.

Add milk, 1 tablespoon at a time, and mix to a stiff dough.

If necessary, add a little water and mix.

Divide into 15 portions and set aside, covered, for 10 minutes.

On the work-board sprinkle a pinch of poppy seeds, if you are using them.

Take one portion of the dough and roll to a ball over the poppy seeds.

Roll or pat each ball with your fingers to a 3-inch disc.

Place one portion of the filling in the middle, gather the edges on top, pinch and seal. Clip off extra dough. If needed, wet edges slightly and seal. Pat into a 2-inch disc.

Make 6 at a time and keep covered with a kitchen towel.

Heat the shortening in a wok on medium heat, but not to smoking point.
Fry a few discs at a time, turning them over without overcrowding the wok.
Fry to a golden-brown and remove with a slotted spoon.

With the same filling rolled into balls dipped in a thin batter and fried in a
kuzhi appam griddle you get a different taste. I associate these treats with both
Poonamallee Athai and Annam Athai.

Drain and serve warm or cool and store in an airtight container.

BANANA HALWA, *chewy caramelized banana fudge. Frequently, in my home, there are no takers for bananas which have turned speckled and brown. I salvage them at this stage when their fructose content also drops, and within half an hour I transform them into a deliciously chewy caramelized fudge which, of course, everyone wants more of.*

## INGREDIENTS TO MAKE 8 SERVINGS

* 6 ripe bananas, peeled and coarsely mashed with fork
* 2 cups brown sugar or grated jaggery
* ½ cup ghee or melted butter (use as much as needed)
* ⅛ teaspoon salt
* 1 teaspoon cardamom powder
* ⅛ teaspoon nutmeg powder
* ¼ cup golden raisins
* ¼ cup pieces of roasted, unsalted cashew nuts
* 2 tablespoons honey

## METHOD

In a heavy wok or saucepan, on medium heat, mix sugar/jaggery and bananas and cook, stirring continuously, till it caramelizes and thickens, about 7 to 10 minutes.

Add ¼ cup ghee, stir and cook till ghee is absorbed.

Lower the heat, add salt, cardamom and nutmeg powders, raisins and stir, scraping the bottom. Cook for 5 minutes, adding two tablespoons of ghee.

Add the cashew nut pieces and honey. Keep stirring for a couple of minutes more to make it chewy.

Serve warm or cold as is, or with a dollop of clotted cream or vanilla ice cream. I prefer mine with plain yogurt.

# *Vaara Shaapaadu with Vermicelli Upma*

'Feeding people and especially the hungry is the greatest gift we can ask for,' my mother said when, on one of my weekend visits to Tanjore from college in 1948, I found her toiling in the kitchen. She was cooking a meal for a dozen children from the Anaathaalaya, a home for orphaned and destitute kids. This she did maybe three or four times a year.

Apart from feeding the children from the Anaathaalaya, she had undertaken to feed three young boys around ten years of age for as long as they needed. The children had left their homes in one of the outlying villages to come and study in Tanjore. They were staying with relatives, who were kind enough to give them shelter in their modest homes but did not have the means to feed them. Two of the boys, Mani and Shiva, came for meals every Tuesday, while Kuppan came every Thursday. On their way to school, they would come to the back door of the house exactly the same time every morning, wash their hands and feet at the garden tap, pick up a banana leaf kept near the door, and squat crosslegged on the cement floor in the verandah adjoining the kitchen, with the leaf placed in front of them. My mother served each one of them with the same care as she would her own children. Steamed rice with sambar and yogurt or buttermilk was the lunch she served them. The institution of vaara shaapaadu (translatable to 'weekly meals') was common when I was growing up; you could call it community service.

Shiva completed the tenth standard board examination, joined the local Serfoji College, and went on to study at the Presidency College in Madras. He was a merit scholarship student in both colleges. On one of my visits to Tanjore many years later, my father handed me an envelope addressed to him and my mother. His eyes were misty with emotion. Shiva was currently living in Washington DC and was working in the World Bank. He was in touch with Mani, who after graduation joined a school in Trichy as a biology teacher, and had brought his parents from his village to live with him. Mani visited my parents one summer, and informed them that Kuppan had joined the postal department and was working in Kumbakonam.

On some days, my mother surprised the youngsters with their favourite tiffin—steamed semia (rice vermicelli) upma. While she made the rice vermicelli at home, soaking and grinding the rice and pressing the fine noodles through a rotating press, I use store-bought rice noodles. They are just as good and save me time and preparation work. Packaged rice, wheat and white flour vermicelli is available in grocery stores in India and abroad. Recently, 'multigrain' vermicelli has made its debut.

## RICE VERMICELLI UPMA, *a satisfying, savoury breakfast or anytime snack.*

### INGREDIENTS TO MAKE 3 SERVINGS

- 4 cups vermicelli (crush the long strips with your fingers to fill 4 cups)
- 6 cups water
- ½ teaspoon salt; more later
- 1 large tomato, chopped in small cubes
- 1 cup mixed vegetables, chopped and boiled soft with a pinch of salt (carrots, beans, peas, bell peppers), drained and set aside
- 2 tablespoons oil
- 1 teaspoon mustard seeds
- 2 teaspoons chana dal
- 3 green chillies, chopped fine
- 10-15 curry leaves, torn in halves
- 2 medium onions, chopped fine

- *1 tablespoon lime/lemon juice*
- *½ cup shredded coconut, fresh or frozen*

## METHOD

Boil the water, adding salt, in a deep pan on medium heat.

Stir in the vermicelli. Turn off the heat and keep covered for 1–2 minutes.

Drain in a colander and run under cold water. Drain, separate with fork, and set aside.

In a wok on medium heat, warm up the oil.

Toss in the mustard seeds, and when they pop, lower the heat.

Add chana dal and stir a couple of times.

Add chillies, onion and curry leaves. Stir till onions are translucent.

Add tomato. Stir a couple of times.

Toss in the cooked vegetables, drained vermicelli, add ½ teaspoon salt, if needed, and turn over with a fork to coat the vermicelli well with the seasoning. Take care not to mash the vermicelli.

Turn the heat off, add lime juice and garnish with coconut. Toss and serve hot.

Coconut chutney and yogurt or buttermilk are tasty accompaniments.

## Dosai and Its Many Avatars

The trump card of south Indian tiffin is the popular rice and lentil crêpe, the dosai. Dosais come in many sizes and shapes, each with its unique colour, flavour, texture and taste. Served in restaurants from the 'set dosai', the smallest two-inch, spongy and soft pancake which comes as a set of three, to the mighty 'family roast', a daunting four-feet-long crisp, cylindrical roll, to the pyramid masala dosai, tall and faceted, inside which is buried the treasure of a smooth, spicy potato filling, dosais along with idlis and filter coffee are the trademark of south Indian tiffin. The list of variations in the dosai genre is endless, each region with its speciality, like the pesarattu, the green gram dosai from the Andhra cuisine, the sheer translucent neer dosai from Mangalore, and the rich killer of a treat, the benne masala from Karnataka, not to mention the 'dollar' dosai, one-inch across and a favourite with children.

The description of the dosai in international culinary dictionaries as a 'crêpe' and pancake fails to do justice to this unique and unparalleled contribution from south India. Ruth, our orthodox Jewish friend, hosted several 'blintz' parties, and was keen that I host a dosai Sunday brunch party for four Jewish academics in her home, when Chamu and I lived in the suburb of Bondi in Sydney. The Greek corner store stocked many of the ingredients I needed. I soaked the grains and ground the batter the previous evening, and left it to ferment in a deep enamelled Dutch oven in Ruth's kitchen. When I arrived early Sunday morning, I found a carton of six eggs helpfully kept out for me. When I spread out the first dosai on the hot skillet, Ruth bustled in, offering to whip up the eggs and add it to the batter, thinking I had forgotten a very crucial ingredient. She found the 'incredible' happening, as she exclaimed, 'But...how is it possible? No eggs, just plain batter! And oh so thin!' Her guests wanted to make the dosais, which they did, and made the magic happen.

Spreading the batter and cooking dosai, the making of ghee (clarified butter), the rolling and frying of wheat flour puri and making paneer (home-made farmer's cheese) continue to be a few of the magical moments filled with fun and surprise in the kitchen for my non-Indian friends.

In most south Indian homes, dosai batter, dosai 'milagai podi' and 'chutney powder', the accompanying spice powders, are kept handy, and the batter stays for three to four days when refrigerated, ready to be cooked and served at very short notice. In the tradition of south Indian hospitality, visitors and guests are offered tiffin and coffee any time of the day, and no snack surpasses dosai accompanied with strong filter coffee.

Mysore prides itself as the home of the 'set dosai', and older residents bemoan the closure of the niche markets of some of the small home eateries. It was brisk business at the Raju Hotel, one such small eatery in Mysore; its fame had spread throughout the state for the delicate 'set dosai' served on banana leaves; a 'set' of three small, spongy, soft pancakes, two inches across, topped with a generous dollop of home-made butter and potato curry. But like many a small 'home eatery', it closed its doors, unable to face competition from the bigger restaurants that offered more varied fare. There was certainly a loss of quality of life here.

In Bangalore, a few restaurants that serve set dosai are so famous that clients come from across town, travelling several miles just for the taste of the dosai. Loyal NRI clients go back to the same small dosai joints that they frequented as students.

Some years back, I visited a dosai 'camp' in Bangalore, a three-day fair where several kinds of dosai were made and consumed. I was amazed at the fifty and more varieties, including dosai with ground bananas in the batter competing with instant dosai, ragi flour dosai, both sweet and savoury, paneer (farmer's cheese) dosai, crisp rava dosai, egg dosai, jackfruit dosai, aval (flattened rice flakes) dosai, jaggery dosai, coconut dosai, neer dosai, green gram pesarattu, Mumbai roadside dosa, a wrap with an innovative filling of spicy stir-fried noodles, cucumber dosai, winter melon dosai, cabbage and other vegetable dosai, as also a Gujarati 'puda' counter, to name a few. Gujarati pudas are made with chickpea batter, and as children growing up in Poona, we called them vegetarian omelettes.

Without exaggeration, every counter in the dosai camp had a long line of enthusiastic customers, the business brisk and efficient, with giant-sized griddles which could make eight dosais at a time! To wash down the dosai, the 'elaneeru' guy was near at hand with a mini hillock of tender coconuts piled on the pavement.

While some dosais are crisp and papery, others are soft, spongy and meltingly soft; some are substantial, others light and wafer-thin, and still others, diaphanous. They come in a range of colours from chocolate brown and creamy yellow to pure white or mottled, and equally varied in taste.

It's funny. Friends of mine in Bangalore, faced with an ornate booklet of an elaborate tiffin menu at a swanky restaurant, would, without even as much as opening it, order 'masala dosai and filter coffee for me'. The 'post-dosai' discussion would be a serious deconstruction seminar, at times poetically sensuous, of a worthy masala dosai and of restaurants that continued to serve the best in town, where good quality ghee is used, where the dosai batter is fermented to sophistication, and where the potato masala filling is temptingly tasty and adequate.

SADA DOSAI, *a rice and lentil crêpe. Sada means ordinary or plain. Plain in appearance maybe, but that does not deter from giving the dosai a delicate taste. Besides it lends itself to many an accompaniment like dosai spice powder, coconut chutney, onion chutney, mint chutney, tomato chutney, tamarind chutney, onion tomato sambar (lentil stew with onions), coconut milk stew, and potato and onion dry curry, to mention a few. My students at the Delhi School of Economics frequented a small shack of an eatery near the college that served sada dosai with tomato ketchup!*

### INGREDIENTS TO MAKE THE BATTER FOR 12-15 SADA DOSAIS

* 1½ cups raw rice
* ¾ cup urad dal
* ½ teaspoon fenugreek seeds (optional)
* ½ teaspoon salt; more if needed
* ¼ cup oil and ¼ cup ghee mixed, for the shortening, to make the dosais
* water, to make the batter

### METHOD TO MAKE THE BATTER

Wash and rinse rice, dal and fenugreek together till the water is clear. Soak in 4 cups of water for 3 hours. Drain water.

Grind soaked ingredients in a blender to a fine smooth fluffy batter. Grind for 2 minutes, adding ¼ cup water, and when the batter is coarsely ground, stop the blender, push down from the sides with a spatula, add another ¼ cup water, and grind for another 2 minutes to a smooth, frothy and light consistency. Test smoothness with fingers. Batter should feel like fine cream of rice.

Empty batter into a deep bowl. Wash out blender with another ¼ cup water and add to bowl.

Add salt, stir briskly and set aside, tightly covered, in a warm place (temperature of 70° F) to ferment for a minimum of 8 hours. The batter, when fermented, increases in volume.

The batter can be refrigerated and used for 3 days.

### METHOD TO MAKE DOSAI

Add water, if needed, to bring the batter to a thick pouring consistency. Taste for salt.

Heat a wrought iron griddle or skillet on medium heat.

Sprinkle a few drops of water on the hot griddle. If it splutters and sizzles, it is ready for you to spread the dosai batter.

Lower the heat, grease the hot griddle with ½ teaspoon shortening.

Immediately pour ⅓ cup batter in the middle, and with the underside of a large ladle or metal cup, spread the batter in a circular motion, from the centre outwards, to form a disc or an oval 8 inches across, and as evenly and thin as you can. The movements of pouring and spreading must be quick, as the batter will start cooking immediately on contact with the hot griddle, and spreading it may be impossible. Drizzle ½ teaspoon shortening on top and around the edges of the dosai. Cook for 1 minute.

Gently ease the edges with a metal spatula and lift the dosai. Flip over and cook the other side for less than 1 minute.

Flip it over again, remove from griddle, and serve either as a disc or folded in half. Best eaten hot off the griddle.

To make crisp dosais, spread the batter out very thin, and drizzle a little more shortening on both sides and cook till the edges turn brown.

To make soft dosais, spread the batter a little thick, use less shortening and cook each side for less than 1 minute.

## MASALA DOSAI, *rice and lentil crêpe wrap with an aromatic potato filling.*

Make the dosai batter as you would for sada dosai.

### INGREDIENTS TO MAKE THE POTATO MASALA CURRY

This curry can also serve as a side dish for a meal with chapattis, puris or rice.

- *3 large potatoes, quartered, boiled soft and peeled*
- *2 tablespoons oil*
- *½ teaspoon black mustard seeds*
- *2 green chillies, slit lengthwise and minced*
- *2 medium onions, quartered and sliced thin*
- *¼ teaspoon turmeric powder*
- *10 curry leaves, torn in pieces*
- *½ teaspoon red chilli powder*
- *1 tablespoon lime or lemon juice*
- *½ cup finely chopped coriander leaves with tender stems*
- *salt to taste*

## METHOD TO MAKE POTATO MASALA CURRY

Heat oil in a heavy wok on medium heat.

Lower heat and add mustard seeds, and when they splutter and pop, stir in the chillies and onions. Sauté till onions are translucent.

Add turmeric powder, curry leaves, red chilli powder, and stir once. Add potatoes and salt. Mix, breaking up potatoes into smaller pieces, mashing some along the way.

Turn off the heat. Stir in lime/lemon juice and chopped coriander.

Cover and set aside.

Potato masala curry can be made a day in advance and refrigerated. Bring to room temperature and warm up for use.

## METHOD TO MAKE MASALA DOSAI

Heat a griddle on medium heat. Lower the heat, grease the griddle, pour and spread the batter. Cook one side as you would for a sada dosai.

Spread 2 tablespoons of potato masala on half the side of the dosai.

Fold the other half over it and press with a spatula.

Lift and serve with coconut chutney on the side.

Alternatively, you could spread the chutney as a first layer over the dosai, and the potato masala over the chutney, fold and serve like a wrap.

## MYSORE SET DOSAI, *porous like a honeycomb, this soft rice and lentil crêpe falls apart even as you pick it up.*

### INGREDIENTS TO MAKE THE BATTER

* ½ cup parboiled rice
* ½ cup raw rice
* ½ cup urad dal
* ½ teaspoon fenugreek seeds soaked soft (optional)
* ¼ cup cooked rice, or ½ cup grated cucumber, peeled and seeds removed
* salt to taste
* water to grind batter

### INGREDIENTS TO MAKE DOSAI

* ½ cup oil
* 1 cup freshly churned butter or ghee to serve with dosais

### METHOD TO MAKE THE BATTER

Combine and rinse rice and dal till the water is clear. Soak in water for 4 hours. Drain.

Grind rice, fenugreek and dal in a blender for 2 minutes, adding ½ cup water. Stop, and with a rubber spatula, scrape and push the batter towards the blades. If needed, add another ¼ cup water and grind till smooth and fluffy.

Add cooked rice or grated cucumber to the batter in the blender and grind for 2 more minutes, adding ¼ cup of water. Stop blender frequently, push down batter towards the blades with a spatula, and grind to a silky smooth, airy batter.

Empty into deep bowl to allow for increase in volume during fermentation.

Add salt, stir briskly and mix. Cover and set aside for a minimum of 8 hours in a warm place (temperature 70° F) for the batter to ferment. The batter should be bubbly and should have increased in volume.

## METHOD TO MAKE THE SET DOSAI

Heat a cast iron griddle on medium heat.

Smear with oil.

Stir the batter and pour 2 tablespoons of batter on the griddle, and spread gently with the underside of a spoon to a 3-inch pancake.

Cover with a lid and cook on medium heat for 1 minute.

Flip over with a metal spatula and cook the other side, uncovered, for half a minute.

Remove before it browns and transfer to plate.

Continue to cook the rest of the batter.

One serving consists of a stack of 3 small dosai with a dollop of butter on top, coconut chutney, potato curry and dosai podi (powder) on the side. Best eaten hot off the griddle and as the butter melts.

Cooked with the same batter, 'dollar dosai', the size of an American dollar coin, is also served as 'cocktail dosai'. The 'dollar dosai' is popular with young children. Dollar dosai were a favourite school lunch tiffin item with me and my sisters.

## DOSAI MILAGAI PODI, *the spice blend powder to accompany dosai. Mixing the powder with ghee makes it richer, but I prefer the nutty aroma of sesame oil.*

Sprinkle the dry dosai podi on boiled potatoes, chopped cucumber, tomato salad or pomegranate salad to liven up the taste. Try a sandwich with a spread of ghee and dosai milagai podi.

### INGREDIENTS TO MAKE ABOUT 1/2 CUP

* *½ cup urad dal*

- 1 teaspoon chana dal (optional)
- 1 teaspoon black sesame seeds
- ½ teaspoon oil
- 3 dry red chillies
- ¼ teaspoon asafoetida powder
- salt to taste
- ⅛ teaspoon grated jaggery or brown sugar

## METHOD

Dry roast each dal separately to a golden brown in a heavy shallow skillet on medium heat. Empty into a bowl.

Dry roast sesame seeds till they start to pop and fly about the wok. Empty into the bowl with the dals.

Turn off the heat, add the oil, red chillies and asafoetida to the hot skillet. Stir a couple of times and add to the bowl.

Cool and grind in a spice grinder to a fine powder. Add salt and sugar, and pulse. Cool and store in an airtight jar.

Stays fresh for several weeks.

## PESARATTU, GREEN GRAM (MOONG BEAN) DOSAI, *from the state of Andhra. With its distinctive colour and taste, it needs no fermentation. Tastes good with tomato chutney.*

### INGREDIENTS TO MAKE 4-6 PESARATTU

- 1 cup whole green gram
- 2 tablespoons rice
- 3 green chillies, minced and divided
- 1-inch piece fresh ginger, grated
- 1 teaspoon cumin seeds, dry roasted and coarsely crushed
- 1 medium sized onion, finely chopped or thinly sliced
- ½ cup oil
- ½ cup ghee
- salt to taste
- ¼ cup chopped fresh coriender leaves

## METHOD

Wash and rinse green gram and rice twice. Drain. Soak in water for 6 hours. Drain.

Grind in a blender to a fine pancake batter adding enough water.

Add half the quantity of chillies and all the ginger, and pulse twice.

Transfer to a bowl. Add salt and cumin. Stir and set aside for 10 minutes.

Heat a cast iron griddle on medium low heat. Grease with ½ teaspoon oil.

Pour ¼ cup batter, and spread evenly to a thin disc with the underside of a ladle, or cup.

Drizzle 1 teaspoon ghee on top. Scatter a few pieces of green chillies, onions and some coriander.

Cover with a lid and cook for 1 minute.

Remove lid, flip over and cook the pesarattu, uncovered, for 1 minute.

Lift and serve hot with ginger-tamarind chutney.

# GINGER-TAMARIND CHUTNEY

**INGREDIENTS TO MAKE ABOUT 1 CUP**

* *1 tablespoon oil*
* *1 tablespoon urad dal*
* *4 red chillies, broken in half*
* *⅛ teaspoon turmeric powder*
* *½ cup grated fresh ginger*
* *1 walnut-size tamarind pulp soaked in ½ cup hot water*
* *2 tablespoons grated jaggery or brown sugar*
* *salt to taste*

**INGREDIENTS FOR THE TEMPERING**

* *1 teaspoon oil*
* *½ teaspoon mustard seeds*

**METHOD TO MAKE THE CHUTNEY**

Warm up the oil in a skillet on medium low heat.

Add urad dal, stir and roast to a golden brown.

Turn off the heat and add red chilli pieces, turmeric powder and fresh ginger. Stir once and empty into blender.

Add tamarind pulp with the water, salt and jaggery to the blender. Grind to a smooth chutney. Empty into serving bowl.

**METHOD FOR THE TEMPERING**

Heat 1 teaspoon oil in a skillet on medium heat.

Toss in the mustard seeds, and when they pop, turn the heat off. Empty into the bowl of chutney. Stir.

# NEER DOSAI, *translates to 'watery dosai'. A simple, thin, unfermented rice batter makes delicious silky crêpes.*

## INGREDIENTS TO MAKE 15-20 DOSAIS

* *1 cup rice*
* *½ cup ghee*
* *1 tablespoon grated coconut, fresh or frozen (optional)*
* *1 tablespoon buttermilk (optional)*
* *water to grind batter*
* *salt to taste*

## METHOD

Rinse rice a few times till the water is clear. Soak for 4 hours.

Grind rice in a blender to a very fine batter, adding salt and coconut, if you are using it. Start by adding ¼ cup water, stop, and using a spatula, push down batter to the centre. Add more water and grind to a smooth thin batter.

Heat a cast iron griddle on medium heat. Smear the surface with a little oil.

Stir the buttermilk, if you are using it, into the batter.

Pour ¼ cup of the batter around the edges of the skillet and let the batter drain to the middle. Gently tilt and rotate to spread and form a disc. Do not spread with spoon.

Cook for 1 minute and remove before edges turn brown. Cook on one side only.

Repeat with the remaining batter and serve hot with ghee on top and chutney on the side.

Chamu, my spouse and companion, Lakshmi and Tulasi's father, passed away in November 1999 in Bangalore, and since February 2000, I have been spending more time with my daughters Lakshmi and Tulasi in Boston, where both are academics. I accepted their invitation to live with them as they expressed their inability to travel to Bangalore, as often as they would have wished, to spend time with me. My life here is as rich and fulfilling as it has been all these years. Boston is a beautiful, multicultural, city with a strong presence of many academic

*(L to R) With Lakshmi, Tulasi,*
*Cherokee the dachshund and Chamu*

institutions of world renown. It is a 'happening' place.

In about a couple of years of my coming to Boston, word got around about my interest in cooking, and I was invited to put together courses on Indian vegetarian cooking for adults at the CCAE, the Cambridge Center for Adult Education. The Center officials knew Tulasi who had, on a few earlier occasions, introduced groups of students to Indian spices. I took this further and designed seven courses,

*Cooking class in session in Boston*

of which four are offered every term; The Indian Vegetarian Harvest Dinner, The Healthy Indian Cuisine, Snacks and Appetizers, Crêpes and Wraps, Indian Pickles, Indian Desserts and A Tour of the Boston Indian Bazaar are participatory courses, with a fixed menu for each class, where I lecture and demonstrate, and students join me in cooking. I introduce them through food and, very often, through 'tiffin' to the rich, multicultural country that is India. As they have often told me, 'Rukka, your narratives of personal experiences spanning several decades with food as the central theme make the classes interesting, and often, when we try cooking at home with your recipes, the stories pop up in our minds and we share them with our families.' The students, young and not so young, both men and women, are enthusiastic and look forward to learning to cook 'home-style' fare, and add, 'It's no surprise, Rukka, that you don't eat out at an Indian restaurant.' I can say with some satisfaction that my classes are fully registered and students want more of the experience and taste of vegetarian India. On hearing the remarks of my students, Lakshmi and Tulasi pointed out to me that their oft-repeated suggestion that I share my memories and stories with a wider audience should now become a reality. Though I am not a food blogger, I now post recipes to former students and friends and

*Lakshmi and Tulasi*

*With Chamu and my son-in-law, Popsi Narasimhan*

sometimes to total strangers via e-mail! I also have friends like Jackie Manne, now ninety years young, who told me just three days ago that she still remembers my teaching her Indian cooking when we spent time in Palo Alto, and I shared some recipes with her, adding, 'Alas, Rukka, I don't cook much anymore but I can still make lassi.' I wish I could cook for her, but she lives in Stanford, California! Jackie and Alan Manne, with their three children, have lived in Delhi whenever Alan was posted in India as a USAID official. But I first met her in 1964 when we lived in Menlo Park, and we have been in touch for half a century. Jackie fondly reminded me of our last meeting in the 1970s in our Benson Town home in Bangalore. She hosted parties in Stanford wearing a saree, looking very comfortable in it. Whenever she cooked Indian vegetarian food, she kept it simple and authentic.

And now requests like, 'Rukka, I have six people coming for tea this Sunday, and I have remnants of hard cheese, zucchini, eggplant and onions; what Indian tiffin can I make?' Quick and easy would be cheese pakodas and vegetable bajjis, would be my response, or a quick vegetable stir-fry, and I e-mail a list of ingredients and the method of preparation. I now meet friends either in my home in Arlington, Boston, or in their homes in the Massachusetts area, for 'cook and eat' Indian tiffin sessions. It's so much fun.

The Cambridge Center hosts a donors' fund raising day every year, with talks, slide shows and food, and for this 'Of Course Day', my class on 'Healthy Indian Vegetarian Cuisine' is one of the few chosen, year after year, to represent the finely tuned, balanced Indian diet. I

*Teaching at the Cambridge Center*

use food as a gateway to our traditional Indian culture, and it works well to introduce and stimulate the senses to explore that which lies beyond, with a sense of sharing, tolerance and empathy.

What started for me as a perceived necessity by mothers for their children in Palo Alto in 1964 is still seen as a need by adults who have travelled widely and would like a cosmopolitan global table at home, and additionally, an informed health-conscious class that shuns diet fads. At the same time, they look for interesting food menus not too elaborate and that are easy to comprehend and replicate. What better food than Indian tiffin?

The TV show, 'The Indian Vegetarian Kitchen: Cooking with Rukka Srinivas', that I host on the local Arlington cable network is one of two series, one on Italian cuisine and mine on Indian vegetarian home-style food. Shot in my kitchen where I am most comfortable, it is a show often repeated during weekends. I wonder what Kunjappa would have to say! Through the food we share, I have met some very interesting people of many nationalities and food preferences, and my students at the Cambridge Center say, 'Rukka, you have much to contribute to the understanding of a global community.' My response is, 'Don't we all do so—in different ways?'

*Acknowledgements*

This book is not an autobiography. Yet the stories and recipes are deeply personal. The manuscript took shape with the help of many people, beginning with my daughters, Lakshmi and Tulasi, who suggested I share my memories, stories and recipes with a wider audience. Thank you both for the idea that encouraged me to go back in time to when I was a schoolgirl. The book is dedicated to both of you.

When I was writing the first few chapters, I was travelling in the UK with Lakshmi and Tulasi. We spent an afternoon with Professor James (Jim) Manor and his wife, Brenda, in their lovely home in Sussex and I casually mentioned my writing project to him. Jim put me in touch with Debbie Reynolds, a much-published cookbook author, who in turn introduced me to her editor, Holly Jennings, who helped me in the early stages of my writing. I also have Jim to thank for putting me in touch with David Davidar. I had met David years ago when he was with Penguin Books and had thought of him when considering possible publishers but wasn't sure if he would remember me, or whether he would be interested in a book of recipes and memories. Jim was instrumental in reconnecting the two of us. I'd also like to thank David for his prompt and encouraging response and for putting me in touch with the editors at Rupa.

My friends Aruna and Krishna Chidambi, Paul Hockings, Nandita Amin, Ira Choudhary and Shubha Chaudhuri, Ram Kumar and Geeta Karthikeyan of Queen Mary's College, my sisters, Leelu, Malu, Challu and Gita, and my nephew, Sanju, for not only cheering me on but also bridging the gap between then and now by sharing their albums of photographs. Kamala, Kanna, Sarasa and Kalyani, I think of you often and of the great times we had growing up. My students at the Cambridge Center for Adult Education with a 'can't wait to see your book, Rukka', gave me much confidence. Thank you all.

Tiffin, which I write about, is made even more appetizing thanks to the photographs of Mahesh Bhat in Bangalore and Nina Gallant in Boston.

I wouldn't have been able to navigate my Apple computer without the steady and capable support of my 'in-house' technical support, my son-in-law, Popsi Narasimhan. Whenever I approached him with what appeared to be an insurmountable problem, Popsi, with a reassuring 'that's simple' tried to train me in tackling the problem. I must confess that I am still confounded and thank him for his patience.

Carney, the African grey parrot, and Monster (Monstu), the green-cheeked conure, kept me busy and in good cheer with their affection, demands and antics. Monster 'helped' with the computer by periodically removing keys on the keyboard and contributed to drawing out the anticipation for the book.

Behind the scenes but always present with me, my parents, aunts, uncles, friends and Chamu, my spouse, have played an undeniably encouraging role throughout the process of writing *Tiffin* and have contributed to its treasured memories.